The
Boundary Waters Canoe Area

Volume 1: The Western Region

Robert Beymer

Wilderness Press

BERKELEY

First edition September 1978
Second edition March 1981
Third edition May 1985
FOURTH EDITION April 1988
Second printing January 1990
Third printing January 1992

Copyright © 1978, 1981, 1985, 1988 by Robert Beymer
All rights reserved
Cover photo by J. Arnold Bolz
Maps by Roger Butler (foldout) and Larry Van Dyke
Design by Thomas Winnett

Library of Congress Card Catalog Number 88-40012
International Standard Book Number 0-89997-098-2

Printed in the United States of America
Published by   Wilderness Press
                2440 Bancroft Way
                Berkeley CA 94704
                (510) 843-8080

                Write for free catalog

⊛ Printed on recycled paper with soybean ink

Library of Congress Cataloging in Publication Data

Beymer, Robert.
  The boundary waters canoe area.

  Includes index.
  Contents: v. 1. The western region.
  1. Canoes and canoeing—Minnesota—Boundary Waters
Canoe Area—Guide-books. 2. Boundary Waters Canoe
Area (Min.)—Guide-books. I. Title.
GV776.M62B6815   1985   917.76   88-40012
ISBN 0-89997-098-2 (v. 1)

Contents

Preface

This book is the result of my nine years of canoeing in the Boundary Waters Canoe Area. I was introduced to the BWCA in June 1967, along with 14 other members of my Explorer Post in Indianola, Iowa. Not a summer since then has gone by without at least one North Woods canoe trip, usually several.

Since my first summer as a guide in the Boundary Waters, I have seen the need for a published trail guide, and as the number of visitors to this aquatic paradise has grown, the need has become even greater.

During the Summer of 1976, the US Forest Service implemented a new Visitor Distribution Program to "protect the water quality and other physical resources of the area and to assure that opportunities for a high-quality wilderness experience are available to its users." Accordingly, from May 1 through September 30, daily limits have been established for the number of overnight permits that may be issued for each of the designated entry points.

With over a million pristine acres of lakes, rivers and forests within its borders, the BWCA is large enough to accommodate the present usage. In 1984 less than ⅓ of the available quotas were actually used. So why do we need a quota system? Because, unfortunately, in 1976 over ⅔ of the visitors to the BWCA used less than 14% of the 73 designated entry points. The result was (and still is) congestion on such popular lakes as Moose, Saganaga, Fall, Trout and Lake One.

It is my firm belief, however, that there would be no need for a quota system if canoeists only knew of the many entry points and routes available to them. Why would anyone want to paddle out of busy canoe "terminals" when he could be entering the BWCA through the winding wilderness of Hog Creek, or the beautiful Granite River, or isolated Bower Trout Lake?

This book is designed to help you discover a better way into the BWCA. It was written for the canoe camper who is capable of taking care of himself in a wilderness environment. It does not take you by the hand and lead you through the often complicated mazes of lakes and portages that characterize the Boundary Waters. It does not always tell you when to turn right, when to veer left, or when to stop and take a picture. You should already possess the understanding and the basic skills that are essential for a canoe trip into a wilderness, particularly the ability to guide yourself along the suggested routes without detailed directions. This book does not include such topics as "what equipment you will need," or "how to plan your food," or "how to shoot a rapids," or "how to pack your gear." Many good "how to" books have been written about canoeing and camping. This guide is a "where to" book. If you need information about techniques, I suggest you read several of the "how to" books and pick out what is appropriate to your needs.

American Red Cross, *Canoeing.* Doubleday: Garden City, NY, 1977.

Boy Scouts of America, *Canoeing.* Irving, B.S.A., North Brunswick N.J.: B.S.A. by Schmidt, Ernest F. (revised 1981).

Cary, Bob, *The Big Wilderness Canoe Manual.* New York: David McKay Company, 1978.

Furtman, Michael, *A Boundary Waters Fishing Guide.* Duluth, MN: Birch Portage Press, 1984.

Jacobson, Cliff, *Wilderness Canoeing and Camping.* New York: E. P. Dutton, 1977.

Mason, Bill, *Path of the Paddle: An Illustrated Guide to the Art of Canoeing.* Toronto and New York: Van Nostrand and Rinehart, 1979.

Riviere, Bill, *Pole, Paddle and Portage: A Complete Guide to Canoeing.* Boston: Little, Brown & Co., 1974.

Preface

Sandreuter, William O., *Whitewater Canoeing.* New York: Winchester Press, 1976.

For a humorous account of one family's explorations, read: Stresau, Marion, *Canoeing the Boundary Waters,* Edmonds, WA: Signpost Books, 1979.

To capture the mood of canoeing in the BWCA, read any of Sigurd F. Olson's vivid accounts: *Reflections from the North Country, The Hidden Forest, Wilderness Days, Open Horizons, Runes of the North, The Lonely Land, Listening Point, The Singing Wilderness.*

This is a *comprehensive* guide, including all entry points that are useful to canoeists in the western half of the Boundary Waters Canoe Area, from Crane Lake east to Kawishiwi Lake. Volume II takes over where this one leaves off, dealing with the entry points in the eastern half of the BWCA.

Preface to the 4th Edition

Since the first edition of Volume I was published in 1978, more than 25,000 copies of both volumes of this book have been sold to inquisitive paddlers in search of routes into the BWCA Wilderness. Over the past nine years, I've received feedback from friends and strangers alike. Most of the comments have been complimentary and quite positive. My work with camping stores in the Twin Cities and in Ely has given me an opportunity to personally encounter many of my readers—a valuable experience available to few writers. Because of the feedback received, and because of the continuing research I have conducted from my current home on the Kawishiwi River, changes have been made in subsequent editions. I've tried to make the books interesting, but above all my goal has been to impart accurate information.

The only major complaints that I have received pertain to my difficulty ratings and to the lengths of the trips that I have recommended. I stand by my difficulty ratings, arbitrary as they may be. Since they are totally subjective, however, perhaps an explanation is in order. Two major factors contribute to the difficulty rating for each route: 1) average distance paddled per day, and 2) length, frequency and difficulty of portages along the route. I consider an "average" day in the Wilderness to include about 10 miles of paddling, interrupted by 5 or 6 portages, averaging 50–100 rods in length. This should challenge most folks. Anything less is usually rated "easy," and days with a great deal more paddling and/or longer, more frequent portages are rated "rugged." The ratings are based on my 20 years of BWCA trips and my experience with all age groups and all experience levels.

Preface to the 4th Edition

As far as the lengths of the recommended routes are concerned, people have requested suggestions for shorter routes. It seems that most paddlers simply don't have more than a week to spare. Consequently, in editions since the first, I've added more route suggestions for 2–4-day trips. These cater to people who intend to do a considerable amount of fishing, perhaps stretching a 3-day route over a full week, as well as to people who simply don't have more than a long weekend to spend in the Boundary Waters.

Both my publisher and I want my guidebooks to serve *you,* the reader. We'll continue to make changes in the future, reflecting new regulations, alterations to existing routes and the wishes of our readers. If you have suggestions, we'd love to hear from you. Thanks! Have a wonderful wilderness experience.

R.H.B.
12/1/87

Acknowledgments

A book like this one could never have been written without the help and encouragement of many people. I could never fully express my appreciation to all of those who had a part in its creation, but it is only fair to at least mention those who offered the greatest contributions.

Herb Evans, former Director of the Voyageur Visitor Center in Ely, who supplied me with the U.S. Forest Service statistical data contained in the original edition of this book.

Earl Fisher, W.A. Fisher Company, who supplied the maps used for research.

Wally Schuette, Lowe Industries, who supplied the 17-foot Loweline canoe used for research during the summers of 1977 and 1978.

Richard A. Smith, Chuckwagon Foods, who supplied the trail food at discount for my research trips.

A.O. Berglund, Jr., Director of Camp Northland, and Skipper Berglund, founder of Camp Northland.

Anne Pomaranc, Betsy Crown and Jo Dunnick, who supplied photographs to illustrate my text.

Tim Bloom, Bill Donald, Fred Brown, Marty Danekind, Tim Nichols, Jeff Ryther and Tom Wilson—my associate guides at Camp Northland.

Jan Baker and Rex Miller—my expedition companions.

Paul W. Loaney, who provided the assistance necessary to complete the ''Geology'' section of Chapter 1.

Bonnie Wilson, Minnesota Historical Society, who assisted me in finding photo illustrations for this volume.

Eddie Bauer, Inc., and Neal Warner, former Manager of the Minneapolis Store, who allowed me the time to conduct field research to revise this volume.

Barb Soderberg, Superior National Forest Headquarters, and Tom Misiano, Isabella Ranger Station, who provided data for the revisions of this volume.

Gerald J. Beymer, who introduced me to the joys of camping experiences.

Ruth E. Beymer, who steadfastly encouraged me to write about these experiences.

Cheryl McFaul Beymer, my favorite canoeing companion.

And all the good people with whom I have tripped into the BWCA and whom I have met on those excursions.

Bob Beymer
St. Paul, Minn.

Ch. 1:
Introduction to the BWCA

The Boundary Waters Canoe Area is paradise for the wilderness canoeist. Stretching for 200 miles along the Canadian border of northeastern Minnesota, this magnificent wilderness offers over 1,200 miles of canoe routes through some of the most beautiful country in the world. That's why over 160,000 persons visit it each year. At over a million acres, it is the second largest unit of our National Wilderness Preservation system, containing the largest virgin forests remaining east of the Rocky Mountains.

HISTORY

The canoe routes on which you will paddle are the very same ones used for hundreds of years by the Sioux and Chippewa Indians and by the French-Canadian Voyageurs. Jacques de Noyons, in about 1688, was probably the first white man to paddle through the lakes and streams that now compose the BWCA. At that time, the Sioux may have still been the dominant Indians in the area. But by the time of the first fur traders in the 18th Century, the Chippewas had moved into the region from the east and had driven the Sioux farther west onto the plains. From then to about 1800, French-Canadian Voyageurs paddled their birch-bark canoes from the hinterlands of northwestern Canada to the shores of Lake Superior, transporting furs from trappers toward the European markets.

During the latter half of the 19th Century, settlers moved into the area, including farmers, loggers and miners. After the railroad penetrated the area, extensive logging and mining operations threatened to devastate the entire region.

The Superior National Forest was designated in 1909, and within it, in 1926, one thousand acres were set aside as a primitive roadless area. This area was enlarged in the 1930's and in 1939 the wilderness area was redesignated the Superior Roadless Primitive Area, establishing boundaries containing over one million acres. In 1958 the current name was adopted. And the BWCA Wilderness Bill of 1978 established the current boundaries, containing 1,075,000 acres. It also prohibits logging, restricts mining operations and limits the use of motorboats to 33% of the water area in 1979 (24% after 1999). The BWCA is regulated by the U.S. Forest Service.

Thanks to the efforts of conservationists throughout the years, this beautiful regions looks almost the same today as it did when De Noyons first viewed it.

WILDLIFE

Nothing represents the Boundary Waters better than the eerie "laughter" of the loon, the Minnesota State Bird. But many other birds are equally at home here, including the bald eagle, the gull, the great blue heron, and the Canadian jay. In the BWCA you will also find the last substantial population of timber wolves in the "lower forty-eight," as well as a large population of moose, white-tailed deer, black bear, beaver and fox. Other mammals include the lynx, fisher, mink, muskrat, otter, marten, weasel, coyote, and a variety of squirrels.

The predominant game fishes are northern pike, walleye, smallmouth bass and lake trout. Crappies and bluegill are also plentiful in some of the lakes. Even rainbow and brook trout have been stocked in some lakes.

The North Woods are covered largely by a coniferous forest, made up of jack pine, Norway pine, white pine, tamarack, black spruce, white spruce, balsam fir and white cedar. There are also extensive stands of deciduous trees, including paper birch and quaking aspen. Very few land areas in the BWCA are not forested.

FIRES

Under a new Forest Service policy implemented in 1987, lightning-caused fires in the BWCA Wilderness will be allowed to burn without suppression if the fires fall within certain "prescribed" limits regarding location, risks to property and public safety, weather factors and other conditions. Fires that are not within prescribed limits, and all human-caused fires, will be suppressed, as they have been in the past.

For centuries, large areas of the Wilderness burned from lightning-caused fires, which reduced fuel accumulations and created diverse wildlife habitats. The new fire policy is intended to partly restore fire to its natural role in the wilderness, whenever it can occur within the limits of safety.

Efforts will be made by the Forest Service to inform the public about ongoing fires. Notices will be posted at canoe landings, and USFS field crews will notify paddlers within the wilderness about threatening blazes.

You may encounter natural fires in the BWCA Wilderness. Forest Service personnel may not be present at the site, although all fires will be under some form of surveillance. If you choose to observe the fire, please do so from a safe distance, and consider the following safety tips:

• Fires normally move in the same direction as the wind. Find a safe location away from the fire's path.

• Be careful while visiting a recently burned area. Ashes may remain hot for days, and there is danger of falling snags and tree limbs.

• Do not attempt to put a prescribed fire out. As a natural fire, it is part of the wilderness. It will cause ecological changes that are consistent with wilderness management.

• Fires may smolder and burn very slowly for days or even weeks without much increase in size. Then weather changes can cause dramatic and dangerous increases in fire size. Respect all fires as potentially dangerous.

Although wilderness fires will bring positive benefits to the forest, fire can also be devastating. Visitors are reminded of their responsibility to prevent human-caused fires. The long-standing Smokey Bear message of fire prevention is still valid. Please be careful!

BEARS

Black bears are common throughout the BWCA. Although they are not normally considered to be dangerous and are usually quite shy around campers, they may be pests when searching for food—your food.

Over the years they have learned that canoe campers always travel with food packs. And where campers are most frequently found camping, bears are most frequently a problem. An unpleasant encounter with a bear could bring an abrupt end to your canoe trip.

There are no hard-and-fast rules to insure protection from a bear. Bear behavior differs under different conditions. The bears you may encounter while visiting the BWCA are wild animals and they *could* be dangerous. Always remember that! Nevertheless, with a few precautions, you will have no problem with these fascinating creatures.

1. Never store food in your tent. And if food has been spilled on your clothes, leave the clothes outside your tent at night.

2. When you are away from your campsite (even just fishing nearby!) and at night, always hang your food pack at least 10 feet above the ground and *away* from tree trunks. Bears are good tree climbers, so the food must be a safe distance (6 feet or more) away from the trunk and from any limbs large enough to support a bear's weight.

3. When you leave your campsite, tie your tent flaps open. Bears are inquisitive animals, and they may want to tour your shelter. If the tent is closed, they could make a new doorway.

4. Keep a clean campsite. Burn all food scraps and leftover grease. Do not dispose of leftovers in the latrine. Bears will find them and destroy the latrine in the process.

5. Don't let an island campsite lull you into a false sense of security. Bears are very good swimmers.

6. Never get between a mother and her cub(s). If you see a cub, you can be sure the mother is nearby. Female bears are extremely protective of their young.

7. If a bear does wander into your campsite, don't panic! They are usually easily frightened off by loud noises. Try

yelling or banging some cooking pots together. Don't charge the bear; it may become defensive.

8. If a stubborn bear does not back off or acts strangely, move to another campsite. It's extremely rare for a bear to attack a human being; but it did happen to two campers in separate incidents (same bear) during the summer of 1987. Neither camper was seriously injured, and the bear was later killed by authorities. (Note: this was the *only* such incident during the 20 years that I've been camping in the BWCA Wilderness.)

9. Finally, with all that said, don't lose any sleep worrying about the sounds you hear outside your tent at night. The noisiest critters are also the smallest—mice among the worst! Bears are among the quietest animals in the woods. If you hear rustling leaves at night, chances are good that it's not caused by a bear. Rest assured!

SAFETY

Risk is an integral part of a wilderness trek. Risks associated with isolation, tough physical challenges, adverse weather conditions and lack of rapid communications are inherent in a visit to the BWCA. At all times exercise caution, use common sense, and consider the following tips:

1) Do not take chances to save time.

2) Always wear a life preserver, even if you can swim.

3) Do not attempt canoe travel during a lightning storm or when waves are running.

4) Never stand in a canoe; keep weight low and centered.

5) If you should capsize, stay with the canoe; it won't sink.

6) Use the portages. Do not run rapids unless you are confident you can do it safely, and only after you have scouted them. Remember that water levels change considerably during the summer months. A rapids that may have been perfectly safe to run during your last trip in August could be a

dangerous, raging torrent during your next trip in June. Canoeing mishaps occur almost every summer in the Boundary Waters. Some result in drownings. Many result in damaged canoes. Most result in spoiled trips.

7) Carry a good first-aid kit and know how to use it. See to it that *every* member of your group knows CPR.

8) In the event of serious accident, send one canoe for help immediately. Or use a heavy smoke signal to attract a Forest Service patrol plane. Evacuation by plane or other motorized vehicle is approved only when there are no other alternatives available and a person needs the immediate services of a doctor. All emergency searches, rescues and evacuations are authorized by the local county sheriff. If an evacuation is necessary, you will be billed for expenses incurred.

9) Boil or treat water before drinking. Even then, if algae are visible, don't drink the water. Although lake water may *look* pure, drinking it without first filtering, boiling or treating it may cause illness. When using a filter or chemicals, be certain that they are designed to remove or kill *Giardia lamblia,* in particular—a nasty parasite that can cause a harsh intestinal illness.

10) Before setting out on your trip, be sure that someone—Forest Service official, outfitter or friend—knows your itinerary and when you expect to return, with instructions to contact authorities if you are overdue.

CLIMATE

In northern Minnesota, spring, summer and fall are crowded into a span of about five months—May through September. Perhaps the best seasons for canoeing in the Boundary Waters are spring (May) and fall (September). At those times, water levels are usually the highest and insects usually the least bothersome. Fishing is also best at these times. But those months are also, normally, the coolest times of the canoeing season. Early June and late August to mid-September are usually the wettest periods.

July and early August normally offer the best weather for

campers. But, because that is a dry time, water levels of some streams may be too low for navigating a loaded canoe, eliminating several excellent route possibilities.

Temperatures and rainfall vary, of course, throughout the BWCA. The following statistics, recorded in International Falls, represent approximations for the western half of the BWCA.

	May	*June*	*July*	*Aug.*	*Sept.*
Average temperature	51°	60°	66°	63°	53°
Average low each day	38°	48°	53°	51°	41°
Average high each day	63°	72°	78°	76°	64°
Precipitation	2.6"	3.9"	3.5"	3.6"	2.9"

Because of its close proximity to Lake Superior, the eastern part of the BWCA sometimes exhibits extremely variable weather. While the lakes in the far eastern region may be blanketed with a cool, misty fog from Lake Superior, nearby lakes to the northwest may be enjoying warm sunshine, thanks to the subtle yet significant effect of the Laurentian Divide. Consequently, no weather data from any one reporting station can accurately represent all of the BWCA's eastern region.

GEOLOGY

It would take another volume to do justice to the geologic history of this incredible country. But it would also be an injustice, perhaps, to not mention it at all.

The rocks in this area are dominantly Precambrian rocks covered by a thin veneer of glacial deposits. For two billion years, during the Precambrian period, vast changes were generated by a large amount of diverse geologic activity that persisted over the area and redefined it many times. Erosion predominated after this until roughly one million years ago, when the great ice sheets of the Pleistocene Epoch began to form. The ice scoured the Precambrian bedrock, gouging out the softer rocks and leaving behind irregular blankets of glacial debris. This created the topography that we see today.

Underneath the Boundary Waters Canoe Area is some of the oldest rock in the world, as old as three billion years. It is part of the vast rock area known as the Canadian Shield, which underlies almost two million square miles of eastern Canada and the Lake Superior region of the United States. In Minnesota this belt of ancient exposed rock extends west from the area of Saganaga Lake on the international border through Ely and International Falls to the northwest part of the state, where the old rocks disappear beneath younger sedimentary deposits. Included in this expanse of ancient rocks are the metavolcanic Ely Greenstone formation, the metasedimentary Knife Lake Group and great granitic *batholiths* like the Vermilion and the Saganaga batholiths. All are known to be older than 2.6 billion years. That date marks the events of the Algoman *orogeny* (mountain-building period), during which the rocks became metamorphosed and strongly deformed, and the granites were intruded from below into the older rocks.

A long period of erosion followed the Algoman orogeny. Rocks that had been formed or altered deep within the earth's crust became exposed at the surface and subjected to erosion. The geologic events that may have been of the most economic significance to the state of Minnesota began with the encroachment of a broad arm of the ocean upon the eroded terrain. Inland seas covered most of what we now call the North Woods. Layers of sedimentary rocks were deposited at the bottom of that enormous sea. Called the Animikie Group, these rocks lie in a belt extending westward along the border lakes from Lake Superior to just south of Saganaga Lake, and then reappearing in the Mesabi Range south of the BWCA. The Animikie rocks include the Pokegama quartzite, the Biwabik iron formation and a sequence of shales and sandstones. Flint, too, is found in abundance in the vicinity of Gunflint Lake. Rich deposits of iron ore are scattered throughout northeastern Minnesota. It is so concentrated in some places that it will cause your compass needle to be deflected from magnetic north. Magnetic Lake, in fact, received its name because of just such a phenomenon.

Around 1.7 to 1.6 billion years ago, another period of mountain building occurred. During the Penokean orogeny the Animikie sedimentary rocks and other existing rocks were folded, faulted, metamorphosed and intruded by granitic *magmas.* Later an outpouring of tens of thousands of feet of lava in and around the area now occupied by Lake Superior created the major rock of the "North Shore." After this volcanic activity subsided, stream erosion and deposition again became the dominant processes in the area.

The inland seas had long since disappeared and new mountains had risen on the continent when the great ice sheet of the Ice Age advanced from the north and began to cover the state of Minnesota. It was the ice sheet that turned this mineral-rich region into the world's best canoe country. During four major periods of glaciation, the glaciers altered the landscape considerably. These periods began perhaps almost one million years ago.

During the last glacial advance and recession (the Wisconsin Glaciation, lasting from about 100,000 to 10,000 years ago), a very distinctive glacial ridge called the Vermilion *moraine* was deposited. The Vermilion Moraine, composed of gray-colored sand and stone, extends from the little town of Isabella to a point southeast of International Falls, bounding lakes Vermilion and Nett. During an earlier advance, the Toimi *drumlins* (isolated oblong hills) were formed in an area south-southeast of the Vermilion moraine and the town of Isabella.

Evidence of the Ice Age is everywhere in the Boundary Waters today. Parallel grooves called *striations* are visible on many rock ledges that were scoured by the ice. Glacial debris unsorted as to size, from small pebbles to huge boulders, is widespread. Here and there one sees large boulders, called *erratics,* which were left "stranded" when the glaciers melted.

Perhaps the greatest distinction of the border lakes area is the domination of exposed bedrock. This region is unlike the rest of the state, which is almost completely covered by glacial deposits, and that explains why there are so many rock-rimmed lakes in the BWCA. The domination of exposed bedrock in the Boundary Waters results in distinctive patterns of lakes and ridges, which reflect the underlying rock structure.

In the eastern third of the area the lakes form a distinctive linear pattern. Long, narrow lakes give the terrain a notable east-west "grain." These lakes are set in two major types of rocks: in the Duluth Gabbro rock, which is a coarse-grained igneous rock, and in the Rove Slate formation, which is a sequence of sedimentary rocks made up mostly of a dark, fine-grained slate.

The lakes on the Duluth Gabbro, which is exposed over an area from Duluth north and east to the Pigeon River, developed their particular pattern because alternating bands of less resistant rock and more resistant rock are oriented east-west. Erosion has removed more of the less resistant rock, creating lake basins. In the area where the Rove Slate formation is exposed—along the international border from Gunflint Lake to Pigeon Point (the Tip of the Arrowhead region)—the east-west linear pattern has a different cause. In this area intervening ridges separate the lakes. These ridges are the exposed edges of south-dipping layers of dark igneous rock that was intruded into the slate after the sedimentary rocks were deposited. The north-facing slopes of the ridges are very steep and form escarpments 200–400 feet high. Huge piles of talus blocks cover the lower parts of many escarpments, the result of erosion by the advancing glaciers as they passed transversely over the ridges. Good examples are found at the northwest end of Brule Lake and at the south end of Gasket Lake.

The lakes set in the Knife Lake group of rocks show a similar linear pattern, but the trend is northeastward. And in the rocks associated with the Ely Greenstone, the pattern is less regular and the depressions in the bedrock are not as deep, resulting in shallower lakes.

In the area underlain by the Saganaga Granite the story is a little different. Here the shapes of the lakes are dictated by cracks in the Precambrian rock. As the cracks were made wider by erosion, they became linear depressions which lakes could occupy. Many of the lakes lie in collections of linear depressions oriented in more than one direction, so that the lakes have zigzag shapes. An overhead view of the area reveals many jagged lakes interconnected by linear channels. Saganaga Lake itself is a good example.

Because of the glaciation of the Ice Age and the characteristic Precambrian rock of the northeastern Minnesota, the

Boundary Waters Canoe Area has the highest concentration of lakes in the state, which itself has the most lakes of any state.

Thanks largely to the Ice Age, the Boundary Waters Canoe Area, with all its interconnected lakes and streams, is one of the most beautiful and certainly one of the most extraordinary recreational wilderness areas of the world.

CAN THE WILDERNESS SURVIVE YOU?

A wilderness, in contrast with those areas where man and his own works dominate the landscape, is hereby recognized as an area where the earth and its community of life are untrammeled by man, where man himself is a visitor who does not remain.

Using this definition, Congress passed the Wilderness Act of 1964 and created the National Wilderness Preservation System. Included as the only water-based wilderness, and the largest wilderness in the lower 48 states, the BWCA is also the most heavily used wilderness in America, visited by as many as 180,000 people each year. Many of these visitors are not familiar with minimum-impact camping techniques and the need to protect the fragile wilderness resource from damage. Litter strewn along portages and left in fire grates; birch trees stripped of bark; red and white pines carved with initials; and fire-blackened areas resulting from campfires left burning are just some of the signs of abuse seen far too often in the BWCA. Other problems caused by the large number of visitors may be less permanent but still inappropriate in a wilderness setting: large, noisy groups shouting across the lake or singing boisterously around a campfire, and bright-colored equipment easily seen from across a lake—all detract from the feeling of quiet and solitude that wilderness visitors seek.

Wilderness areas are managed to protect and maintain the environment in its natural state for our enjoyment and for the enjoyment of generations to come. The responsibility for protecting these areas lies not only with professional managers, however. As a visitor, *you and your group also share in this responsibility.* You must realize your place within the wilderness not as a conqueror, but as a wise keeper and a good steward of this land and water. By simply utilizing the following suggestions of the United States Forest Service and adhering to the rules and regulations of the BWCA, you will ensure a quality wilderness experience for yourself and others, as well as preserve the area for generations to come.

Pre-Trip Planning

A safe, enjoyable wilderness experience starts at home with careful planning. First, ask yourself and members of your group if you really *want* a trip into the wilderness—a place where you'll find no piped water, prepared shelters, predictable weather or easy travel. Wilderness travelers cannot count on signs to direct the way; they must know how to read a map and use a compass. In an area which is unfamiliar and sometimes downright hostile, you must be your own doctor, guide and entertainer—prepared for accidents, changes in weather and such obstacles as high winds on large lakes.

Vacationing with a group of people is always challenging, because of variations in skills, interests and physical strength. Get your group together ahead of time to plan your trip. Talk about what each person is looking for and expects on the trip. Decide as a group where to go, when to go, what equipment to take along and what to eat. By looking at these things ahead of time, the group will have a better idea of what to expect from the trip, and there will be fewer ''surprises'' to dampen spirits. Consider not only the good aspects of BWCA canoe trips— warm sun-drenched afternoons on sky-blue lakes, cooled slightly by a mere whisper of a breeze—but also the dreaded conditions that plague many trips—hordes of hungry flying insects, fish with no appetite at all, long and muddy portage trails, prolonged periods of cold rain, and gale-force winds that make canoe travel extremely difficult or virtually impossible. Both trip scenarios are possible—indeed likely—at one time or another. Be psychologically and physically prepared for the worst.

If at all possible, keep your group size small. Few camp-sites have tent pads for more than two or three tents. Some are barely large enough for one tent. If your group will be large, plan to split up and travel separately. Better yet, plan completely different routes. You'll have more pictures and experiences to share when you get home. A small group has much less impact on the wilderness and on other visitors.

Equipment: When selecting equipment for your trip, choose environmentally ''natural'' colored tents, packs and clothing to help you travel and camp inconspicuously. Bright colors contribute to a crowded feeling. Carry a small stove and fuel to use when dry wood is hard to find. Stoves heat more cleanly, quickly and evenly than campfires. Axes and hatchets are not necessary. There is plenty of suitable firewood which can easily be broken or cut with a small camp saw. See that at least one person in each canoe carries a map and a compass, and knows how to use both. Kept in a plastic case and tied to the canoe, the map is readily available for quick and constant reference. Line your packs with large, heavy plastic bags, to keep all the contents dry. And, by all means, practice packing before you leave home. Remember, everything you pack will have to be carried—by *you.*

Clothes: Clothing needs may vary somewhat from season to season, but always plan for all extremes. *Layering* is the most efficient method to stay warm and dry. Lightweight cotton is ideal for warm weather, while wool, even when wet, provides warmth on chilly days and at night. Good raingear is essential, and it can also serve as a great windbreaker on cold, windy days. Bring two pairs of footwear, boots or sturdy walking shoes for portaging, and sneakers or moccasins for walking around the campsite. Wearing the latter at the campsite is not only kind to your feet; it also causes less soil-compaction damage to the site.

Food: Since cans and bottles are not allowed in the BWCA, some foods will have to be repacked in plastic bags or in other plastic containers. If possible, pack each meal's food together in a larger bag to make meal preparation easier.

Travel

When planning your trip route, make sure you aren't overly ambitious. Consider all members of the group, and plan to travel at the speed of the least experienced paddler. It's a good idea to plan for a layover day or two. You'll have more time to fish or relax, and, if you run into rough weather, you won't have to worry about taking unnecessary chances just to stay on schedule.

Respect for other wilderness visitors starts before you ever leave home. Practice picking up a canoe and other canoeing skills before you head out on your trip. The first portage is no place to try to figure out how to get the canoe up on your shoulders.

If a portage is crowded, patiently wait on the water for your turn. Load and unload your canoe as quickly as possible, keeping your gear together off to the side and out of the way of any other people. Avoid dragging your canoe across rocks. Not only does it damage the canoe, but the noise can also be heard a great distance away. Move as quickly as possible across portages; don't stop for rest breaks or for lunch. Know who is responsible for each pack, each canoe and each piece of miscellaneous equipment *before* setting foot on the trail. Accountability reduces the possibility of leaving something behind.

Wildlife Precautions

While traveling throughout the BWCA, always treat the wildlife with respect. Remember, you are a visitor in the wilderness but the wildlife are residents. You can help the wildlife stay wild and healthy by not feeding the creatures and not interfering with their normal routines. Where campsites are kept clean and food packs are suspended between trees properly, bears are generally not a problem. Nor are the smaller pests that might otherwise depend on humans for their sustenance (i.e., chipmunks, mice and their cousins). Seeing a bear on a canoe trip should be a treat, not a tragedy. (See BEARS above.)

If you are fortunate enough to see loons on your wilderness trip, keep your distance. Don't chase them down the lake or holler to them. Should you find yourself near any nesting birds (loons, bald eagles, herons, gulls, etc.), observe the nesting area from a distance. Human disturbance at a nest site may lead to nest abandonment and loss of eggs.

Moose, deer, beavers, otters, mink, owls, hawks and ospreys are just a few of the many kinds of animals that may be seen by peaceful paddlers. The more quietly a group travels, the greater its chances of seeing wildlife.

Dogs: Though dogs are not banned from the wilderness, they are better off left home. Many dogs become real barkers, even if they never bark at home. Other visitors don't want to listen to barking all night long. Other dogs may charge wild animals, including bears. If you choose to bring your dog, it must be kept on a leash at landings and on portages.

Camping

Plan to make camp early enough in the day to assure finding an available campsite. Consider sites that are off the main travel routes and in back bays. They are used less often and offer a better opportunity for privacy.

Most wilderness visitors are there for solitude... quiet... to seek respite from the hustle and bustle of day-to-day urban living. Each person wants the sensation of being the first and only person in an area. Loud shouting, singing and dogs barking from across the lake are not appreciated.

Tent pads are provided at each developed campsite. Trenching and cutting pine boughs for "mattresses" (once accepted practices) are not only *not* necessary; they are illegal in the BWCA, because of the environmental harm they inflict. If your tent is bright-colored, set it up as far from the shore as possible, so that it cannot be seen by other campers across the lake.

Remember that noise travels a great distance across water. Keep group noise to a minimum, and you'll improve the quality of the wilderness experience for yourself and for others. You will also greatly improve your chance of seeing wildlife.

Dead, downed wood for campfires is abundant in the BWCA—though not always at the campsites. The best place to look is back from the shore, away from campsites. Usually the driest wood is found on fallen trees that are leaning against other windfalls, and not lying directly on the ground. The best wood for campfires comes from dead, dry jack pine, white pine, spruce, tamarack, white cedar, aspen and ash. Paper birch is excellent firewood when cut green, split and dried, but it is usually very poor when found lying on the ground, because it rots quickly. Red pine and balsam fir are also poor fire-woods. DO NOT CUT LIVE TREES! Green wood from any tree burns very poorly, if at all. Damage to live trees (cutting, carving or peeling bark) is not only unsightly: it also causes irreparable damage to the forest and it's illegal. Carry some fire ribbon or other starting material to ignite fires in wet weather.

Before heading for the lake to wash dishes, remember: you will get the water for tomorrow morning's coffee from the same place. Soapy water should *never* end up in the lake. Take your dishes and hot water back away from the lake to wash them. Rinse them well and dump all the water at least 150 feet from the lake to avoid polluting it. Likewise, when you feel the urge to wash yourself, jump in the lake to get wet, then soap up and rinse off at least 150 feet from the shore.

Burn all left-over food in a HOT fire. If you must bury leftovers or fish entrails, paddle along the shore away from campsites, go into the woods at least 150 feet from the water and bury it in six to eight inches of soil. *Do not use the latrine as a garbage can,* since bears will tear the toilet box out to get at leftovers.

Put your fire *dead* out anytime you leave it unattended—even if you just go fishing for a while. Pour water over the fire while stirring the ashes. Then, if you feel any warmth in the ashes with your bare hand, douse the ashes again.

Leave No Trace

The general rule for disposal of litter and leftovers is *eat it, burn it* or *pack it out.* When leaving a campsite, leave no trace of your presence there. After a fire is dead out, sift through the ashes for twist ties, foil and other debris not completely burned. Pack them in your litter bag, along with any cigarette filters or other trash, and carry them out. Add to that any litter found on portages and at canoe landings. Always leave an area cleaner than you found it. Fortunately, that isn't hard to do.

A TRUE WILDERNESS?

There are those purists who would not classify the BWCA as a true wilderness. In one sense, they are right. Regulations dictate that you must camp only in Forest Service campsites, which are equipped with stationary fire grates and box latrines. There are obvious signs all around you that other people have camped at the very same spot many, many times before.

There are also those who declare that you must paddle for weeks before you can truly feel a sensation of "wilderness." Regarding the BWCA, I must disagree. Seldom are more than one or two long portages necessary for the BWCA visitor to perceive the true wilderness around him. The disquieting drone of motors fades into the past, and one enters a new world of only natural sensations. Depending on your point of entry, it could take a day, or maybe two, to find your wilderness. On the other hand, it may be waiting only minutes from your launching site, scarcely more than a stone's throw away from the road's end. Wherever you start, a magnificent wilderness is not far away in the BWCA.

Wilderness involves emotions. A wilderness experience is an emotional experience. If a person cannot sense deep emotion while camped on the shores of some placid wilderness lake, hearing the cry of a loon, he will never understand the pleas of those who would save the Boundary Waters Canoe Area.

—Charles Ericksen

Ch. 2:
How to Use This Guide

This book is an accumulation of *suggestions*. It does not give all possible routes into the BWCA. Quite the contrary, the routes that you could take are virtually infinite in number. Furthermore, you may wish to follow only a part of one route, or you may wish to combine two or more routes. Most of the routes suggested are "round trip"—they begin and end at (or within walking distance of) the same location. There is no need for car shuttles between two points.

Any group entering the Boundary Waters must have in its possession a travel permit, granting permission to enter through one of the 83 designated entry points. Since this guide treats only the western half of the Boundary Waters, and since not all entry points are well suited for canoeists, only 28 entry points are discussed in this book:

1	Trout Lake	25	Moose Lake
4	Crab Lake	26	Wood Lake
6	Slim Lake	27	Snowbank Lake
7	Big Lake	30	Lake One
8	Moose River (South)	31	Farm Lake
9	Sioux River (South)	32	South Kawishiwi River
12	Little Vermilion Lake	33	Little Gabbro Lake
14	Sioux River (North)	34	Island River
16	Moose River (North)	35	Isabella Lake
19	Stuart River	36	Hog Creek
20	Angleworm Lake	37	Kawishiwi Lake
21	Mudro Lake	75	North Kelly Road
22	Range Lake	77	South Hegman Lake
24	Fall Lake	84	Snake River

Twenty other entry points exist in the western half of the Boundary Waters, but they are not included in this guide for the following reasons.

Some are used mostly by hikers.

3 Pine Lake Trail	15 Sioux Hustler Trail
10 Norway Trail	74 Snowbank Trail
18 Stuart Lake Trail	76 Big Moose Lake Trail
13 Herriman Lake Trails	85 Angleworm Trail
	86 & 87 Pow Wow Trails

Some are redundant, serving parts of the Boundary Waters that are better served by other entry points that *are* included in this guide.

2 Phantom Lake (served by Crab Lake)
5 Cummings Lake (Crab Lake)
11 Blandin Road (Moose River)
17 Portage River (Moose River)
29 North Kawishiwi River (South Kawishiwi River)
63 Four Mile Portage (Fall Lake)

One leads nowhere, and is not suitable for inclusion in a canoe trip guidebook:

67 Bog Lake

Some are from Canada.

71 From Canada into lakes east of Basswood Lake
72 From Canada into Basswood Lake
73 From Canada into lakes west of Basswood Lake

The routes included in this guide are grouped according to accessibility: 1) those accessible from the Echo Trail, 2) those accessible from the Fernberg Road, and 3) those accessible from State Highway 1.

Using statistical data and personal observations, each entry point is briefly discussed. Statistics given pertain to the Summer of 1986, the most current data available when this book was revised.

1) **Permits:** The estimated number of overnight travel permits issued to groups using the entry point in 1986, using all modes of transportation.

2) **Popularity Rank:** The relative popularity of the entry point, compared with all other entry points (77 categories in 1986).

3) **Daily Quota:** The maximum number of overnight travel permits that can be issued each day to groups using the entry point.

Further discussion includes the entry point's location (airline distance from Ely), how to get there, public campgrounds nearby, amount of motorized use through the entry point, and other comments of interest to canoeists.

Following the discussion of an entry point are the suggested routes that use that entry point. Introductory remarks tell you: 1) how many days to allow; 2) the approximate number of miles; 3) the number of different lakes, rivers and creeks to be encountered, as well as the number of portages en route; 4) the difficulty (easy, challenging or rugged), based largely on the frequency, length and difficulty of portages; 5) Fisher maps that cover the route; 6) the travel zones through which the route passes; and 7) general comments, including fishing opportunities. Then each route is broken down into suggested days, giving the sequence of lakes, streams and portages, followed by points of special interest.

Example: DAY 2: **Little Trout Lake,** p. (portage) 376 rods, **Little Indian Sioux River,** p. 40 rods, **river,** p. 35 rods, **river,** p. 20 rods, **river,** p. 120 rods, **Otter Lake,** p. 5 rods, **Cummings Lake.**

Explanation: On the hypothetical second day of this route, you will paddle across Little Trout Lake, and portage 376 rods to the Little Indian Sioux River. You will follow the river to Otter Lake, negotiating four portages along the way. Finally, you will portage 5 rods from Otter Lake to Cummings Lake and make camp there at one of the campsites marked by a red dot on the Fisher map.

A word about travel zones: In the introduction to each canoe route are listed the numbers of the travel zones through which that route passes. In order to acquire statistical data about the travel patterns of canoeists, the Forest Service designated 49 zones in the BWCA. For several years, information was compiled at year's end to statistically summarize the visitation patterns of the previous summer. This has been condensed into Appendix II at the end of this book. It offers you a quick "look" at the regions through which your canoe route will pass. This information, combined with that found in Appendix III (Travel Permit Data) will give you a fairly good idea of just how "busy" your proposed route is. And that might be a factor in determining whether the route is suitable for you.

A word about the use of rods: One rod equals 16½ feet. Since this is roughly the length of most canoes, it is the unit of linear measurement used in canoe country. The Forest Service has posted wood signs indicating the number of rods at the beginnings of most portage trails in the BWCA, and the Fisher maps also use this unit of measurement. Although the F-Series maps are topographic, the indicated number of rods tells little about the difficulty of the portages to be encountered. Long ones may be quite easy, and short ones may be extremely tough. This guide will warn you about the tough ones.

Of course, any route may be made more difficult by completing it in fewer days than recommended, or made easier by adding days. If you plan to do a great deal of fishing, you should probably add at least one day for each three days suggested. For longer trips, you may also want to add layover days to your schedule, in the event that wind, foul weather, sickness or injury should slow you down. (Always carry an extra day's supply of food too, for just that reason.

MAPS

It would be nearly impossible to show detailed maps on the pages of this book. Instead, you will find a foldout map of the entire western region inside the back cover. When taking your trip, however, I recommend the waterproof-parchment maps published by the W. A. Fisher Company. The new "F Series" of maps combine to cover all the Boundary Waters Canoe Area and Canada's Quetico Provincial Park. Campsites are updated annually on these maps, which are designed specifically for the canoeist and the fisherman. The campsites are indicated by red dots on the maps.

The discussion of each route tells you which maps cover it. You can order them from:

W. A. Fisher Company
Box 1107
Virginia, MN 55792-1107

They cost $2.50 each, plus sales tax for Minnesota residents and a shipping charge. Or you can buy your maps from any one of many canoe-trip outfitters when you arrive in northern Minnesota. They are also available at many camping stores in the Twin Cities area, as well as in some other upper-Midwestern cities.

OBTAINING TRAVEL PERMITS

Any overnight visitor in the BWCA Wilderness between May 1 and September 30 must have a BWCA travel permit in possession. It allows a party of up to 10 people to enter the wilderness only on the date and through the entry point specified on the permit. Once in the wilderness, a party is free to travel where it desires, as long as motor-use restrictions are not violated. The permit is free. It may be picked up as early as 48 hours ahead of the scheduled trip at any Superior National Forest office or cooperating business (outfitter, resort, camp, etc.). Permits are also required for daytime visitors using motors (except at the Little Vermilion Lake entry point). However, permits are *no* longer necessary for *non*motorized *day* users in the BWCA.

Entry quotas have been established for overnight campers in order to reduce competition for the limited number of established campsites and to avoid unauthorized camping on undeveloped sites. The daily limits (which range from only one to as many as 35) are based on the number of campsites on the routes served by each entry point. The quotas do not apply to day users, for which there is no limit established, except for motorists. The quotas are in effect only during the five-month period when permits are required. There are no limits on the number of overnight permits issued after September 30 and before May 1.

Reservations

All overnight travel permits are available through advance reservations, for a nonrefundable fee of $5 per reservation. You do not *have* to make a reservation before arriving at the BWCA, but it is advisable, since quotas at some entry points fill up early. There is no charge for the permit—only for the reservation. A reservation simply assures that a permit to enter the wilderness on a specific day and at a certain entry point will be available.

Beginning on each February 1, reservations may be made for the following summer. Reservations may be made *only* at the central reservation office of the Superior National Forest in Duluth. Mail your requests to:

BWCA Reservations
Superior National Forest
P.O. Box 338
Duluth, MN 55801
Or phone: (218) 720-5440

Phone reservations will be accepted only with the use of a valid VISA or MasterCard during normal business hours. Prior to mid-May and after mid-September, the office is open from 8:00 a.m. to 4:30 p.m. weekdays. During the summer season, reservations will be taken from 7:00 a.m. to 6:00 p.m. daily. Reservation requests must include the following: 1) the name, address and phone number of the party leader, 2) the desired entry point, 3) the desired entry date, 4) the planned exit point, 5) the planned exit date, 6) the party size, 7) the name of at least one other group member, 8) the method of travel (paddle canoe, motorboat, hiking, etc.) and 9) payment (check, money order or charge-card number with expiration date). Alternate starting dates and entry points may also be listed on the application in case the first choices are not available.

Travel permits will be mailed to people who make their reservations at least one week before their departure dates. Reservations made within the last seven days will be processed, but no confirmation will be sent to the applicant, and these permits will have to be picked up at any Forest Service office or cooperating business. A permit may be obtained only by the party leader or the alternate whose name appears on the application. Identification is required, and periodic checks may take place in the wilderness.

Information

The Forest Service personnel at the reservation office are available *only* for reservations. For *information* about the BWCA contact one of the Forest Service offices listed below. They can answer your questions, but cannot process reservations. Normal business hours are from 8:00 a.m. to 4:30 p.m. weekdays before May 10 and after Labor Day. During the summer, these offices are open daily from 7:00 a.m. to 5:00 p.m.

Entry Points	Closest Ranger Station & Address	Telephone #
1,9,12,14,16	La Croix Ranger Station Box 1085 Cook, MN 55723	(218) 666-5251
4–33,77	Kawishiwi Ranger Station 118 S. 4th Ave. E. Ely, MN 55731	(218) 365-6126
34,35,75,84	Isabella Ranger Station 2759 Highway 1 Isabella, MN 55607	(218) 323-7722
36–37	Tofte Ranger Station Tofte, MN 55615	(218) 663-7280

If you have not secured a permit in advance of your trip, you may pick it up at any ranger station or cooperating business. It is advisable, however, to drop by one that is closest to your entry point, because the people there are likely to be more familiar with your proposed route. They can alert you to high water or low water conditions, bear problems, suitable campsites, road conditions and other particulars.

HEAVY USE PERIODS

When planning your trip, you may increase your chance of obtaining a BWCA permit by considering the following guidelines.

1. The busiest days for entry are Saturday, Sunday and Monday. You will have a better chance on one of the other four days of the week.
2. Memorial Day weekend, Independence Day weekend, Labor Day weekend and the first three weeks of August are the busiest times.
3. Consider using an entry point that has, in the past, ranked low in popularity. A majority of visitors use a very small minority of the entry points.

RULES AND REGULATIONS

The following regulations apply to all users of the BWCA.

1. Travel permits must be obtained before entering the BWCA and must be in your possession while in the BWCA.
2. Party size is limited to 10 people. No more than 10 may use a campsite at one time.
3. Camping is permitted only at Forest Service campsites that have steel fire grates and box latrines, or within certain designated "remote areas."
4. Open campfires are permitted only within constructed fireplaces at developed campsites, or as specifically approved on the BWCA permit.
5. Nonburnable, disposable food and beverage containers are not permitted. Containers of fuel, insect repellent, medicines, personal toiletry articles, and other items which are not foods or beverages are permitted.
6. Camping is limited to a maximum of 14 consecutive days at one campsite.
7. Fires must be drowned with water and be dead out before a campsite may be vacated.
8. It is unlawful to cut live trees, shrubs or boughs.
9. Motorized travel and mechanical portaging are permitted only on certain specified routes.
10. No watercraft, motor, mechanical device or equipment not used in connection with the current visit may be stored on or moored to National Forest land and left unattended.

11. No motorized or mechanical equipment of any type is permitted within the BWCA, except as specified above.
12. Trenching is not permitted. It disturbs soil and causes erosion.
13. The use of firearms is discouraged.
14. The use of moss or boughs for a bed is not allowed.
15. Use cord instead of nail and wire.
16. Airplanes must maintain an altitude of 4000 feet above sea level.
17. All state and local laws and regulations must be obeyed.
18. Demonstrate common courtesies. Leave clean campsites for those who follow. Preserve and respect the solitude of the BWCA. Sound carries far across open water—especially on a quiet evening.
19. Use wilderness latrines. If no latrine is available, bury human waste at least 100 feet from shore.
20. Keep soaps, dishwater and grease away from lakes and streams. Use biodegradable soap instead of detergents.
21. Use the bottom of a canoe for a table, rather than constructing one from native materials.
22. Since 1985, the use of metal detectors in the BWCA is allowed *only* when there is specific authorization by the Forest Service. Unauthorized use is strictly forbidden.
23. Camping is restricted to *one night only* on the following lakes: Moose, Newfound, Sucker, Birch, Carp, Knife (to Thunder Point) and Ogishkemuncie.

A FINAL WORD

Believe it or not, these age-old routes *do change*. In fact, they may change several times each year. A rock-strewn rapids that requires a portage in mid-August may be a navigable channel three weeks later, after the autumn rains. A portage indicated as 15 rods on the map may turn out to be 35 rods in reality, when the water level is so low that you must walk an extra 20 rods before the water is deep enough to set your canoe down. When a portage becomes too eroded from over-use, the Forest Service sometimes constructs a new one, which is usually longer than the original. And occasionally an author's memory and notes fail him and a mistake is made. So if you have any comments, suggestions or corrections to make pertaining to this guide, please write the author (in care of the publisher). Thank you.

Ch. 3:
Provisions of the BWCA Wilderness Act

In the fall of 1978 Congress enacted legislation that drastically altered the regulations governing the BWCA. The Boundary Waters wilderness does not *appear* any different now than it did before 1979, but it may *sound* different in places.

Before January 1, 1979, the Boundary Waters was administered in accordance with the 1964 Wilderness Act. Logging was allowed within the Wilderness and motorboats were permitted on 60% of the water surface area.

The BWCA Wilderness Act of 1978 added 20 small additions totalling 45,000 acres to the existing BWCA, and it established the current boundaries to include 1,075,000 acres of wilderness. It also prohibited logging anywhere in the BWCA, closed most of the interior motor routes, and restricted motorboats to 33% of the water surface area (24% after 1999)—mostly perimeter lakes served directly by access roads. Some of those lakes will remain open to motorized use indefinitely; others will be phased out by 1999. A few have no horsepower limits, but most are limited to either 10 or 25 horsepower.

The 1978 BWCA Wilderness Act also includes the following provisions.

1. Additions to the BWCA protect portions of following areas: Sioux R., Oriniack L., Moose R., Portage R., Stuart R., Baldpate L., Hegman Lks., Little Bass L., Big Moose L., Duck

L., Bear Crk., Fourtown L.-Range R. area, Wood L., Parent L., Delta L., L. One, N. Kawishiwi R., South Kawishiwi R., L. Isabella, Hog Crk., Kinogami L., East Pipe L., Juno L., Brule L., Eagle Mt. Trail, Bower Trout L., Ram L., Brant L., South L., Duncan L., Daniels L., Caribou L., Deer L., Pine L., Stump L., East Pike L., John L., Royal R., Moose L.

2. Mining is restricted and the Secretary of Agriculture has the authority to acquire mineral rights in the wilderness and along three road corridors in a 222,000-acre Mining Protection Area. No other federal land controls are involved in the MPA.

3. Motorboats are prohibited in the wilderness except on the following lakes and rivers:

   a. No horsepower limits, indefinite use: Little Vermilion L., Loon R., Loon L., SW end of Lac LaCroix to Wilkins Bay. (Loon Falls and Beatty Portage trams will remain.)

   b. 25 h.p. limit, indefinite use: Trout, Fall, Moose, Newfound, Sucker, Newton, Basswood (except portion NW of Washington Is. and N. of Jackfish Bay to the Basswood R.), South Farm, Saganaga (except W. of American Pt.), E. Bearskin, Snowbank.

   c. 10 h.p. limit, indefinite use: Sea Gull E. of Threemile Is., Clearwater, N. Fowl, S. Fowl, Island R., Alder, Canoe.

   d. 10 h.p. limit until 1999: Sea Gull W. of Threemile Is.

4. There are no horsepower limits on portions of lakes outside the Wilderness. (parts of Fall, Moose, Snowbank, Sea Gull, Clearwater, E. Bearskin, etc.)

5. Some major routes previously open to motorboats were closed in 1979: Lac LaCroix from Snow Bay to Iron L., Sioux R., Moose R., Big Moose L., Oriniack and Pine Lks., Hegman Lks., Fourtown-Range R. area, Wood L., N. Kawishiwi R., Ensign-Vera chain, L. One-Four-Insular-Alice-Thomas-Ima-Disappointment chain, S. Kawishiwi R., Gabbro-Bald Eagle Lks., Parent and Perent Lks., Sawbill-Cherokee-Kelly-Peterson-Burnt-Smoke chain, Cone-Winchell-Gaskin-Horseshoe-Caribou chain, Tuscarora L., Alpine-Red Rock Lks., Cypress-Swamp-Cache Bay, Pine R.-Granite R.-Maraboef L. chain, South-Rose-Mountain-Moose chain, Duncan L., Daniels L., Caribou-Moon-Deer Lks., Pine L., E. Pike-John-Royal R. chain. In 1984 the following lakes and

rivers were also closed to motorboats: Basswood River, Crooked Lake, Carp Lake, Knife River, Knife Lake, Birch Lake, and the part of Basswood Lake north of Jackfish Bay and Washington Island.

In 1986 Brule Lake was added to the list.

6. There will be quotas on how many motorboats will be allowed on each lake, including day use (average of 1976, '77, '78 use). Resorts, cabin owners and their guests are exempt on their lakes. Overnight camping by motorboat is allowed.

7. Towboats in excess of 25 h.p. may not be used in the BWCA after January 1, 1984.

8. Snowmobiles are prohibited in the wilderness except for: Permanent use of the Crane L.-Little Vermilion winter portage to Canada, and the Saganaga winter route to Canada (access to homes).

9. The Secretary of Agriculture is allowed to permit grooming by snowmobile of a limited number of cross-country ski trails near existing resorts.

10. Resorts will be protected through assistance programs, expanded recreational facilities outside BWCA, new hiking trails near resorts and voluntary sale. A voluntary sale program applies to the following lakes only: Fall, Moose, Snowbank, L. One, Ojibway, Jasper, Sawbill, E. Bearskin, Clearwater, Saganaga, Sea Gull, McFarland, North Fowl, South Fowl. Owners of resorts on lands riparian to any of these lakes may require the Federal Government to purchase their resort.

11. After a resort has been sold under these conditions on a given lake, other property owners on that lake who wish to sell must first offer their property to the government (they may, however, sell or give their property to family members).

12. Old and deteriorating dams within the Wilderness may be maintained only to protect Wilderness values or public safety.

13. The government is given authority to enforce the motorboat and snowmobile regulations of the act on state water. No other federal jurisdiction over state waters is asserted. The state is allowed to impose more stringent regulations.

Ch. 4:
Entry from the Echo Trail

The Far Western Area

The western region of the Boundary Waters Canoe Area contains most of the entry points included in this guide. Thirteen entry points are easily accessible from the Echo Trail. Another entry point (#1-Trout Lake) is most easily accessible from State Highway 1–169, but because of its proximity to the other entry points in the western region, it fits much better in this category than with the other entry points accessible from State Highway 1, which are southeast of Ely.

Ely is the largest of the small northern Minnesota towns that serve visiting canoeists in the BWCA's Western Region. Originally the commercial center for iron mining and logging operations, Ely has evolved gradually—sometimes reluctantly—into the Canoe Capital of America. It's a modern, bustling community with supermarkets, motels, restaurants, bars, laundromats, service stations, and surely, the most canoe-trip outfitters per capita of any town in the world. Until recently, headquarters for visiting canoeists was the Voyageur Visitor Center on the eastern outskirts of town. That was closed for renovations in 1986 and will remain closed until it is incorporated with the International Wolf Center in a new multimillion dollar complex at the same location.

Meanwhile, the U.S. Forest Service and the Ely Chamber of Commerce are sharing a log cabin at the intersection of Highways 1 and 169 in Ely. This attractive building is now the place to go for up-to-date tourist information about Ely and surrounding Superior National Forest, including Western Region canoe routes. Even if you've been on a particular route before and intend to follow it again, it's always a good idea to stop in for the latest information about water levels, pesky bears, campsite closings, new regulations and the like.

The Echo Trail is a winding, hilly, scenic drive that most people find delightful, if they don't have to drive it every day. To get to it from the Chamber of Commerce building, drive 1 mile east on State Highway 169 to its junction with County Road 88. Turn left here and follow this good highway for 2½ miles to its junction with County Road 116, which is commonly called the Echo Trail.

The Echo Trail winds its way north and west for about 50 miles to County Road 24, near Echo Lake and south of Little Vermilion Lake (#12), the westernmost entry point for the Boundary Waters. The road surface is blacktop for the first 10 miles, but it is gravel the rest of the way. It does straighten out, however, near the Moose River entry point, and from there on it is not a bad gravel road. Most of the "trail" is treacherous, though, so drive with care.

Entry Point 1—Trout Lake

Permits: 736

Popularity Rank: 9

Daily Quota: 14 (3 beyond Trout Lake)

Location: Trout Lake is accessible from Lake Vermilion, about 15 airline miles due west of Ely. From Ely follow State Highway 1-169 west for 26 miles to the junction of 1-169 and County Road 77, about 4½ miles west of Tower, Minnesota. Turn right on County Road 77 and follow this black-topped road northwest for 11.8 miles to the public landing on Moccasin Point. After 10 miles, at the "Y" intersection of the Arrowhead Point and Moccasin Point roads, veer left and continue for the final 1.8 miles to the public access. There you'll find a large private parking lot operated by Moccasin Point Resort, with gasoline pumps, telephone booth, snack bar and store. If you haven't secured your BWCA permit in advance, it may be picked up at the resort.

Description: Public campgrounds on or near Lake Vermilion's south shore are located at Tower-Soudan State Park, McKinley Park and Tower Park. Any of these will provide you with a convenient place to spend the night prior to the canoe trip. All are less than twenty miles from the public access on Vermilion. Camping fees are charged at all of them.

Vermilion is a very popular lake, dotted with private cabins and resorts. It is particularly attractive to aquatic motorists, many of whom travel into Trout Lake, where there is a 25-horsepower limit on motor size. Of all entry points into the BWCA, Trout Lake boasts the highest percentage of motor boats and the lowest percentage of paddlers. Of the 736 overnight permits issued in 1986, only 88 went to paddlers—a mere 12% of the total. Since motorboats are restricted to Trout Lake, and since Trout is the 9th busiest entry point in the BWCA, this all means that you may find some congestion, mostly in the form of motorboats, on Trout Lake.

Nevertheless, it also means that very few permits are issued to groups that can penetrate the lakes and rivers beyond Trout Lake. The conclusion: you can quickly pass through one of the busiest and noisiest lakes in the Boundary Waters and into one of the least traveled and most pristine areas within the BWCA, offering as much solitude and bountiful wildlife as you should ever hope to encounter. If you can tolerate the first and last days, you will surely find a wilderness trip from this entry point to be outstanding.

Route #1: The Pine Creek Loop

3 Days, 22 Miles, 3 Lakes, 1 Creek, 4 Portages
Difficulty: Easy
Fisher Maps: F-1, F-8
Travel Zone: 8

Introduction: This little loop will give you an excellent taste of what the Boundary Waters is all about. Large lakes where motorboats are permitted quickly lead to a more isolated region restricted to paddlers—an area that receives relatively few human visitors and is home to much wildlife. From the boat landing on Vermilion, the route first leads northeast to Trout Lake, then follows tiny Pine Creek to Pine Lake, and finally returns to the south end of Trout Lake and backtracks to Vermilion. Longtime favorite of anglers, Trout Lake contains lake trout, walleyes and smallmouth bass, while Pine Lake is a good source of walleyes and northern pike. Stretching the loop over three full days should allow plenty of time to fish.

Experienced canoeists with little interest in fishing could easily complete the loop in two days. Avid anglers and explorers, however, may want to add a fourth day to allow time to ply the waters of the more remote lakes just east of the loop.

DAY 1: **Lake Vermilion,** p. 60 rods, **Trout Lake.** Unless wind is a problem across the vast expanses of Vermilion and Trout lakes, this will be a very easy beginning to this 3-day outing. The only portage of the day climbs over a low hill, with one canoe rest near the midpoint. Along the route you'll see many private cabins and (probably) numerous motorboats. Most of the motor use on Trout Lake, however, is "day use" only.

There are many fine campsites on Trout Lake. One of the loveliest is at Norway Point, about two-thirds of the way up the east shoreline, 8 miles from your origin.

DAY 2: **Trout Lake,** p. 40–65 rods, **Pine Creek, Pine Lake.** When the water level in Pine Creek is high enough, you may paddle 25 rods from Trout Lake into the mouth of the creek, necessitating a portage of only 40 rods. And unless the beavers are active, there may be no other obstructions along the course of the creek. When the water level is low, however, the portage must begin at the sandy shore of Trout Lake, requiring a 65-rod carry. It's an easy carry, regardless of the length. Less than a mile up the creek, you may have to lift your canoe across a shallow, boulder-strewn section. You may also "bottom out" at the source of the creek, near Pine Lake. Of course, beavers may entirely alter the character of Pine Creek at any time. Expect the unexpected!

You'll find a scenic overlook at the summit of a high rock slope adjacent to the Chad Lake portage trail. A short climb there reaches a panoramic view across Pine Creek valley. In mid-July you might also find a wealth of blueberries.

There are several good campsites (9 total) on Pine Lake. The best are in the northwest part of the lake; the most private are in the southeast end. A couple of small sand beaches along the eastern shoreline will, no doubt, be enticing to the swimmers in your group.

Be alert for wildlife. In July 1987 my party witnessed three deer, one moose, two mink, several great blue herons, two loons and a soaring bald eagle. And that was on the "busy" 4th of July weekend!

DAY 3: **Pine Lake,** p. 260 rods, **Trout Lake,** p. 60 rods, **Vermilion Lake.** The 260-rod portage is not a particularly tough one, but the length makes it a challenge to inexperienced trippers. Five canoe rests may help. After negotiating the second portage, you may want to reward your efforts by soaking your body in the gentle, scenic rapids that separate Trout and Vermilion lakes.

Route #2: The Cummings Lake Loop

4 Days, 47 Miles, 14 Lakes, 1 River, 4 Creeks, 22 Portages
Difficulty: Rugged
Fisher Maps: F-1, F-8, F-9
Travel Zones: 8, 11, 9, 10

Introduction: This route will take you from Lake Vermilion north through Trout and Little Trout lakes to the lengthy portage into the Little Indian Sioux River. You will paddle east up this tiny, winding stream, through marshy terrain teeming with wildlife, to its headwaters from Otter and Cummings lakes. From the east end of Cummings Lake, you will turn south and then west, navigating the tiny lakes and streams that will return you to the busy motor route from which you began.

Your first and last days will probably be shared with many others, but solitude will be yours to cherish in the remote eastern portion of this interesting loop. Moose and deer are plentiful along the Little Indian Sioux River, and fishing is good in many of the lakes along the route. Try for bass in Otter, Cummings, Chad and Trout lakes. Or catch a walleye breakfast in Pine, Buck, Little Trout or Trout Lake. Northern pike are found in nearly all the lakes on this route. And, by all means, don't forget the NAME of your entry point; there are lake trout to be found in the depths of Trout Lake.

DAY 1: **Lake Vermilion,** p. 60 rods, **Trout Lake, Little Trout Creek, Little Trout Lake.** Your first day won't be too exciting, unless you are run over by a motorboat, or unless a strong northwest wind makes crossing Trout Lake very difficult or impossible. (If the latter is the case, I suggest you reverse this route and portage 260 rods into Pine Lake. You will bypass the main portion of Trout Lake, and a west wind will be no problem until you reach Cummings Lake and begin your journey back to Trout Lake.) Even if you arrive at Little Trout Lake early in the day, I suggest you stop there and make camp. There are no designated USFS campsites on the Little Indian Sioux River, and very few places that could even be MADE into campsites.

DAY 2: **Little Trout Lake,** p. 376 rods, **Little Indian Sioux River,** p. 40 rods, **river,** p. 35 rods, **river,** p. 20 rods, **river,** p. 30 rods, **river,** p. 40 rods, **river,** p. 20 rods, **river,** p. 28 rods, **river,** p. 120 rods, **Otter Lake,** p. 5 rods, **Cummings Lake.** You will find this day to be a sharp contrast from the prior day of paddling on big lakes. With seven short portages scattered along the meandering Sioux River, travel is deceivingly slow. Relax and enjoy the bountiful wildlife and absence of other canoes along its course. I once witnessed six deer and a cow moose leisurely drinking from the river's swampy bank. Who knows how many other creatures watched US paddle silently through this winding wilderness? The 376-rod portage from Little Trout Lake to the river is not well traveled and may be muddy. But there are no major inclines over which to pass. Several nice campsites are near the east end of Cummings Lake.

DAY 3: **Cummings Lake,** p. 35 rods, **Korb Creek, Korb Lake, Korb Creek,** p. 1–3 rods, **Creek, Little Crab Lake, Lunetta Creek, Lunetta Lake,** p. 60 rods, **Lunetta Creek,** p. 100 rods, **Schlamm Lake,** p. 210 rods, **Glenmore Lake,** p. 195 rods, **Western Lake,** p. 80 rods, **Buck Lake,** p. 250 rods, **Chad Lake.** It is primarily because of this day that this route is labeled "rugged." You will be carrying your load across eight portages totalling over 850 rods, four of which are well over half a mile each! None is difficult, however, just long. The 100-rod portage into Schlamm Lake follows an old logging road for about 8 rods. Should you wish to get back to Trout Lake sooner, a good short-cut is possible by portaging 480 rods from Cummings Lake directly into Buck Lake. This trail is virtually flat, and there are sixteen canoe rest along the way. But this will eliminate a scenic series of small lakes and streams between Cummings and Schlamm lakes. Chad is known to contain bluegills, northern pike and largemouth bass; Buck and Western are two of the best walleye lakes in the area, so eat well!

   DAY 4: **Chad Lake,** p. 260 rods, **Pine Creek, Pine Lake,** p. 260 rods, **Trout Lake,** p. 60 rods, **Lake Vermilion.** Your first 260-rod portage gradually ascends 83 feet from the shore of Chad Lake before dropping steeply to Pine Creek. From the top of the steep rock slope adjacent to the end of the portage, you may enjoy a panoramic view across the Pine Creek valley. In mid-July, too, you may find a wealth of blueberries there. In low-water periods, Pine Creek may be quite shallow at its source near Pine Lake. There may also be beaver dams obstructing the course of the creek, necessitating occasional liftovers. The second portage climbs 92 feet above Pine Lake before descending to the shore of Trout Lake. Once again, you will be back on the heavily traveled motor route from whence you came.

Route #3: The Winding River Route

7 Days, 88 Miles, 17 Lakes, 4 Rivers, 2 Creeks, 33 Portages
Difficulty: Rugged
Fisher Maps: F-1, F-8, F-9, F-16
Travel Zones: 8, 11, 3, 6, 5

   Introduction: This strenuous route will take you north from Lake Vermilion through Trout and Little Trout lakes and north down the meandering Little Indian Sioux River, across the Echo Trail to the Pauness lakes. From Lower Pauness you will paddle and portage east through the Shell chain of lakes to Oyster Lake. Then you will turn south and re-enter the unique world of small rivers, as you paddle down the Oyster River and up the Nina-Moose and Moose rivers, across the Echo Trail, to Big Moose Lake. With river travel behind you, you will now work your way (and I mean WORK) through the tranquil lakes and long portages leading back to Trout and Vermilion lakes. Nearly half of your route will be on small, winding rivers. Most of the other half will be on portages, the last five totalling 1,830 rods, or an average of 366 RODS EACH! Nine of your portages will be in excess of 200 rods, the longest nearly two miles. It all adds up to a route that I call RUGGED.

If portaging does not scare you and rivers "turn you on," you will surely find this loop delightful. The portions of the Little Indian Sioux and Moose rivers that lie north of the Echo Trail are rather heavily traveled at times. They are among the 15 most popular entry points for the BWCA. The region between Trout Lake and the Echo trail is used much less than the northern sector, and you will find no one but dedicated wilderness enthusiasts here. The only parts of the route where motors are allowed are at the beginning and end, on Trout and Vermilion lakes.

DAY 1: **Lake Vermilion,** p. 60 rods, **Trout Lake, Little Trout Creek, Little Trout Lake.** If strong westerly winds prohibit navigation across Trout Lake, an alternate route bypasses the main portion of this huge lake: portage 260 rods into Pine Lake, and follow Pine Creek around to the 40-rod portage back into the northeast corner of Trout. This will obviously take longer. Regardless of the time, however, you should go no farther than Little Trout Lake, as there are no designated campsites on the Little Indian Sioux River.

DAY 2: **Little Trout Lake,** p. 376 rods, **Little Indian Sioux River,** p. 20 rods, **river,** p. 120 rods, **river,** p. 8 rods, **river,** p. 120 rods, **river,** p. 60 rods, **river, Upper Pauness Lake.** This will be a long day of paddling down the gradually widening, deepening and straightening channel of the Little Indian Sioux River. Between portages it is virtually impossible to know EXACTLY where you are. Use the portages as landmarks, and alert yourself to the GENERAL direction of travel. Watch out for traffic as you cross the Echo Trail at the 120-rod portage. From that point on, the number of canoes you will see will greatly increase. You will be wise to claim the first campsite you see on Upper Pauness Lake. The 120-rod portage at the Echo Trail is seldom used and may be overgrown and very difficult to follow during the latter part of summer. There are no portage rests, but at the midpoint is a scenic lunch spot next to a cascading rapids.

DAY 3: **Upper Pauness Lake,** p. 8 rods, **Lower Pauness Lake,** p. 216 rods, **Shell Lake,** p. 15 rods, **Little Shell Lake,** p. 4 rods, **Lynx Lake,** p. 280 rods, **Ruby Lake,** p. 10 rods, **Hustler Lake,** p. 240 rods, **Oyster Lake.** When your trip is over, you may look back at this day as one of the roughest. Of the three portages over 200 rods, though, only one is really wicked. The 216-rod trail from Lower Pauness Lake to Shell Lake is merely long, and not too steep. It intersects the Sioux-Hustler Foot Trail. The 280-rod path from Lynx Lake to Ruby Lake, on the other hand, climbs steeply to an elevation 128 feet above Lynx before gradually descending 72 feet to Ruby Lake. And, alas, the trail from Hustler Lake to Oyster Lake is mostly downhill; after gaining 64 feet across a third of the portage, it then descends 141 feet throughout the last half mile to Oyster Lake. Take time at the beginning of this day to paddle to the northwest end of Lower Pauness Lake and hike down into the scenic granite gorge through which Devil's Cascade plunges toward Loon Lake. Unless the water level is extremely low, you can probably avoid the 4-rod portage to Lynx Lake by negotiating the tiny channel connecting it with Little Shell Lake.

All the portages this day will be on good trails, and portage rests are located about every 40 rods.

Hang your food pack high tonight (and tomorrow night on Nina-Moose Lake). Bears are known to be nuisances in this area, where they have prematurely ended many a canoe trip. After the food pack is secured, if you have any energy left this evening, try your luck at catching one of the lake trout, northern pike or smallmouth bass that inhabit Oyster Lake.

DAY 4: **Oyster Lake,** p. 60 rods, **Oyster River,** p. 20 rods, **Oyster River, Nina-Moose River,** p. 96 rods, **river,** p. 70 rods, **river, Nina-Moose Lake.** This day is intended to be short and easy. Nina-Moose is far from being the most scenic lake in the North Woods, but there are no designated USFS campsites beyond it until you reach Big Moose Lake, nine portages and a lot of winding river away. Pick a campsite early, as this is on a heavily used route, and relax while fishing for some of the northern pike, walleye or bass that inhabit this shallow lake. Along the western shoreline, you will see evidence of the 1971 forest fire that scourged nearly 25 square miles of woodland between here and the Little Indian Sioux River.

DAY 5: **Nina-Moose Lake, Moose River,** p. 25 rods, **river,** p. 20 rods, **river,** p. 160 rods, **river,** p. 77 rods, **river,** p. 40 rods, **river,** p. 40 rods, **river,** p. 17 rods, **river,** p. 160 rods, **river,** p. 60 rods, **Big Moose Lake.** The Moose River is another narrow, winding little stream through marshy terrain. Almost choked with vegetation during prime summer months, visibility along your route is frequently hardly more than a few yards in front of the canoe. Travel is slow, as you paddle against the current and meander considerably. Big Moose Lake is most impressive after a full day on this tiny stream. You should have little or no competition for the four campsites here, unless during a busy holiday weekend. Anglers may find northern pike and smallmouth bass nearby.

DAY 6: **Big Moose Lake,** p. 580 rods, **Cummings Lake,** p. 480 rods, **Buck Lake,** p. 250 rods, **Chad Lake.** Your first trek of the day (and longest of the whole trip) crosses several small hills at both ends, but the major portion of the path follows a nearly level ridgetop. Hiking is quite easy, and there are 19 canoe rests along the way. The next 1½-mile portage is even more level, with 16 canoe rests at regular intervals along the path. The third portage will seem like nothing after the first two, although it does gently surmount a 50-foot hill. Notice how the stream between Chad and Buck lakes changes direction midway across the portage.

DAY 7: **Chad Lake,** p. 260 rods, **Pine Creek, Pine Lake,** p. 260 rods, **Trout Lake,** p. 60 rods, **Lake Vermilion.** (See comments for Day 4, Route #2.)

Entry Point 4—Crab Lake

Permits: 286
Popularity Rank: 22
Daily Quota: 6

Location: Crab Lake is accessible from big Burntside Lake, a very popular and populated lake located about 4 miles northwest of Ely. Several public accesses are situated around Burntside, of which two are the most practical for the suggested routes. SOUTH SHORE: From a junction of Highway 1–169 about 3 miles west of Ely, drive north on County Road 88 2½ miles to the public access road (sign pointing to Burntside Lodge). Or, from the southeast end of the Echo Trail, follow County Road 88 5 miles west to the Burntside Lake road. The boat access and parking lot are located just south of Burntside Lodge, about 200 yards north of County Road 88. There is space for about a dozen cars; don't use the lodge's private parking areas. NORTH ARM: Follow the Echo Trail (Co. Rd. 116) north and west from County Road 88 for 9 miles. Turn left onto County Road 644, and follow this winding gravel road southwest for 2⅓ miles to the public access on the left (and the Slim Lake portage on the right). You will find this located just past the entrance to YMCA Camp Widjiwagan.

Description: Camping is prohibited at both accesses. Fenske Lake Campground, located just 3 miles from the North Arm access on the Echo Trail (toward Ely) is a good place to camp the night before departing from the North Arm access. It takes about a 20-minute drive to reach the South Shore access from this campground. A campsite fee is required.

Although Burntside is a lake laden with motor boats, motors are prohibited through the Crab Lake Entry point. Even if they were legal, I doubt that many would enter, as it requires crossing a one-mile portage. The trail ascends about 100 feet and passes through a wet area that has been flooded by beaver dams. It's hard not to get your feet wet.

Not many canoeists enter the BWCA this way, either. Consequently, Crab Lake provides one of the quickest escapes into solitude of any BWCA entry point. Here you can "easily" retreat for a three-day weekend and see few, if any, people beyond Crab Lake itself.

Adventurous souls with extra time who will do almost anything to avoid a 1-mile portage may consider an alternative. Crab Creek also joins Burntside Lake with Crab Lake, but it's not an easy alternative. The mouth of the creek is in another bay of Burntside Lake just north of the portage. Paddling into the mouth, you'll immediately encounter a small obstacle—a small rapids that requires a 1-rod liftover. After nearly a mile of meandering through the narrow, shallow creek, where beaver dams occasionally spring up, you'll encounter a larger rapids. A half mile further upstream is yet another, even longer and more precipitous rapids. There are no maintained portage trails around these two rapids—just the vague paths of other hardy explorers. Above the final rapids the creek may be too dry for navigation during low-water periods. If you like canoeing through regions where few others dare, and you don't mind bushwhacking your way across portages, then you'll surely enjoy the Crab Creek alternative. The one-mile portage, however, is much quicker and actually much easier, in spite of its length.

Route #4: The Buck Lake Loop

3 Days, 34 Miles, 10 Lakes, 2 Creeks, 12 Portages
Difficulty: Rugged
Fisher Maps: F-9, F-8
Travel Zones: 9, 10

Introduction: This interesting little route will take you from the south shore access of Burntside through one of the most populated lakes "serving" the BWCA and into one of the least traveled sections of the Boundary Waters—within a time span of less than a day! You'll head north from beautiful big Burntside, across Crab Lake and west through small lakes and tiny streams to Buck Lake. From Buck you'll portage 1½ miles northeast to Cummings Lake, and then travel the length of this pretty lake to Korb Creek. After a side trip to seldom visited Coxey Pond, you'll return to Crab Lake via swampy Korb Creek, and then portage out of this tranquil scene and back into busy Burntside to the boat landing from which you started.

When finished, you will have carried your canoe and packs across portages totalling 1,931 rods (over 6 miles!) Or, if each portage takes TWO trips to get all of your gear across, that means over 18 miles of walking during this weekend outing! That's why this "interesting route" is called RUGGED. The only people you will see in the interior portion of this route, therefore, are dedicated canoeists: a nice difference from those encountered along the Moose chain of lakes (and others).

Walleye, northern pike, lake trout, bass and bluegill are all found in lakes along this route. Crab and Cummings lakes, in particular, are good spots to try your luck for northerns, bass and bluegill. The experienced angler might find lake trout and smallmouth bass in the depths of Burntside Lake. But those who are hungry for walleye should paddle straight for Buck Lake.

Regardless of your fishing luck, you'll surely find the isolated lakes and streams along this route to be a delightful escape for three days full of healthy exercise.

DAY 1: **Burntside Lake,** p. 320 rods, **Crab Lake,** p. 20 rods, **Little Crab Lake, Lunetta Creek, Lunetta Lake,** p. 60 rods, **Lunetta Creek,** p. 100 rods, **Schlamm Lake,** p. 210 rods, **Glenmore Lake.** You will be portaging over 2 miles this day, so don't begin this route unless you are physically ready. Burntside Lake, with well over 100 picturesque islands, could be confusing to even an experienced map reader. Keep constant count of the islands and bays as you weave through them to the Crab Lake portage. None of the portages is difficult, however—just long. The 100-rod portage into Schlamm Lake follows an old logging road for about 8 rods. Don't be worried if campsites are occupied on Crab Lake. Most weekend traffic either stops here or proceeds on north to Cummings Lake. Nevertheless, remember that campsites are infrequent between Crab and Buck—only one per lake.

DAY 2: **Glenmore Lake,** p. 195 rods, **Western Lake,** p. 80 rods, **Buck Lake,** p. 480 rods, **Cummings Lake.** The westernmost tip of this loop is not shown on Fisher Map 112. So here is what you are missing: After the 195-portage from Glenmore Lake, follow the western shore of Western Lake to the northwest corner, where an 80-rod portage will take you to Buck Lake. Paddle to the right (northeast) on this long, narrow lake, to the 480-rod portage that is shown on Map 112. This portage is long, but nothing to worry about. The trail is virtually flat, and there are 16 canoe rests along the way. There are several nice campsites on the east end of Cummings.

DAY 3: **Cummings Lake,** p. 35 rods, **Korb Creek, Korb Lake, Korb Creek,** p. 1–3 rods, **creek, Little Crab Lake,** p. 20 rods, **Crab Lake,** p. 320 rods, **Burntside Lake.** If the water level is high enough and your time permits, you may enjoy a side trip from Korb Creek to Silica Lake and Coxey Pond. These lakes are probably visited more by hikers than canoeists, as the Cummings Lake Trail passes between them. It is about three miles from that point to the North Arm Road (County Road 644).

Route #5: Canadian Border Route

10 Days, 107 Miles, 29 Lakes, 3 Rivers, 7 Creeks, 48 Portages

Difficulty: Challenging

Fisher Maps: F-9, F-8, F-16, F-17, F-10

Travel Zones: 9, 11, 3, 4, 7, 2, 13, 16, 15

Introduction: This route will lead you from the North Arm of Burntside Lake through Crab and Cummings Lakes to the marshy wilderness of the Little Indian Sioux River. Down this meandering little creek, across the Echo Trail and on north to Loon and Slim Lakes, you will then paddle east through the chain of lakes and creeks paralleling Lac La Croix just to the south of this mammoth lake. From the east end of Lac La Croix, you'll continue east across Iron Lake, around impressive Curtain Falls, through the many bays of Crooked Lake, and up the legendary Basswood River. From beautiful lower Basswood Falls you will point your canoe southwest and forge on up the scenic Horse River to Horse Lake and leave the Boundary Waters via Mudro Lake. You'll end this trip at the Nels Lake landing. Unless you have made prior arrangements to have a vehicle waiting there, you must walk the final four miles back to the North Arm access.

This challenging route will require 10 full, strenuous days for the average group of canoeists, without a layover day. Strong winds, however, could slow travel considerably on portions of Burntside Lake, the Little Indian Sioux River, Lac La

Croix and Crooked Lake. The Little Indian Sioux River offers a fine opportunity to view moose, deer, beaver and other forms of wildlife, as it flows through a region in the BWCA seldom visited by tourists. Early summer is usually the best season in which to make this journey, since the Sioux River could be too dry for navigation later in the summer, especially during a dry year. Furthermore, your last day (Fourtown to Nels) could be more walking than paddling when the interconnecting creeks are too low for loaded canoes.

Although there are numerous portages along the route, few are longer than 100 rods. Most of the route is well traveled, with the exception of the Sioux River south of the Echo Trail, where portage trails may be difficult to see. In addition to the abundant wildlife and generally good fishing, voyagers may also find two fine displays of prehistoric Indian pictographs adorning the sheer granite cliffs of Lac La Croix and the Basswood River. Splendid waterfalls, treacherous rapids, beautiful big lakes and quaint little ones all interconnect to create a fascinating variety of canoeing terrain.

DAY 1: **Burntside Lake,** p. 320 rods, **Crab Lake,** p. 20 rods, **Little Crab Lake, Korb Creek,** p. 1–3 rods, **creek, Korb Lake, Korb Creek,** p. 35 rods, **Cummings Lake.** Caution: Burntside Lake can be confusing to even the experienced guide, so watch carefully for the portage to Crab Lake, in the third bay west of the "narrows" from the North Arm, along the north shore of the lake. Several good campsites can be found near the east end of Cummings Lake. You'll find northern pike, bass and bluegill inhabiting Crab and Cummings lakes, trout and bass in Burntside Lake.

DAY 2: **Cummings Lake,** p. 5 rods, **Otter Lake,** p. 120 rods, **Little Indian Sioux River,** p. 28 rods, **river,** p. 20 rods, **river,** p. 40 rods; **river,** p. 30 rods, **river,** p. 20 rods, **river,** p. 35 rods, **river,** p. 40 rods, **river.** Campsites are few and far between on this swampy, winding little river, so start looking while the sun is still high in the sky. In fact, you will find NO designated USFS campsites unless you portage 376 rods into Little Trout Lake or 200 rods into Bootleg Lake (both portages are not only long but hard to find). The nine short portages and considerable meandering make travel deceivingly slow. Between portages it is virtually impossible to know

EXACTLY where you are. Use the portages as landmarks, and alert yourself to the GENERAL direction of travel. A decent campsite may be found on the river between the beginnings of the portages into Little Trout and Bootleg lakes.

DAY 3: **Little Indian Sioux River,** p. 20 rods, **river,** p. 120 rods, **river,** p. 8 rods, **river,** p. 120 rods, **river,** 60 rods, **river, Upper Pauness Lake.** This will be a long day of paddling, down the gradually widening, deepening and straightening channel of the river. Watch out for traffic as you cross the Echo Trail at the 120-rod portage. The 120-rod portage at the Echo Trail is seldom used and may be overgrown and difficult to follow during the latter part of the summer. There are no portage rests, but a scenic lunch spot next to a cascading rapids marks the midpoint. From that point on, the number of canoes you see will greatly increase. You'll be wise to take the first campsite you see on Upper Pauness Lake.

DAY 4: **Upper Pauness Lake,** p. 8 rods, **Lower Pauness Lake,** p. 160 rods, **Loon Lake, East Loon Bay, Little Loon Lake,** p. 173 rods, **Slim Lake,** p. 52 rods, **creek, Section 3 Pond,** p. 52 rods, **South Lake.** Take time to view the scenic granite gorge through which Devil's Cascade plunges 75 feet from Lower Pauness Lake to Loon Lake. Though mostly downhill, this ½-mile portage does climb to a summit overlooking the Cascade, where you'll find a portage rest and sunny campsite for hikers using the Sioux-Hustler Trail. The other half-mile portage this day is uphill, rising 65 feet from Little Loon Lake to Slim Lake. It's steep in some places, and muddy in others, but five canoe rests along the way make portaging a *little* easier. A nice campsite on South Lake is located on a rocky point just to the left of the muddy landing for the portage from Section Three Pond.

DAY 5: **South Lake,** p. 120 rods, **Steep Lake,** p. 45 rods, **Eugene Lake,** p. 50 rods, **Little Bear Track Lake,** p. 30 rods, **Bear Track Lake,** p. 200 rods, **Thumb Lake,** p. 9 rods, **Finger Lake,** p. 90 rods, **Finger Creek, Pocket Lake.** A good, hearty breakfast is a prerequisite this day, as it begins with a steep, uphill portage that climbs 125 feet to Steep Lake. You'll find it to be much tougher than the 200-rod trail between Bear Track and Thumb lakes, which descends 81 feet on a good path with eight canoe rests. You'll find three good campsites on Pocket Lake, and good fishing for northern pike, walleye and bass.

DAY 6: **Pocket Lake,** p. 20 rods, **Pocket Creek** p. 25 rods, **creek, Lac La Croix.** If you wish, you can probably avoid the 20-rod portage out of Pocket Lake by running, lining or walking the shallow rapids into Pocket Creek. Lac La Croix is the longest and most beautiful of the international lakes bordering the BWCA, dotted with over 200 islands. Pocket Creek will lead you into the most scenic area of the lake, and numerous good campsites are located near the southeast end. This will be your easiest day of the trip, allowing plenty of time to explore the Indian pictographs (rock paintings) and Warrior Hill (see the Fisher map) found on the Canadian shore. Both monuments are reminders of an ancient civilization that once flourished in this aquatic wilderness. Legend says that Ojibway braves used Warrior Hill to test their strength and courage by racing from the lake's edge to the summit of the precipice. You will truly appreciate this feat after climbing it yourself—and the incredible view from the top will make your effort worthwhile!

DAY 7: **Lac La Croix,** p. 80 rods, **Bottle Lake, Iron Lake,** p. 140 rods, **Crooked Lake.** In addition to the beautiful Curtain Falls between Iron and Crooked lakes, you may also wish to see Rebecca Falls, which slice through two narrow gorges on each side of the island on which the portage into McAree Lake lies. The waterfalls are on both sides of the island, and to view Rebecca, you must first land at the portage and then hike on either side of the island to its north end. Because of the precarious location of this portage, caution must be exercised when approaching it. The swift current flows to either side of the island, and, unless your approach is dead-center to the island, your canoe could be drawn down this dangerous falls. If you are here in July, look for blueberries on the island. But *please note:* As soon as you set foot on land you are illegally entering Canada, unless you have received clearance from Canadian authorities to do so, back at the La Croix Ranger Station.

Curtain Falls, on the other hand, will be approached from the bottom. The portage on the US side is not difficult, but steadily uphill. You may put in at the very brink of the falls, or about 100 feet farther into Crooked Lake. The choice is yours, but I prefer the second as the safest one during normal water conditions for a group that may not be strong enough to fight the swift current at the top of the falls. Use your own judgment and be careful!

A beautiful campsite is located on the eastern tip of the large island near the entrance to Saturday Bay. Several good sites are scattered throughout the lake.

DAY 8: **Crooked Lake, Basswood River.** This easy day of paddling will enable you to enjoy the many interesting bays of Crooked Lake and the historic sites along the Basswood River. At least one eagle's nest is located near the east end of Crooked Lake, and it is not unusual to see eagles soaring overhead. Table Rock is a campsite popular among the French-Canadian voyageurs of two hundred years ago. A display of Indian paintings may be seen along the west shore of Basswood River, about a mile downstream from Lower Basswood Falls. Several fine campsites are located near here.

DAY 9: **Basswood River,** p. 32 rods, **Basswood River, Horse River,** p. 70 rods, **river,** p. 50 rods, **river, rapids, river,** p. 50 rods, **river, rapids, river, rapids, Horse Lake,** p. 70 rods, **pond,** p. 10 rods, **Fourtown Lake,** p. 1–3 rods, **Fourtown Lake.** After portaging around Basswood Falls before entering the Horse River, you may enjoy paddling beyond this confluence to scenic Wheelbarrow Falls, about ¾ mile up the Basswood River. While traveling up the Horse River, you will encounter at least three short, shallow rapids up which you will have to pull your canoe. These are located near the source of the river. Horse and Fourtown Lakes are both popular among fishermen. In them you'll find northern pike, walleye and bluegill. Since the BWCA Wilderness Act took effect on January 1, 1979, Fourtown is no longer a motor-designated lake. Nor may sea planes land at its southern end, since *all* of the lake is now in the BWCA. The beautiful campsites found there should now be more appealing to the wilderness canoeist.

DAY 10: **Fourtown Lake,** p. 10 rods, **Fourtown Creek,** p. 110 rods, **pond,** p. 30 rods, **Mudro Lake, Mudro Creek,** p. 30 rods, **Picket Lake,** p. 30 rods, **Picket Creek,** p. 185 rods,

Nels Lake. Beware the creeks connecting these four lakes when the water level is down. They can make life miserable for the voyager with a heavily loaded canoe. When the water level is up, on the other hand, you may be able to eliminate the 30-rod portage between Mudro and Picket by paddling or walking your canoe through this shallow stretch and under the Cloquet Road (Forest Route 457). Watch your step on that last portage: a log bridge crosses a creek midway through the carry, and it is slippery when wet.

Entry Point 6—Slim Lake

Permits: 58
Popularity Rank: 45
Daily Quota: 2

Location: Slim Lake is 8 miles northwest of Ely, 2 miles west of the Echo Trail and a scant ½ mile north of Burntside Lake. To get there, follow the Echo Trail (County Road 116) 9 miles north and west from County Road 88. Turn left onto County Road 644 (North Arm Road) and follow this winding gravel road southwest for 2⅓ miles to the public access of Burntside Lake on the left.

Description: On the right side of the road here, you will see a primitive road leading northwest up a gentle slope into the woods. That one-lane forest road dead-ends about ¼ mile north of County Road 644, where a beaver dam has flooded the road. A small parking area there accommodates 3–4 vehicles. A board walk across the shallow beaver pond marks the beginning of an easy 80-rod portage to the east shore of Slim Lake. It is a wide and easy trail, and it ascends quite gently.

Motors are prohibited through the Slim Lake Entry Point. Although it is close to one of the most popular lakes in the area—Burntside—you will quickly escape into a genuine feeling of wilderness solitude and will experience a high-quality expedition via either of the two routes suggested below.

Camping is prohibited at the access to Slim Lake. But Fenske Lake Campground, located just 3 miles from here, toward Ely on the Echo Trail, provides a good place to spend the night before your trip. It will cost you to camp there.

Route #6: The Big Moose Loop

3 Days, 34 Miles, 12 Lakes, 1 River, 1 Creek, 13 Portages
Difficulty: Rugged
Fisher Map: F-9
Travel Zones: 11, 9

Introduction: This short, rugged journey will take you northwest from the Slim Lake portage, through half a dozen seldom-visited lakes, to the northern edge of this portion of the BWCA at Big Moose Lake. Turning south then, you will cross your longest portage (580 rods) to enter Cummings Lake. Continuing south, you will meander through a series of fascinating little creeks and lakes and exit the Boundary Waters across a mile-long portage into beautiful, big Burntside Lake. Following its northern shoreline, you will soon return to your origin at the Slim Lake portage near the upper end of the North Arm of Burntside.

When finished, you will have spent as much time walking on portage trails as you did paddling on the adjoining scenic lakes. Three portages are in excess of 1½ miles and a fourth is exactly 1 mile. It is largely BECAUSE of these portages, however, that this route is so enticing to the wilderness enthusiast. Only the dedicated canoeist will tackle the route, and it is not unusual to see no other canoeists along that portion of the route contained within the BWCA, where motors are not allowed. You'll feel truly isolated from the rest of the world, even though you will never be more than 5 miles from a road or resort.

Populated Burntside Lake will nearly always be bustling with motorized traffic, and you will witness private cabins, resorts and camps throughout the final 5 miles of your expedition. Were it not for the exceptional beauty of this island-studded lake, the accompanying activity might prove to be a dismal end for an otherwise high-quality wilderness trip.

Fishermen will find northern pike, bass and pan fish along

much of the route, and the persistent angler may even pull lake trout from Burntside.

DAY 1: p. 80 rods, **Slim Lake,** p. 77 rods, **Rice Lake,** p. 130 rods, **Hook Lake,** p. 540 rods, **Big Rice Lake.** Portages total 887 rods this day—that's 2,600 rods of walking if you cannot transport all of your gear in one carry! Don't attempt this route unless you are in the *best* of shape! All portages, except the first, are very lightly traveled. And you may have trouble seeing the pathway during your 540-rod carry to Big Rice Lake. Use the 11 portage rests to guide you! If time permits, I suggest yet another ½ mile of walking (without loads this time). An outstanding panorama can be seen from a high, rocky ridge ¼ mile south of Slim Lake, affectionately named "Old Baldy" by the summer residents of nearby Camp Northland. A blazed trail begins at a Forest Service campsite on the southeast shore of Slim Lake and winds up the thickly wooded hillside. Watch for a spur trail to the left that leads up to the rocky summit. If you miss it and continue walking on the main path, you will eventually find yourself back at County Road 644, near the shore of Burntside's North Arm.

Also if time permits and the season is right, you will find "fields" of blueberries atop the rocky cliffs just north of the Slim Lake end of the portage from Burntside.

DAY 2: **Big Rice Lake,** p. 8 rods, **Portage River, Lapond Lake,** p. 30 rods, **Portage River,** p. 150 rods, **Duck Lake,** p. 480 rods, **Big Moose Lake,** p. 580 rods, **Cummings Lake.** If you thought day 1 was unbearable, you might as well stay on Big Rice Lake another night and then backtrack to your origin, because this day is even tougher: 1,248 rods of portages! The last three portages are *very* seldom used, and windfalls may slow your treks considerably, particularly during spring. The first 25 rods of both the 150- and 480-rod carries are over muskeg. The 150-rod portage was nearly impassable with windfalls during the early summer of 1978. And the lake to which it leads is no treat, with muskeg bordering most of the southern and western shorelines. The 480-rod trail crosses over numerous small hills, but there are 10 portage rests along the way to help out. If you are exhausted by the time you reach Big Moose Lake, rest awhile, but don't give up. The next portage is not as bad as it looks. It begins and ends on a rather hilly note, but follows a rather level ridgetop along most of its course. There are 19 canoe rests along the way.

Several good campsites can be found at the east end of Cummings Lake, including one very large, beautiful site on the east shore, near the Cummings Lake Trail.

DAY 3: **Cummings Lake,** p. 35 rods, **Korb Creek, Korb Lake, Korb Creek,** p. 1–3 rods, **creek, Little Crab Lake,** p. 20 rods, **Crab Lake,** p. 320 rods, **Burntside Lake, North Arm Burntside Lake.** Your last day will be the easiest, by far, so take time to enjoy the pretty little lakes and streams leading toward Burntside. The only major challenge of the day is the 320-rod portage into Burntside Lake, but it will seem like nothing after the ordeal you have already been through. After an initial short climb, the trail slopes gently downhill, and passes through a wet area flooded by beaver dams. The next 2 miles of paddling will surely be the most confusing stretch on this route. Watch carefully for the narrow channel leading northeast into the North Arm.

Route #7: The Meandering Moose Loop

7 Days, 72 Miles, 17 Lakes, 4 Rivers, 39 Portages

Difficulty: Rugged

Fisher Maps: F-9, F-16

Travel Zones: 11, 5, 2, 13, 12

Introduction: This week-long journey will provide a smorgasbord of scenic terrain, from the tiniest of creeks to the largest of lakes. From the Slim Lake portage, you will paddle north and west through a series of small lakes and streams to Big Moose Lake. Then you will leave the BWCA for a day and head down the meandering Moose River, across the Echo Trail and on north to Nina-Moose Lake. Continuing north, you'll glide down the placid Nina-Moose River to Lake Agnes and eventually to giant Lac La Croix on the Canadian border, where you will stop to view old Indian rock paintings and climb atop legendary Warrior Hill. From beautiful Lac La Croix, you will point southeast and paddle into Iron Lake, where you will have an opportunity to view two scenic water-falls before leaving the Canadian border and traveling south-west to Stuart Lake. Up the Stuart River, you will paddle south, again crossing the Echo Trail, to Big Lake. From there you will retrace your path through the lakes and streams that lead to the Slim Lake portage to the North Arm road.

You will see few other travelers in that portion of the BWCA south of the Echo Trail or along the Stuart River. From the Moose River, north of the Echo Trail, to Lac La Croix, however, you will share the waterway with others—but not so many as to spoil it. Lac La Croix itself will probably be the busiest lake on the route, as it receives considerable traffic originating at Crane Lake. Resorts and an Indian reservation are located along its northern shore, and motorboats are not an uncommon sight-sound! Nevertheless, this is one of the most beautiful lakes in all the Boundary Waters, and you will surely enjoy your short visit there. Motors are permitted only on Big Lake, the Canadian side of Lac La Croix, and the part of the Moose River that is outside the BWCA.

Several LONG portages greet you at the beginning and end of this large loop, the longest being nearly 600 rods. However, none in the middle portion is excessive.

If the water level is low, you may find the going rough along the upper part of the Moose River and on the Stuart River, but the lower part of the Moose and all of the Nina-Moose are nearly always navigable.

Anglers will find northern pike and bass along much of the route, as well as lake trout in Lac La Croix and walleye in Lac La Croix and Iron Lake. If you really like fishing, stretch this rugged trip into eight days, instead of seven. You will have much more time to search for the elusive critter.

DAY 1: p. 80 rods, **Slim Lake,** p. 77 rods, **Rice Lake,** p. 130 rods, **Hook Lake,** p. 540 rods, **Big Rice Lake.** (See comments for Day 1, Route #6.)

DAY 2: **Big Rice Lake,** p. 8 rods, **Portage River, Lapond Lake,** p. 30 rods, **Portage River,** p. 150 rods, **Duck Lake,** p. 480 rods, **Big Moose Lake.** Although one LONG portage awaits you this day, you are not expected to go far. The first 25 rods of both the 150- and 480-rod carries are across muskeg. The 150-rod portage was nearly impassable with windfalls during the early summer of 1978. And the lake to which it leads is no real treat, either. Duck is a shallow, unimpressive lake, with muskeg bordering most of the southern and western shorelines. The 480-rod trail crosses over numerous small hills, but offers 10 portage rests along the way. Both pathways are *very* seldom used. Big Moose Lake will offer you several attractive campsites. But there are no Forest Service sites designated along the Moose River. Make camp early, and plan to break camp early the following morning.

DAY 3: **Big Moose Lake,** p. 60 rods, **Moose River,** p. 160 rods, **river,** p. 17 rods, **river,** p. 40 rods, **river,** p. 40 rods, **river,** p. 77 rods, **river,** p. 160 rods, **river,** p. 20 rods, **river,** p. 25 rods, **river, Nina-Moose Lake.** Travel is deceivingly slow in this meandering little stream. Without an early start, you may not make it to Nina-Moose Lake before dusk. You will cross under a spur of the Echo Trail and the Echo Trail itself, and be outside the BWCA part of the day. Canoe traffic is bound to increase beyond the Moose River parking lot north of the Echo Trail, which serves the most popular entry point along the Echo Trail. Find a campsite early on Nina-Moose Lake and try your luck at catching the northern pike, walleye and bass that inhabit this shallow lake. Along the western shoreline you will see evidence of the 1971 fire that ravaged nearly 25 square miles of woodland between here and the Little Indian Sioux River.

DAY 4: **Nina-Moose Lake, Nina-Moose River,** p. 70 rods, **river,** p. 96 rods, **river, Lake Agnes,** p. 24 rods, **Boulder Bay,** p. 65 rods, **Lac La Croix.** This will be the easiest day of your trip, but there is plenty to see and do, so you won't get bored! You'll find a fascinating display of ancient Indian pictographs adorning the sheer granite cliffs along the Canadian shore, about 2 miles north of Boulder Bay. Less than a mile south, you will find "Warrior Hill," where legends tell of Indian braves racing to the summit of this awesome cliff to prove their strength and courage. A climb to the top will reveal a spectacular panorama, and you will develop an instant respect for the Indians who could RUN to the top.

DAY 5: **Lac La Croix,** p. 80 rods, **Bottle Lake, Iron Lake,** p. 72 rods, **Dark Lake,** p. 67 rods, **Rush Lake,** p. 60

rods, **Fox Lake,** p. 320 rods, **Stuart Lake.** If time permits, you will surely enjoy making a short side trip to view two of the more spectacular waterfalls in this part of the BWCA. Rebecca Falls are located at the northern outlet of Iron Lake, where they plunge 23 feet across jagged rocks into McAree Lake. Use caution as you approach these falls. The swift current above them flows to either side of a narrow island, upon which is located the portage to the bottom. You must land on the island at the top of the split falls and hike along its perimeter to view the spectacle. If the season is right, you will find literally thousands of blueberries decorating the island. Remember, though, in order to legally set foot on Canadian soil, you must have secured authorization from the Canadian Government, at a Ranger Station. Curtain Falls, on the other hand, is quite safe, since you will be approaching it from the bottom. It drops a total of 29 gorgeous feet on its way from Crooked Lake to Iron Lake. An outstanding lunch spot is found about midway up the torrent on an outcropping of rock below the main drop of water.

Beware the series of hilly portages between Iron and Stuart lakes. The first three are short, but steep; the last is a mile long! It follows a good path, however, across level to gently rolling terrain. Eleven portage rests line the trail.

DAY 6: **Stuart Lake,** p. 74 rods, **Stuart River,** p. 14 rods, **river,** p. 74 rods, **river,** p. 52 rods, **river,** p. 85 rods, **river,** p. 600 rods, **Big Lake.** The Stuart River is a shallow, weedy, meandering stream, with beaver dams scattered generously along its entire course. Thanks to Nature's "corps of engineers," the northernmost stretch of the river (just after your portage from Stuart Lake) may be too low for navigation during dry spells; so plan on wet feet. If you can make it to the 14-rod portage, the worst is behind you.

The last portage of the day is the longest one of the whole route, and it is mostly uphill. It follows a good path, though, and has six canoe rests along the way. After 513 arduous rods of walking, you'll pass through a small parking lot, cross over the Echo Trail, and then gradually descend for 73 rods to Big Lake.

Big Lake is entirely outside the BWCA, and two resorts

are located at the northeast and northwest corners of the lake. Should you wish to end your trip here, you could buy a ride at one of these resorts.

DAY 7: **Big Lake,** p. 150 rods, **Lapond Lake, Portage River,** p. 8 rods, **Big Rice Lake,** p. 540 rods, **Hook Lake,** p. 130 rods, **Rice Lake,** p. 77 rods, **Slim Lake,** p. 80 rods. Beyond the first portage of this day, the route should all look familiar to you. (See comments for Day 1, Route #6.)

Entry Point 7—Big Lake

Permits: 12
Popularity Rank: 67
Daily Quota: 2

Location: Big Lake is located 12 miles northwest of Ely, just south of the Echo Trail. To get there, follow the Echo Trail for 17.1 miles from County Road 88, 7.4 miles past the point at which it turns to gravel and one mile past the access road to Whispering Pines Resort. Drive with caution on this narrow, winding road, particularly for the last 7.4 miles. Traffic is not heavy, but there is always some, because two resorts are located on Big Lake.

Turn left onto Forest Road 1027, which leads 0.3 mile down to the north shore of Big Lake. Forest Road 1027 was constructed in 1985 to replace a more primitive access road that was suitable for only 4-wheel-drive vehicles. A new boat ramp and a small parking area were also constructed at that time. The long portage trail from the Stuart River merges with the new road about 20 rods from the public landing.

Description: The public campground at Fenske Lake, 10 miles closer to Ely on the Echo Trail, provides a good place to spend the night before your canoe trip. There is a campsite fee.

Very few people use Big Lake to enter the Boundary Waters, and most of the BWCA south of the Echo Trail is very lightly used. You will find a high quality wilderness experience using either of the routes mentioned below. Motors are prohibited through this entry point, although they *are* allowed on Big Lake itself.

Route #8: The Slim-Crab Loop

3 Days, 38 Miles, 13 Lakes, 1 River, 2 Creeks, 13 Portages
Difficulty: Rugged
Fisher Map: F-9
Travel Zones: 11, 9

Introduction: This difficult route will take you south from Big Lake through a series of small lakes and streams to big Burntside Lake, located south of the BWCA. You will follow the north shore of Burntside southwest to the long portage into Crab Lake. Through another series of small scenic lakes and streams, you will paddle northward to the longest portage of the trip, into Big Moose Lake. From Big Moose you will take another long walk, to Duck Lake, and continue to work your way east back to your origin on Big Lake. When finished, you will think that you walked as much as you paddled—and perhaps you did! Three portages are in excess of 1½ miles! Because of these long treks, only the dedicated canoeist will tackle the route, and it is not unusual to see no other canoeists along that portion of the loop contained within the BWCA, where motors are not allowed. You feel worlds away from your nearest neighbor, when, in fact, you will never be more than 5 miles from a road or resort.

Populated Lake Burntside will nearly always be bustling with motorized traffic, however, and you will witness private cabins, resorts and camps throughout your stretch on this beautiful, island-studded lake. Fishermen will find northern pike, bass and pan fish along much of the route, and the persistent angler may even pull lake trout from the depths of Burntside Lake.

DAY 1: **Big Lake,** p. 150 rods, **Lapond Lake, Portage River,** p. 8 rods, **Big Rice Lake,** p. 540 rods, **Hook Lake,** p. 130 rods, **Rice Lake,** p. 77 rods, **Slim Lake.** The 540-rod portage is *very* seldom traveled, and you may have trouble following the path. There are 11 canoe rests along the way. If you are not in the best of shape, be prepared for mighty sore muscles at day's end. But if you still have some energy, you'll find two treats at the south end of Slim Lake. A blazed trail begins at a Forest Service campsite on the southeast shore of

Slim Lake that winds up the thickly wooded hillside to a trail that spurs off to the left and leads to a high, rocky ridge ¼ mile south of Slim Lake. Affectionately named "Old Baldy" by the summer residents of nearby Camp Northland, this summit affords an outstanding panorama of the surrounding woodlands. Watch for the spur trail. If you continue on the main trail, you will eventually find yourself on County Road 644, a mile to the south.

If you have arrived here during the right season, you will find blueberries atop Old Baldy, as well as along the rocky cliffs just north of the Slim Lake end of the portage from Burntside.

DAY 2: **Slim Lake,** p. 140 rods, **North Arm Burntside Lake, Burntside Lake,** p. 320 rods, **Crab Lake,** p. 20 rods, **Little Crab Lake, Korb Creek,** p. 1–3 rods, **creek, Korb Lake, Korb Creek,** p. 35 rods, **Cummings Lake.** 10 rods from Slim Lake the portage trail widens into a primitive road and continues sloping downhill to Burntside Lake, just after crossing the Echo Trail. Watch for traffic! You will find the mile-long portage into Crab Lake to be mostly uphill and wet from beaver activity, but it slopes gently, and 11 canoe rests are situated evenly along the trail. A very nice campsite for a large group is located on the west shore of Cummings Lake, near the Cummings Lake Trail.

DAY 3: **Cummings Lake,** p. 580 rods, **Big Moose Lake,** p. 480 rods, **Duck Lake,** p. 150 rods, **Portage River, creek, Big Lake.** Your three big portages total 1,210 rods; and if you can't carry all of your gear in one trip, that means over *11 miles* of walking. Your friends back home will never believe it! Fortunately, your longest portage of the route (between Cummings and Big Moose) is mostly level, with only a few small hills at each end. Nineteen canoe rests are useful in determining how far you have walked, even if you don't need them for rests. The last two portages are *very* seldom used. The 480-rod path passes over several small hills before ending with 25 rods of muskeg, adjacent to Duck Lake. The 150-rod trail was plagued with a plethora of windfalls in the spring of 1978, rendering it almost impassable. And, similar to the previous portage, the end of this one is across soggy, sometimes treacherous, muskeg.

From the end of the 150-rod portage, paddle left onto the Portage River and follow it northeast for about 25 rods. From that point a small creek meanders eastward to Big Lake.

Route #9: The Grassy-Beartrap Route

6 Days, 54 Miles, 31 Lakes, 5 Rivers, 1 Creek, 45 Portages
Difficulty: Rugged
Fisher Maps: F-9, F-10, F-17, F-16
Travel Zones: 11, 15, 14, 12

Introduction: This large, fascinating loop will take you south from Big Lake to Burntside Lake, and then northeast through many picturesque small lakes and streams to two popular fishing lakes, Horse and Fourtown. From Fourtown Lake you will angle off to the northwest and paddle through several small lakes to the Beartrap River. About halfway down the Beartrap River you will branch off on Sterling Creek and follow it west to Sterling Lake and eventually on to Stuart Lake. Then you will turn south and paddle up the Stuart River to your origin at the Echo Trail.

Much of your trip will be spent on small, winding streams and scenic little lakes, most of which are off limits to motorists. Nearly two full days of travel, however, will be outside of the Boundary Waters, as you cross through the Echo Trail between the Slim Lake and Range Lake entry points. This region is the only portion of the route where motors are permitted. Most of the loop receives light to moderate use, the immediate vicinity of Burntside Lake being the only exception.

Water level is a critical factor for the navigation of this route. Passage could be difficult or impossible in most of the rivers and creeks during periods of extremely low water.

Fishermen will find walleye, northern pike and pan fish along much of the route. Fourtown and Horse lakes, in particular, are popular among anglers.

DAY 1: **Big Lake,** p. 150 rods, **Lapond Lake, Portage River,** p. 8 rods, **Big Rice Lake,** p. 540 rods, **Hook Lake,** p. 130 rods, **Rice Lake,** p. 77 rods, **Slim Lake.** (See comments for Day 1 of Route #8.)

DAY 2: **Slim Lake,** p. 140 rods, **North Arm Burntside Lake,** p. 250 rods, **West Twin Lake, East Twin Lake,** p. 14 rods, **Everett Lake,** p. 120 rods, **Fenske Lake,** p. 10 rods, **Little Sletten Lake,** p. 70 rods, **Sletten Lake,** p. 120 rods, **Tee Lake,** p. 48 rods, **Grassy Lake.** None of the portages is difficult, but their frequency slows travel considerably. The only uphill challenge is the 70-rod path between Little Sletten and Sletten lakes. You will see several cabins and resorts from Burntside to Fenske Lake, but the small lakes east of the Echo Trail are quite uncivilized.

DAY 3: **Grassy Lake, beaver pond,** p. 24 rods, **Grassy River, Range River,** p. 1 rod, **river,** p. 23 rods, **river,** p. 10 rods, **river, Range Lake,** p. 109 rods, **Sandpit Lake,** p. 117 rods, **Tin Can Lake.** The 1-rod portage on the Range River is merely a liftover where the Cloquet Road crosses the river. (See the sketch of the Range River area on next page.) Beaver dams are not uncommon on portions of the Range River. If you wish, you may walk all of the way from Range Lake to Tin Can Lake, a total walking distance of 301 rods. You will be following an old railroad bed most of the way, offering an easy pathway.

DAY 4: **Tin Can Lake,** p. 90 rods, **Horse Lake,** p. 70 rods, **pond,** p. 10 rods, **Fourtown Lake,** p. 1–3 rods, **Fourtown Lake,** p. 35 rods, **Boot Lake,** p. 15 rods, **Fairy Lake,** p. 50 rods, **Gun Lake,** p. 30 rods, **Gull Lake,** p. 40 rods, **Mudhole Lake,** p. 60 rods, **Thunder Lake.** Since 1978, Fourtown Lake is no longer a designated motor route. Beyond it, too, the lakes are "paddle only," and rather lightly traveled. You should encounter no difficulty on the portages this day.

DAY 5: **Thunder Lake,** p. 9 rods, **Beartrap Lake,** p. 200 rods, **Beartrap River,** p. 65 rods, **river,** p. 20 rods, **river, Sunday Lake,** p. 17 rods, **Beartrap River, Sterling Creek,** p. 160 rods, **creek,** p. 8 rods, **Sterling Lake,** p. 148 rods, **Bibon Lake,** p. 10 rods, **Nibin Lake,** p. 180 rods, **Stuart Lake.** Your first long portage is mostly downhill, with 4 canoe rests. You will descend nearly 100 feet in all between Beartrap and Sunday lakes. The Beartrap River is shallow, weedy, and extremely tiny until it joins with Spring Creek and acquires a width of about 4–5 rods. You may encounter several beaver dams between the 20-rod portage and Sunday Lake, with a few requiring lift-overs.

The Range River

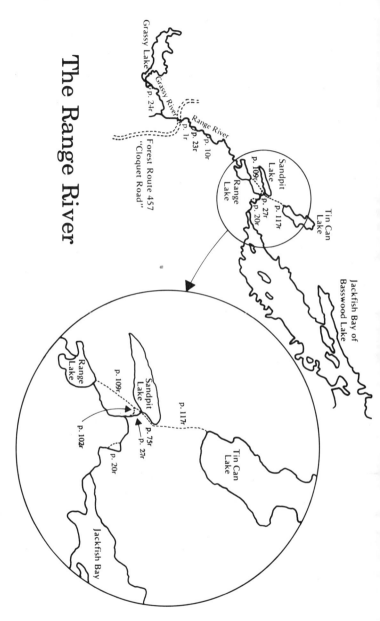

Grassy Lake

Grassy River

p. 24r

Range River

p. 1r

p. 10r

p. 23r

Forest Route 457
"Cloquet Road"

Sandpit
Lake

p. 109r

Range
Lake

p. 117r

p. 27r

p. 20r

Tin Can
Lake

Jackfish Bay of
Basswood Lake

Range
Lake

p. 109r

Sandpit
Lake

p. 117r

p. 102r

p. 75r

p. 27r

p. 20r

Tin Can
Lake

Jackfish Bay

During dry periods, Sterling Creek may be too low to carry a loaded canoe. In fact, my wife and I had to portage right down the middle of the sandy creek bed in August of 1979.

All the portages between Sunday and Stuart lakes are *very* seldom used by people, and their paths are often quite difficult to see. You'll see far more moose tracks than human ones!

The roughest of the carries is the 148-rod portage, which climbs a steep hill separating Sterling and Bibon lakes. Four portage rests will help somewhat. The other two ½ mile carries are not as exhausting as the shorter one, but the portage rests may be broken down.

DAY 6: **Stuart Lake,** p. 74 rods, **Stuart River,** p. 14 rods, **river,** p. 74 rods, **river,** p. 52 rods, **river,** p. 85 rods, **river,** p. 600 rods to the Big Lake landing. Before leaving Stuart Lake, you may want to hike to the top of a scenic overlook near the portage from Nibin Lake. About 5 rods east of the first portage rest, away from Stuart Lake, the Stuart Lake Trail crosses your path. Follow it south for about 80 rods to a rocky clearing where a couple of rock cairns have been built. From this point, head west through the sparsely wooded terrain to a rock ridge that overlooks Stuart Lake. The panorama is well worth the extra effort!

Beaver dams are scattered along the river's course, and during low-water periods you may find it necessary to step out of the canoe on occasion, particularly at the lower (northern) end of the shallow, winding, weedy stream. Your last long portage of the trip follows a good path, but climbs steadily for ⅔ of its length. There are six canoe rests to ease your weary shoulders.

Should you get a late start this morning or find it necessary to make an early camp, there is a campsite on White Feather Lake, accessible through a short stream that connects to the Stuart River just south of the 52-rod portage. The connecting stream may be partly (or totally) blocked by a beaver dam. By standing up in your canoe, however, you can easily see the not-so-distant lake, which offers a pleasant change of scenery from the marsh through which the Stuart River flows.

Portage between Seagull and Saganaga Lakes

A beaver palace in the Moose River

Portaging from Big Moose Lake to Duck Lake

The Painted Rocks on Lac La Croix   *George Miles Ryan*

Lunch break beside the Kawashiwi River

Lower Basswood Falls tempted many a foolish Voyageur

Paddling up the Moose River toward Big Moose Lake

Curtain Falls between Crooked Lake and Iron Lake
Walking the Kawashiwi River rapids

Basswood River   *Donald Holmquist*

A moose on the banks of the Isabella River

Putting in at Duck Lake

Exercise caution where the portage crosses the Echo Trail. From the Stuart River parking area, veer toward the right to find the beginning of the 73-rod portage connecting the Echo Trail with the Big Lake public landing.

Entry Point 8—Moose River—South

Permits: 40

Popularity Rank: 51

Daily Quota: 2

Location: The Moose River begins its course at the northwest corner of Big Moose Lake, 15 miles northwest of Ely, and slowly winds its way north for about 10 miles to Nina-Moose Lake. The Echo Trail crosses the river about midway between the two lakes. One access, a mile north of the Echo Trail, serves trippers paddling toward Nina-Moose Lake, via the Moose River-*North* entry point. To find the public access for canoeists who wish to paddle *south* to Big Moose Lake, drive 23½ miles on the Echo Trail from County Road 88 to its intersection with Forest Route 464. Turn left and drive an additional 3½ miles to the Moose River.

Parking space is rather limited, but there is seldom much competition for it.

Description: The Moose River is a narrow, shallow, meandering stream. During dry periods, its navigation could be awkward. Because of its remote location, and undoubtedly because of the difficult portages leading east and south from Big Moose Lake, the Moose River-South entry point is used by few canoeists. Among those few who do use it, only a small percentage continue beyond Big Moose Lake, which is a beautiful weekend destination in itself.

The nearest Forest Service campground is at Lake Jeanette, 13½ miles farther west on the Echo Trail from its junction with Forest Route 464. Or, perhaps you would like to stop at the Fenske Lake Campground, 8 miles from County Road 88 on the Echo Trail. There is a campsite fee at either Forest Service campground.

A high-quality wilderness experience can be found on either of the excellent routes described below.

Route #10: The Crab-Slim Loop

4 Days, 37 Miles, 12 Lakes, 2 Rivers, 1 Creek, 17 Portages
Difficulty: Rugged
Fisher Map: F-9
Travel Zones: 11, 9

Introduction: This exhausting route is recommended for only the hardiest of voyagers. From big Moose Lake you will portage nearly 2 miles south to Cummings Lake. Continuing south through a series of small, picturesque lakes and streams, you will then portage another mile, out of the BWCA into beautiful Burntside Lake. Weaving your way through the confusing maze of islands and into the North Arm of this populated lake, you will then portage back into the Boundary Waters via the Slim Lake entry point. You will continue paddling northwest through the small lakes and tiny streams and carrying your gear across the LONG portages that lead back to Big Moose, from which you will retrace your path back down the Moose River to the landing at Forest Route 464.

When finished, you will have spent as much time walking on portage trails as you did paddling on the adjoining scenic lakes. Three portages are longer than 1½ miles and a fourth is exactly 1 mile. It is largely BECAUSE of these portages, however, that this route is so enticing to the wilderness enthusiast. Only the truly dedicated canoeist will tackle the route, and it is not unusual to see no other canoeists along that portion of the route contained within the BWCA, where motors are not allowed. You will feel truly isolated from the rest of the world, even though you will never be more than 5 miles from a resort or road.

Nevertheless, Burntside Lake will nearly always be bustling with motorized traffic, and you will pass private cabins, resorts and camps throughout this portion of your trip. Were it not for the exceptional beauty of this island-studded lake, the accompanying activity might prove to be a dismal part of an otherwise high-quality wilderness trip.

Fishermen will find northern pike, bass and pan fish along much of the route, and the persistent angler may even pull lake trout from Burntside Lake.

DAY 1: **Moose River,** p. 160 rods, **river,** p. 60 rods, **Big Moose Lake,** p. 580 rods, **Cummings Lake.** Don't let the 580-rod portage scare you; it's long, but not too difficult. Although the beginning is uphill and overgrown in places, the path soon levels off, and then follows a ridgetop along most of its course. Nineteen canoe rests make life a little easier, too. Several good campsites are at the east end of Cummings Lake, including a very large, nice site on the east shore near the Cummings Lake Trail.

DAY 2: **Cummings Lake,** p. 35 rods, **Korb Creek, Korb Lake, Korb Creek,** p. 1–3 rods, **creek, Little Crab Lake,** p. 20 rods, **Crab Lake,** p. 320 rods, **Burntside Lake,** p. 140 rods, **Slim Lake.** This will be the easiest day of the trip, by far. The only major challenge is the one-mile portage into Burntside Lake. After an initial short climb, the wide, smooth trail slopes gently downhill and passes through a wet area that has been flooded by beaver dams. The next 2 miles of paddling will be the most confusing stretch of this route, so watch carefully for the narrow channel leading northeast into the North Arm of Burntside.

If time permits at the day's end, you may wish to visit "Old Baldy," a high, rocky ridge ¼ mile south of Slim Lake. (See comments for Day 1, Route #8.)

DAY 3: **Slim Lake,** p. 77 rods, **Rice Lake,** p. 130 rods, **Hook Lake,** p. 540 rods, **Big Rice Lake,** p. 8 rods, **Portage River, Lapond Lake.** (See comments for Day 1, Route #6.)

DAY 4: **Lapond Lake,** p. 30 rods, **Portage River,** p. 150 rods, **Duck Lake,** p. 480 rods, **Big Moose Lake,** p. 60 rods, **Moose River,** p. 160 rods, **river.** If an emergency arises or if for any other reason you decide to terminate your expedition early, portage 150 rods from the north shore of Lapond Lake into Big Lake. Two resorts are located on the north shore, and there you will find easy access to the Echo Trail. The 150-rod and 480-rod portages are not often traveled upon, and windfalls may slow your treks considerably, particularly in spring. The first 25 rods of both are over muskeg. The 480-rod trail crosses several small hills, but there are 10 canoe rests along the way.

Route #11: The Sioux-Border Loop

8 Days, 82 Miles, 20 Lakes, 3 Rivers, 3 Creeks, 42 Portages
Difficulty: Rugged
Fisher Maps: F-9, F-8, F-16
Travel Zones: 11, 9, 13, 4, 7, 2, 5

Introduction: This elongated loop will first take you south from Big Moose Lake across the long 580-rod portage to Cummings Lake. From there you will turn west and paddle into the headwaters of the Little Indian Sioux River, which will continue meandering to the west for several miles before bending northward, crossing the Echo Trail and eventually entering the Pauness lakes. You will portage around scenic Devil's Cascade and proceed into Loon Lake and then northeast to South Lake. Then you will point eastward and navigate the small lakes and streams that lead to the southwest portion of beautiful Lac La Croix, where you will have an opportunity to see Indian pictographs and climb legendary Warrior Hill. After going southwest to Lake Agnes, you will paddle up the Nina-Moose River to Nina-Moose Lake. Continuing south, you will re-enter the Moose River and follow its course across the Echo Trail to Forest Route 464 and the point where this journey originated.

The whole route will require eight full, strenuous days for the average group of canoeists, plus any layover days. If strong winds prevail, you may find the going slowed considerably on portions of the Indian Sioux River. Early summer is usually the best time to make this trip, since the Sioux and Moose rivers could be too shallow later in the summer, especially during a dry year.

Most of the route south of the Echo Trail is not heavily used, and the portage trails may sometimes be hard to see. Along the Indian Sioux River, wildlife is plentiful, including moose, deer and beaver. North of the Echo Trail, however, you will see many more canoes. But even there, use is moderate, except on the ever-popular Lac La Croix. In general, if you like to paddle on slow, meandering little streams, and you don't mind frequent—and occasionally long—portaging, you will find this route delightful.

DAY 1: **Moose River,** p. 160 rods, **river,** p. 60 rods, **Big Moose Lake,** p. 580 rods, **Cummings Lake.** (See comments for Day 1, Route #10.)

DAY 2: **Cummings Lake,** p. 5 rods, **Otter Lake,** p. 120 rods, **Little Indian Sioux River,** p. 28 rods, **river,** p. 20 rods, **river,** p. 40 rods, **river,** p. 30 rods, **river,** p. 20 rods, **river,** p. 35 rods, **river,** p. 40 rods, **river.** Campsites are few and far between on this swampy, winding little river, so start looking while the sun is still high in the sky. In fact, you will find NO designated Forest Service campsites unless you portage 376 rods into Little Trout Lake or 200 rods into Bootleg Lake (both portages are not only long but also hard to find). The nine short portages and considerable meandering make travel deceivingly slow. Between portages it is virtually impossible to know EXACTLY where you are. Use the portages as landmarks, and alert yourself to the GENERAL direction of travel. A decent campsite may be found on the river between the portages into Little Trout and Bootleg lakes.

DAY 3: **Little Indian Sioux River,** p. 20 rods, **river,** p. 120 rods, **river,** p. 8 rods, **river,** p. 120 rods, **river,** p. 60 rods, **river, Upper Pauness Lake.** This will be a long day of paddling down the gradually widening, deepening and straightening channel of the river. Watch out for traffic as you cross the Echo Trail at the 120-rod portage. This trail is seldom used and may be overgrown and difficult to follow during the latter part of summer. There are no portage rests, but a scenic lunch spot next to a cascading rapids marks the midpoint. From that point on, the number of canoes you see will greatly increase. You will be wise to grab the first campsite you see on Upper Pauness Lake.

DAY 4: **Upper Pauness Lake,** p. 8 rods, **Lower Pauness Lake,** p. 160 rods, **Loon Lake, East Loon Bay, Little Loon Lake,** p. 173 rods, **Slim Lake,** p. 52 rods, **Creek, Section Three Pond,** p. 52 rods, **South Lake.** Take time to view the scenic granite gorge through which Devil's Cascade plunges 75 feet from Lower Pauness Lake to Loon Lake. The portage here is mostly downhill, with three canoe rests along the way. But there is a fairly steep rise to the second rest, which marks the midpoint of the trail, and offers the best view of the gorge below. The other half-mile portage this day is uphill, rising 65 feet from Little Loon Lake to Slim Lake. It is steep in some places and muddy in others, but five canoe rests along the way make portaging a LITTLE easier. A nice campsite on South Lake is located on a rocky point just left of the muddy landing for the portage from Section Three Pond.

DAY 5: **South Lake,** p. 120 rods, **Steep Lake,** p. 45 rods, **Eugene Lake,** p. 50 rods, **Little Bear Track Lake,** p. 30 rods, **Bear Track Lake,** p. 200 rods, **Thumb Lake,** p. 9 rods, **Finger Lake,** p. 90 rods, **Finger Creek, Pocket Lake.** This day starts out with a steep portage that climbs 125 feet to Steep Lake. You may need to use all 4 canoe rests to catch your breath! You will find it much tougher than the 200-rod trail between Bear Track and Thumb lakes, which descends 81 feet on a good path with eight canoe rests. There are three good campsites on Pocket Lake, and good fishing for northern pike and walleyes.

DAY 6: **Pocket Lake,** p. 20 rods, **Pocket Creek,** p. 25 rods, **creek, Lac La Croix.** If you wish, you can probably avoid the 20-rod portage out of Pocket Lake by running, lining, or walking the shallow rapids into Pocket Creek. Lac La Croix, dotted with over 200 islands, is the longest and one of the most beautiful of the international lakes bordering the BWCA. This will be the easiest day of your trip, allowing plenty of time for you to explore the Indian rock paintings and Warrior Hill, found on the Canadian shoreline. Both monuments are reminders of an ancient civilization that once flourished in this aquatic wilderness. Legend says that Ojibway braves used Warrior Hill to test their strength and courage by racing from lake's edge to the summit. You will appreciate this feat only after climbing it yourself, and the incredible view from the top will make your effort worthwhile.

DAY 7: **Lac La Croix,** p. 65 rods, **Boulder Bay,** p. 24 rods, **Lake Agnes, Nina-Moose River,** p. 96 rods, **river,** p. 70 rods, **river, Nina-Moose Lake.** This day takes you through the most heavily traveled portion of the entire route. Be psychologically prepared for company, both the 2-legged and the 4-legged varieties. Bears are known to be nuisances in this area, where they have prematurely ended many a canoe trip. After the food pack is secured, try your luck at catching one of the walleyes, northern pike or smallmouth bass that inhabit Nina-Moose Lake.

DAY 8: **Nina-Moose Lake, Moose River,** p. 25 rods, **river,** p. 20 rods, **river,** p. 160 rods, **river,** p. 77 rods, **river,** p. 40 rods, **river,** p. 40 rods, **river,** p. 17 rods, **river.** The Moose River is another narrow, winding little stream through marshy terrain. Almost choked with vegetation during prime summer months, your route is frequently visible scarcely more than a few yards in front of the canoe. Travel is slow, as you are paddling against the current and meandering considerably. The 160-rod portage will take you into the parking lot serving the Moose River entry point. Bear to the right (west) and you will find the river again just past the parking area. Four canoe rests are situated along the smooth, sandy trail, which slopes gently uphill. When the water level is down, during the latter part of the summer, be prepared for your canoe to scrape the river's sandy bottom. South of the parking area, you'll be outside of the Boundary Waters all of the way back to your origin.

Entry Point 9—Little Indian Sioux River-South

Permits: 18

Popularity Rank: 62

Daily Quota: 1

Location: The Little Indian Sioux River begins its winding course about 15 miles northwest of Ely. It flows west for about 6 miles and then turns north and eventually flows into Loon Lake on the Canadian border. All the river except that part in the immediate vicinity of the Echo Trail is contained within the BWCA. The upper part of the river (south of the Echo Trail) is accessible via the Sioux River-South entry point (#9), while the lower, northern part is served by the Sioux River-North entry point (#14). To get to the accesses, follow the echo Trail for 31½ miles from County Road 88. The South access is below the bridge on the left side of the road. A small parking lot on the north side of the road will accommodate half a dozen autos.

Description: You may wish to spend the night before

your trip at a public campground 5½ miles west on the Echo Trail, at Jeanette Lake. This will enable an early start the following morning—and you will need it! There is a fee to camp there.

This entry point leads into one of the least traveled, most pristine areas within the Boundary Waters, offering as much solitude and bountiful wildlife as you would ever hope to encounter. the Little Indian Sioux River provides a good opportunity to view moose, deer, beaver and other wildlife. It is most suitable early in the summer, when the water level is usually up. During dry spells, the river could be too shallow for navigation with loaded canoes. Regardless of the date, you will surely see few if any other canoes on this slow and weedy stream.

Route #12: Trout-Cummings Lakes Loop

5 Days, 55 Miles, 12 Lakes, 1 River, 4 Creeks, 26 Portages
Difficulty: Rugged
Fisher Maps: F-8, F-9
Travel Zones: 11, 8, 10, 9

Introduction: This high-quality wilderness expedition will take you up the Little Indian Sioux River and into Little Trout Lake. Continuing south, you will paddle into giant Trout Lake, and then turn east and follow a chain of interesting little lakes and streams to Little Crab Lake. From there, you will paddle north into Korb and Cummings lakes, before turning west and re-entering the Little Indian Sioux River, which leads you back north to your origin on the Echo Trail.

You will find fishing good in many of the lakes along this route. Try for northern pike or bass in Cummings, Otter, Little Trout and Trout Lake. Or, if the thought of lake trout sounds especially good, take time to fish the lower depths of Trout Lake.

You will feel truly isolated throughout most of this route. But during your brief swing through the northeastern corner of Trout Lake, you may see dozens of motor boats with anglers testing their luck for lake trout. The motor route through Trout Lake is one of the busiest in the BWCA. But, rest assured, the commotion won't extend beyond Trout Lake. The rest of this route will be shared with few, if any, other canoeists.

DAY 1: **Little Indian Sioux River,** p. 8 rods, **river,** p. 120 rods, **river,** p. 20 rods, **river,** p. 376 rods, **Little Trout Lake.** Get an early start this day, as you will surely find the going to be slow on this winding little stream. And if a strong south wind prevails, you will have that to contend with too. There are no Forest Service campsites on the river, so it is important that you reach Little Trout Lake in time to find a site. Watch carefully for the 376-rod portage, as it may pass by unnoticed. If you come to a 40-rod portage on the river, you will know you have just passed the long one, which is not well-traveled and may be muddy, but has no major inclines.

DAY 2: **Little Trout Lake, Little Trout Creek, Trout Lake, Pine Creek,** p. 40 rods, **creek,** p. 260 rods, **Chad Lake,** p. 250 rods, **Buck Lake,** p. 80 rods, **Western Lake.** Be prepared for the first long portage. It steeply climbs nearly 100 feet above Pine Creek before descending gradually to Chad Lake. On the 250-rod portage between Buck and Chad lakes over a 50-foot hill, notice how the interconnecting stream changes direction midway across the portage.

DAY 3: **Western Lake,** p. 195 rods, **Glenmore Lake,** p. 210 rods, **Schlamm Lake,** p. 100 rods, **Lunetta Creek,** p. 60 rods, **Lunetta Lake, Lunetta Creek, Little Crab Lake, Korb Creek,** p. 1–3 rods, **creek, Korb Lake, Korb Creek,** p. 35 rods, **Cummings Lake.** None of the portages this day is difficult, although the 210-rod trail between Glenmore and Schlamm lakes climbs 84 feet over a hill. On the 100-rod portage from Schlamm Lake, the path veers off to the right on a gravel road for about 8 rods up a small creek that flows into it. Occasional beaver dams may obstruct your passage on the creek leading into Little Crab Lake. These will require nothing more than a quick liftover, however. The short rapids on the creek leading into Korb Lake may be tempting, but beware the rocky ledge over which it passes. You will find several good campsites at the east end of Cummings Lake, including a large, nice site on the east shore near the Cummings Lake Trail.

DAY 4: **Cummings Lake,** p. 5 rods, **Otter Lake,** p. 120 rods, **Little Indian Sioux River,** p. 28 rods, **river,** p. 20 rods, **river,** p. 40 rods, **river,** p. 30 rods, **river,** p. 20 rods, **river,** p.

35 rods, **river,** p. 40 rods, **river.** There are no Forest Service campsites along the Little Indian Sioux River, so unless you portage back into Little Trout Lake or tackle the 200-rod portage into Bootleg Lake, you had better start looking for suitable sites while the sun is still high in the sky. The nine short portages and the river's considerable meandering make travel deceivingly slow. Between portages it is virtually impossible to know exactly where you are. Use the portages as landmarks, and alert yourself to the GENERAL direction of travel. A decent campsite may be found on the river between the portages to Little Trout and Bootleg lakes.

DAY 5: **Little Indian Sioux River,** p. 20 rods, **river,** p. 120 rods, **river,** p. 8 rods, **river.** All of your last day will be spent backtracking the part of the river that you paddled on the first day. If you prefer a change of scenery, portage 200 rods into Bootleg Lake and then follow the Little Pony River north to its junction with the Indian Sioux just above the 120-rod portage.

Route #13: The Crooked-Oyster Route

10 Days, 110 Miles, 29 Lakes, 6 Rivers, 1 Creek, 49 Portages
Difficulty: Rugged
Fisher Maps: F-8, F-9, F-10, F-17, F-16
Travel Zones: 11, 9, 15, 17, 16, 13, 2, 5, 6, 3

Introduction: This long loop will first take you south and east up the Indian Sioux River to Cummings Lake. Continuing south, you'll paddle through several small lakes and creeks and leave the BWCA via the Crab Lake portage into Burntside Lake. Through the Dead River you will then pass into a plethora of tiny lakes and adjoining portages leading northeast to the Range River, which continues northeast back into the BWCA and on to Jackfish Bay, the westernmost bay of enormous Basswood Lake. From the northwest corner of mighty Basswood, you will follow the Canadian border down the beautiful Basswood River, past three lovely waterfalls and a display of Indian rock paintings, to Crooked Lake, a challenge for any map reader. Continuing west along the border you will pass yet another scenic waterfall on your way to island-studded Lac La Croix. From here you will leave the land of the Maple Leaf and turn southwest through a chain of less-traveled lakes and streams connected by rugged portages, to the Pauness lakes. Here you will turn south and again paddle up the lazy Little Indian Sioux River to your origin at the Echo Trail.

When finished, you will have paddled through one of the most varied and beautiful routes in all the BWCA—tiny lakes and mammoth ones, narrow streams and meandering rivers, gorgeous waterfalls, lovely rapids and menacing beaver dams all join together for an unforgettable journey into the domain once inhabited by the Chippewa and woodland Sioux Indians. Motors are prohibited on most of the route, and at times you will see no other canoeists. But during your brief interlude outside of the Boundary Waters, you will surely encounter numerous motorboats, cabins and resorts from Burntside Lake to Fenske Lake, where you must also cross the Echo Trail. But you should not find this part of the route dull, for Burntside is dotted with countless islands that enhance the beauty of this popular lake and the tiny lakes just east of the Echo Trail are as attractive as any found within the designated wilderness area.

Most of the route is easily navigable during any season. The Indian Sioux and Range rivers, however, may offer difficult passage when the water level is low. Normally, the best time for such a trip is in early summer or after the autumn rains. Parts of the route may be impassable during the dry month of August. Wind may also be a potential hazard on this route, particularly on Jackfish Bay. Basswood Lake is notorious for its high, dangerous waves on windy days.

Fishing is generally good throughout most of the route for walleye and northern pike. You will also have an opportunity to fish for lake trout in Basswood, Burntside and Oyster lakes and Lac La Croix. One of the largest northern pike I have seen caught was pulled out of the Basswood River, a ways below Lower Basswood Falls.

DAY 1: **Little Indian Sioux River,** p. 8 rods, **river,** p. 120 rods, **river, Little Pony River,** p. 60 rods, **river,** p. 60 rods, **Bootleg Lake.** (See comments for Days 4 and 5, Route #12.)

DAY 2: **Bootleg Lake,** p. 200 rods, **Little Indian Sioux River,** p. 40 rods, **river,** p. 35 rods, **river,** p. 20 rods, **river,** p. 30 rods, **river,** p. 40 rods, **river,** p. 20 rods, **river,** p. 28 rods, **river,** p. 120 rods, **Otter Lake,** p. 5 rods, **Cummings Lake.** (See comments for Days 4 and 5, Route #12.) Several nice campsites are found near the east end of Cummings Lake.

DAY 3: **Cummings Lake,** p. 35 rods, **Korb Creek, Korb Lake, Korb Creek,** p. 1–3 rods, **creek, Little Crab Lake,** p. 20 rods, **Crab Lake,** p. 320 rods, **Burntside Lake, Dead River, East Twin Lake.** If you are tired of paddling on small streams by now, bypass lower Korb Creek and nearly all of Korb Lake by portaging 70 rods from the south bay in Cummings Lake into the west end of Korb Lake. Your only real challenge of this day is the 1-mile portage into Burntside Lake. It starts out climbing a small hill, but most of the trail is downhill, on a wet path that has been flooded by beaver dams. With well over 100 islands, Burntside Lake may be confusing to even the experienced map reader. Watch carefully for the bay from which the Dead River flows toward Twin Lakes. You will find three small, relatively new Forest Service campsites bordering East Twin Lake, but the largest and best site is an undeveloped one on the north side of the portage between East Twin Lake and Everett Lake.

DAY 4: **East Twin Lake,** p. 14 rods, **Everett Lake,** p. 120 rods, **Fenske Lake,** p. 10 rods, **Little Sletten Lake,** p. 70 rods, **Sletten Lake,** p. 120 rods, **Tee Lake,** p. 48 rods, **Grassy Lake, Beaver Pond,** p. 24 rods, **Grassy River, Range River,** p. 1 rod, **river,** p. 23 rods, **river,** p. 10 rods, **river, Range Lake,** p. 102 rods, **Range River,** p. 20 rods, **river, Jackfish Bay.** Of the many portages you will walk today, the only exhausting one is the 70-rod trail which surmounts a steep hill between Little Sletten and Sletten lakes. There may be beaver dams between Grassy Lake and the pond thereafter, as well as on the upper portion of the Grassy River and the lower stretches of the slow, winding, marshy Range River, near Range Lake. When portaging out of Range Lake, bear to the right as the trail divides. This will lead you directly to the Range River, on your way to Jackfish Bay. (Otherwise you will portage 109 rods to Sandpit Lake and then must come back and cross another 27-rod trail to get to the same location reached by the 102-rod portage.) (See detailed sketch of the Range River region in Route #9.)

DAY 5: **Jackfish Bay, Basswood Lake,** p. 340 rods, **Basswood River,** p. 30 rods, **river,** p. 32 rods, **river,** p. 32 rods, **river.** Three portages this day circumnavigate three scenic waterfalls: Basswood Falls, Wheelbarrow Falls, and Lower Basswood Falls. The upper portion of the Basswood River is considered "Dangerous Water." The 340-rod portage bypasses this section. It follows a good, well-traveled path and has six canoe rests along the way. It is the safest route, and I recommend it. If you prefer, however, you may flirt with the dangerous rapids by taking shorter portages instead of the one long one. Use your own discretion, based on the water conditions and your own skill. But keep these two historic facts in mind as you proceed: 1) many a foolish voyageur has lost his life on this portion of the Voyageurs' Highway trying to avoid the burdensome carries; and 2) as "Skipper" Berglund used to remind me, "No Indian ever lost his life on a portage."

You will find several nice campsites just below Lower Basswood Falls. Because of the heavy use of this area, you would be wise to get there as early as possible and make camp while sites are still available.

DAY 6: **Basswood River, Crooked Lake.** No need to put your boots on this morning. You won't encounter a single portage, just a LOT of paddling. A display of Indian rock paintings may be seen about a mile downstream from Lower Basswood Falls. Farther north, near the entrance to Wednesday Bay of Crooked Lake, you will pass Table Rock, a campsite long ago used by voyageurs carrying furs from the Northwest to outposts on Lake Superior. Keep your map handy on Crooked Lake. You will need it every minute! Watch for eagles soaring overhead: at least one nest is located near the east end.

DAY 7: **Crooked Lake,** p. 140 rods, **Iron Lake, Bottle Lake,** p. 80 rods, **Lac La Croix.** Curtain Falls, with a drop 29 feet, separates Crooked and Iron lakes. Use caution and stay close to the left shoreline as you approach the misty brink of the beautiful falls. You will see two possible portage landings on the US shoreline, one a hundred feet away from the falls and one on the very edge. It appears from the portage trail that a good many people prefer the safer landing, several rods from the fall's edge.

When crossing Iron Lake, take time to go a short distance out of your way to visit Rebecca Falls, at the northern outlet into McAree Lake. (See comments for Day 5, Route #7.)

Two points of historical interest await you on Lac La Croix. Barely more than a mile past the portage from Bottle Lake is Warrior Hill, once the testing ground for the bravery and strength of Ojibway braves, who ran from the lake's edge to the top of the rocky summit. If you climb to the top, you will be rewarded with an outstanding panorama of the surrounding area. Farther up the Canadian shoreline, you will soon come to a fine display of ancient Indian rock paintings. There are several outstanding campsites in the vicinity. Find one early, as this portion of the border is usually heavily traveled by Canadian motor boats and American canoeists alike. The scenic splendor of this area makes the buzz of the motors tolerable.

DAY 8: **Lac La Croix,** p. 65 rods, **Boulder Bay,** p. 24 rods, **Lake Agnes,** p. 160 rods, **Oyster River,** p. 60 rods, **Oyster Lake.** If the water level is high enough and you prefer a few miles of extra paddling to eliminate 205 rods of portaging, you may wish to consider two alternatives. When leaving the south end of Lac La Croix, paddle past the 65-rod portage trail and continue through winding, shallow Boulder Bay to the 24-rod portage, into Lake Agnes. Then, instead of portaging 160-rods, to the Oyster River, exit Lake Agnes via the Nina-Moose River at the south end. Paddle upstream for half a mile to the mouth of the Oyster River on the right. You will soon come to a 20-rod portage, but the 160-rod one is not necessary.

DAY 9: **Oyster Lake,** p. 240 rods, **Hustler Lake,** p. 10 rods, **Ruby Lake,** p. 280 rods, **Lynx Lake,** p. 4 rods, **Little Shell Lake,** p. 15 rods, **Shell Lake.** Your first long portage is mostly uphill, climbing more than 140 feet above Oyster Lake. The 280-rod trail ascends very gradually, but then quickly drops nearly 130 feet to Lynx Lake. The first long trek has five portage rests and the second has six. Both follow good paths. You can probably avoid the 4-rod portage by paddling through the tiny channel that connects Lynx and Little Shell lakes. Be sure to safely elevate your food pack at night, as bears are a common nuisance around Shell Lake.

DAY 10: **Shell Lake,** p. 216 rods, **Lower Pauness Lake,** p. 8 rods, **Upper Pauness Lake, Little Indian Sioux River,** p. 60 rods, **river,** p. 40 rods, **Public Access.** If time permits you will surely enjoy a visit to Devil's Cascade, which plunges 75 feet down through a scenic granite gorge from Lower Pauness Lake to Loon Lake.

Entry Point 12—Little Vermilion Lake

Permits: 265

Popularity Rank: 24

Daily Quota: 16

Location: Little Vermilion Lake is the westernmost entry point for the BWCA, located 40 miles northwest of Ely. It is accessible from popular Crane Lake, two miles to the west (five miles by water trails), at the north end of County Road 24. To get there from Ely, follow the Echo Trail 49 miles to its terminus and junction with County Road 24. Turn right and follow 24 north for 8 miles to the public access at the south end of Crane Lake. From Orr, Minnesota, drive east on County Road 23 for seventeen miles to the junction with County Road 24 at Buyck. Crane Lake is 12 miles north of Buyck on County Road 24. Parking is available only on private lots where daily fees are charged.

Description: Public campgrounds are located near Orr and Buyck, and at Echo Lake, just east of the junction of the Echo Trail with County Road 24. The one at Echo Lake is the closest place to your trip's point of departure. There is a fee to camp there.

Although Little Vermilion Lake ranks high in popularity overall, only about 10% of the summer use permits are issued to parties using canoes without motors. Most of the traffic consists of fishermen in motor boats on their way to ever-popular Lac La Croix, a Canadian border lake where motors are allowed by international agreement. Accordingly, you will find little peace and quiet during your first day on either of the suggested routes that follow. A major portion of each route, however, still maintains a high degree of wilderness character because it is beyond the popular motor routes leading to and along the Canadian border.

Wind can be a problem before you even reach Little Vermilion Lake, as both Crane and Sand Point lakes are highly susceptible to the effects of a strong northwest wind. Normally, however, winds are nearly calm early in the morning, when you will be crossing these two large lakes.

Crane Lake is well-populated with resorts and cabins along its southern shoreline. The north shore of Crane and the west shore of Sand Point mark the southeast boundary of Voyageurs National Park, which is another reason for Crane Lake's popularity. Near the public access, you'll find a post office, gas stations, a grocery store, and an American Customs station for trippers returning from Canada. Sea planes and large motor boats may be a hazard to your tiny craft, so watch out!

Route #14: The Finger-Lac La Croix Loop

7 Days, 70 Miles, 16 Lakes, 1 River, 3 Creeks, 15 Portages
Difficulty: Challenging
Fisher Maps: F-15, F-22, F-23, F-16
Travel Zones: 1, 4, 2, 7

Introduction: This generally easy route takes you north from Crane to Sand Point Lake and then follows the international boundary south through Little Vermilion Lake and up the Loon River to Loon Lake. Continuing along the Canadian Border, you will paddle north into beautiful Lac La Croix and follow this giant horseshoe for 25 miles north, then east, and then south to its very scenic southeastern corner. After viewing the Indian rock paintings and climbing to the top of legendary Warrior Hill, you will point back to the west and return to Loon Lake via the series of interesting lakes and streams that parallel the border a couple miles south of Lac La Croix. From Loon, you will retrace your path down the Loon River and through Little Vermilion Lake back to your origin at Crane Lake.

Although most of the route is easy, the series of frequent portages between Thumb and Little Loon lakes give this loop a rating of "Challenging." During the first half of the trip, only two portages will be encountered, but 13 of these obstacles will loom before you on your return trip from the southeast end of Lac La Croix. Water level should not be a critical factor on this route, except that very low water may necessitate a portage around "56 Rapids" on the Loon River. Finger and Pocket creeks could also be problems for heavily loaded canoes in very low water.

Most of this route is heavily used during summer months. Only that part between Pocket Creek and Little Loon Lake, which is the only part of the route where motors are prohibited, receives light-to-moderate use. Attractive scenery and several points of historical interest combine to compensate for the noise and congestion found along much of the route.

Anglers will find that northern pike predominate throughout most of the lakes on the loop. Walleye may also be found in Crane, Little Vermilion and Loon lakes, as well as in Lac La Croix, where lake trout and bass are also present.

DAY 1: **Crane Lake, Sand Point Lake, Little Vermilion Narrows, Little Vermilion Lake, Loon River, rapids, river,** p. 80 rods, **Loon Lake.** Because of the popularity of this motor route, and because Loon Lake is also accessible from another popular entry point, the Little Indian Sioux River— North, you will be wise to start your trip early so as to get one of the campsites on Loon Lake. If the wind cooperates, you should encounter no major obstacles this day, but it is a lot of paddling for a first day out!

At "56 Rapids," an 11-rod portage exists, although, when the water is high, paddling up the rapids is no problem.

DAY 2: **Loon Lake,** p. 50 rods, **Lac La Croix.** In the western half of Lac La Croix, you will see countless small islands that make navigation difficult at times. If necessary, use your compass to establish a general heading and forget about accounting for every little island you see, many of which are not even shown on the map. Don't miss the display of Indian rock paintings along the US shoreline, just north of the 50-rod "Beatty Portage" from Loon Lake. Along the Canadian shoreline, you will see a couple of resorts, and an Indian village farther east at the source of the Namakan River, in the Neguaguon Lake Indian Reservation, adjacent to

Quetico Provincial Park. You should plan to spend the night somewhere near the northwest end of Coleman Island.

If you can make it a little farther, Lady Boot Bay offers a lovely setting in which to camp. One last note: **beware of sunburn.** On a day of continuous paddling, such as this one so early in your trip, it is very easy to absorb too many rays. Don't let it happen to you.

The BWCA Wilderness Act of 1978 greatly restricted motorized use of Lac La Croix on the US side of the international border. Since January 1, 1979, motors are not allowed in US waters from Snow Bay (at the northwest corner of the lake) all of the way to its southeast end. The southwest end of the lake, however, may still receive motorboats of any size without restrictions on horsepower. This regulation, of course, does not apply to the Canadian half of the lake. So you are still likely to hear motorboats in nearly all parts of the lake, except in the immediate vicinity of Lady Boot Bay.

DAY 3: **Lac La Croix.** Because of the ever-present threat of wind on Lac La Croix, it is best to allow for two full days to paddle from one end to the other. A strong head wind is always a retarding menace, but also beware the strong TAIL wind. When starting across a wide-open expanse of water with a strong wind at your back, the lake ahead of you may appear to be quite safe. But, as you proceed farther and farther out from the shoreline or islands from which you were originally protected, you will find that the waves continue to build up, higher and higher, until suddenly you find your canoe swamped or capsized. Wind can be either a friend or a foe, depending on how much respect you have for it and how much good judgment you demonstrate in its presence.

Two fascinating points of historical interest await you in the southeast end of Lac La Croix. On the west shore of Canada's Irving Island, you will first pass another fine display of old Indian pictographs. About a mile further south, then, you will come to Warrior Hill, once the testing ground for the bravery and strength of Ojibway braves who ran from the lake's edge to the summit of the rocky precipice. You will be rewarded with an outstanding panorama of the surrounding area if you climb to the top. There are several outstanding campsites in the vicinity. Find one early, as this portion of the border is still heavily traveled by motor boats (on the Canadian side) and canoeists alike. The incredible beauty of this area makes the buzz of the motors tolerable.

You will find that Lady Boot Bay offers a lovely setting in which to camp this night. Several excellent campsites are also located near the pictographs.

DAY 4: **Lac La Croix, Pocket Creek,** p. 25 rods, **creek,** p. 20 rods, **Pocket Lake, Finger Creek,** p. 90 rods, **Finger Lake,** p. 9 rods, **Thumb Lake,** p. 200 rods, **Bear Track Lake.** All your portages this day are uphill. The 200-rod trail from Thumb to Bear Track follows a good path and has eight canoe rests along the way, but it climbs rather steeply at first. You may be able to eliminate the 20-rod portage into Pocket Lake by paddling or walking your canoe up the shallow rapids draining Pocket Lake.

DAY 5: **Bear Track Lake,** p. 30 rods, **Little Bear Track Lake,** p. 50 rods, **Eugene Lake,** p. 45 rods, **Steep Lake,** p. 120 rods, **South Lake,** p. 52 rods, **Section 3 Pond, creek,** p. 52 rods, **Slim Lake,** p. 173 rods, **Little Loon Lake, East Loon Bay.** The only uphill portage this day is the 72-rod trail from South Lake to Section 3 Pond. The 120-rod path out of Steep Lake is quite steep, but downhill.

DAY 6: **East Loon Bay, Loon Lake,** p. 80 rods, **Loon River, Little Vermilion Lake.** This day is short enough to allow plenty of time for a visit to one of the area's most scenic attractions. Paddle to the far south end of Loon Lake, leave your canoe and gear at the base of the 160-rod portage, and hike up into the beautiful granite gorge through which Devil's Cascade plunges 75 feet from Lower Pauness Lake—a great place for a gorp break.

DAY 7: **Little Vermilion Lake, Little Vermilion Narrows, Sand Point Lake, Crane Lake.** This should all be familiar from your first day of paddling.

Route #15: The Iron-Horse-Hustler Route

12 Days, 130 Miles, 41 Lakes, 6 Rivers, 4 Creeks, 51 Portages

Difficulty: Challenging

Fisher Maps: F-15, F-22, F-16, F-17, F-10, F-9

Travel Zones: 1, 4, 7, 2, 13, 16, 15, 12, 5, 6, 3

Introduction: This scenic route will lead you to a smorgasbord of large and small lakes, winding little rivers and tiny creeks, half a dozen lovely waterfalls and several points of historic interest. From Crane Lake you will first head north to Sand Point Lake, and then turn southeast and paddle along the Canadian border through Little Vermilion Lake and up the Loon River to Loon Lake. From East Loon Bay you will again travel north into a chain of small lakes and streams that lead east to the beautiful southeast end of giant Lac La Croix. Then, again you will follow the international boundary southeast through Iron and Crooked lakes and up the Basswood River, pausing to view lovely waterfalls en route. From Lower Basswood Falls you will leave the Land of the Maple Leaf and point your canoe southwest, up the placid Horse River to two popular fishing lakes, Horse and Fourtown. Paddling and portaging your way through another chain of small lakes, you'll plot a northwestward route that leads you down the Beartrap River and up Sterling Creek, eventually to Stuart Lake. From the west shore of Stuart Lake you will portage to the Dahlgren River and follow it down to the southernmost bay of Lac La Croix, only to jump quickly from it to Lake Agnes. From this heavily traveled lake, you will meander your way via the Oyster River to Oyster Lake. From Oyster, through Hustler and Lynx, to Lower Pauness Lake you will encounter many a long and arduous portage before re-entering familiar Loon Lake, where you camped the first night. From here on, you will backtrack down the Loon River and through Little Vermilion and Sand Point lakes to your origin at Crane Lake.

When finished, you will have seen virtually every kind of canoeing terrain in the BWCA. You will have seen two fine displays of old Indian rock paintings and several of the most scenic waterfalls in the Boundary Waters, and you will have had an excellent opportunity to see many of the species inhabiting the area: moose, deer, black bear, bald eagle, beaver and who knows what else.

While traveling along the Canadian border, you will doubtless see numerous other voyagers, as well as on Fourtown Lake and Lake Agnes. Along the rest of the route—the majority of it—however, you will see far fewer people.

In addition to the fishing opportunities mentioned for Route #14, you will also find northern pike, walleye and pan fish in the border lakes, Horse, Fourtown and Agnes, and you might try for lake trout in Oyster Lake.

DAY 1: **Crane Lake, Sand Point Lake, Little Vermilion Narrows, Little Vermilion Lake, Loon River, rapids, river,** p. 80 rods, **Loon Lake.** (See comments for Day 1, Route #14.)

DAY 2: **East Loon Bay, Little Loon Lake,** p. 173 rods, **Slim Lake,** p. 52 rods, **creek, Section 3 Pond,** p. 52 rods, **South Lake,** p. 120 rods, **Steep Lake,** p. 45 rods, **Eugene Lake,** p. 50 rods, **Little Bear Track Lake,** p. 30 rods, **Bear Track Lake.** Your first half-mile portage climbs about 65 feet from Little Loon Lake to Slim Lake. It is steep in some places and muddy in others, but five canoe rests along the way make the portaging a little easier. The one-third-mile portage into Steep Lake climbs an exhausting 125 feet—perhaps the toughest portage you'll run into until your last couple days. It has four canoe rests.

DAY 3: **Bear Track Lake,** p. 200 rods, **Thumb Lake,** p. 9 rods, **Finger Lake,** p. 90 rods, **Finger Creek, Pocket Lake,** p. 20 rods, **Pocket Creek,** p. 25 rods, **creek, Lac La Croix.** If you wish, you can probably avoid the 20-rod portage out of Pocket Lake by running, lining or walking your canoe down the shallow rapids of Pocket Creek. Lac La Croix is the longest and one of the most beautiful of the international lakes bordering the BWCA, dotted with over 200 rocky, picturesque islands. Pocket Creek will lead you into the most scenic part of the lake, and numerous good campsites are located near the southeast end.

DAY 4: **Lac La Croix,** p. 80 rods, **Bottle Lake, Iron Lake,** p. 140 rods, **Crooked Lake.** Before leaving Lac La

Croix in the morning, take time to explore the Indian rock paintings and Warrior Hill found on the Canadian shoreline. (See comments for Day 3 of Route #14.) Also take time, while crossing Iron Lake, to visit Rebecca Falls, at the outlet into McAree Lake. (See comments for Day 5, Route #7.)

Curtain Falls, with a total drop of 29 feet, separates Crooked and Iron lakes. Unlike Rebecca Falls, it will be approached from the bottom, and the portage around it is not difficult. Until 1984, motorboats were allowed on Crooked Lake and the Basswood River from Basswood Lake. They are no longer allowed in the region between Lac La Croix and Basswood Lake.

DAY 5: **Crooked Lake, Basswood River.** Laced with countless islands and protruding peninsulas, Crooked Lake may be confusing to even an experienced guide. On an overcast day, a compass is mandatory. Watch overhead as you wind your way through this fascinating lake, for at least one bald-eagle nest is located near the east end, and eagles are occasionally seen soaring above the lake. Between Wednesday and Moose bays, you will paddle past Table Rock, a campsite long ago popular among French-Canadian Voyageurs and still used today. Three miles south of that point, you will pass another good display of Indian pictographs. Several nice campsites are located near the base of Lower Basswood Falls, the final drop (12 feet) in the Basswood River.

DAY 6: **Basswood River,** p. 32 rods, **river, Horse River,** p. 70 rods, **river,** p. 50 rods, **river, rapids, river,** p. 50 rods, **river, rapids, river, rapids, Horse Lake,** p. 70 rods, **pond,** p. 10 rods, **Fourtown Lake,** p. 1–3 rods, **Fourtown Lake,** p. 35 rods, **Boot Lake.** After your portage around Lower Basswood Falls and before entering the Horse River, you may enjoy paddling beyond this confluence to scenic Wheelbarrow Falls, about ¾ mile up the Basswood River, where the river drops another 12 feet.

While paddling up the Horse River, you will come to at least three short, shallow rapids, up which you will have to pull your canoe. These are located near the head of the river.

Horse and Fourtown Lakes are both popular among fishermen. In them you will find northern pike, walleye and bluegill. Sea planes that once brought fishermen to the south end of Fourtown, when it was outside the Boundary Waters, are no longer permitted on this lake, since the BWCA Wilderness Act of 1978 took effect.

DAY 7: **Boot Lake,** p. 15 rods, **Fairy Lake,** p. 50 rods, **Gun Lake,** p. 30 rods, **Gull Lake,** p. 40 rods, **Mudhole Lake,** p. 60 rods, **Thunder Lake.** This will be an easy day, but since campsites are scarce between Thunder and Stuart lakes, it's best to stop here.

DAY 8: **Thunder Lake,** p. 9 rods, **Beartrap Lake,** p. 200 rods, **Beartrap River,** p. 65 rods, **river,** p. 20 rods, **river, Sunday Lake,** p. 17 rods, **Beartrap River, Sterling Creek,** p. 160 rods, **creek,** p. 8 rods, **Sterling Lake,** p. 148 rods, **Bibon Lake,** p. 10 rods, **Nibin Lake,** p. 180 rods, **Stuart Lake.** (See comments for Day 5, Route #9.)

DAY 9: **Stuart Lake,** p. 118 rods, **Dahlgren River,** p. 140 rods, **Boulder Bay,** p. 24 rods, **Lake Agnes, Nina-Moose River, Oyster River,** p. 20 rods, **Oyster River,** p. 60 rods, **Oyster Lake.** If you are tired of river paddling by now portage 160 rods from Lake Agnes to the Oyster River and eliminate a couple miles of paddling. Be sure to hang your food pack safely off the ground this night, as bears are known to raid campsites in this region.

DAY 10: **Oyster Lake,** p. 240 rods, **Hustler Lake,** p. 10 rods, **Ruby Lake,** p. 280 rods, **Lynx Lake,** p. 4 rods, **Little Shell Lake,** p. 15 rods, **Shell Lake.** Psych yourself up for the first long portage of the day, which is mostly uphill, climbing more than 140 feet above Oyster Lake. The 280-rod trail from Ruby Lake ascends very gradually, but then drops nearly 130 feet to Lynx Lake. The first has five portage rests; the second has six. Each follows a good path. Unless the water level is very low, the 4-rod carry will probably not be necessary. Shell Lake is also in an area known for bear problems, so again, be sure you elevate your food at night, and when you are away from the camp.

DAY 11: **Shell Lake,** p. 216 rods, **Lower Pauness Lake,** p. 160 rods, **Loon Lake,** p. 80 rods, **Loon River, Little Vermilion Lake.** Your first long portage passes over a low ridge between Shell and Lower Pauness lakes, and it is not too difficult. The second is mostly downhill, through a scenic granite gorge where Devil's Cascade plunges 75 feet from Lower

Pauness Lake to Loon Lake. There is a fairly steep incline, however, to the second canoe rest, which marks the midpoint of the portage, and offers the best view of the gorge below. A sunny campsite is located here for hikers using the Sioux-Hustler Trail. The third portage also bypasses a waterfall, where the Loon River drops 20 feet into Loon Lake. From that point on, you are back in what should be familiar territory.

DAY 12: **Little Vermilion Lake, Little Vermilion Narrows, Sand Point Lake, Crane Lake.** Welcome home!

Entry Point 14—Little Indian Sioux River-North

Permits: 569

Popularity Rank: 13

Daily Quota: 7

Location: The Little Indian Sioux River begins its winding course about 15 miles northwest of Ely. It flows west for about 6 miles and then turns north and eventually flows into Loon Lake on the Canadian border. All the river except that part in the immediate vicinity of the Echo Trail is contained within the BWCA. The upper part of the river (south of the Echo Trail) is accessible via the Sioux River-South entry point (#9), while the lower, northern part is served by the Sioux River-North entry point (#14). To get to the accesses, follow the Echo Trail for 29.6 miles from County Road 88. About 0.1 mile past the Sioux River bridge, turn right and follow an access road 0.3 mile north to the 40-rod portage leading to the river. A large parking lot has recently been constructed next to the portage.

Description: A public campground at Jeanette Lake, 5½ miles farther west on the Echo Trail, provides a good place to spend the night before your trip, enabling an early start the following morning. There is a charge to camp there.

In spite of its remote location, this entry point is one of the more popular ones, providing easy access to beautiful, big Lac La Croix on the Canadian border. Although it was a designated motor route prior to 1979, 84% of the permits were given to groups using canoes without motors. Although motors are no longer allowed on the river, it continues to be a busy entry point.

In addition to the two routes suggested below, you can also reverse Route #13 from the Little Indian Sioux River-South entry point (#9).

Route #16: The Pocket-Hustler Loop

6 Days, 60 Miles, 22 Lakes, 2 Rivers, 3 Creek, 29 Portages
Difficulty: Challenging
Fisher Map: F-16
Travel Zones: 3, 4, 7, 2, 5, 6

Introduction: This circular loop begins with a portage and then follows the Little Indian Sioux River north to the Pauness lakes and on to Loon Lake on the Canadian border. It then turns east and follows a chain of fascinating little lakes and streams that parallel the Canadian border seldom more than 2 miles south of the international boundary. You will then enter the scenic southeast end of Lac La Croix, where you will have an opportunity to view old Indian rock paintings and climb legendary Warrior Hill. From the southeast tip of this mammoth lake, you will portage into Lake Agnes and then turn west through a series of rugged portages connecting lakes used less than any others on this route. Through Oyster, Hustler and Shell lakes, you will re-enter the Pauness lakes and then retrace your path up the Little Indian Sioux River to your origin at the Echo Trail.

Motors are prohibited on most of the lakes and streams on this route. However, the Canadian side of Lac La Croix is often buzzing with traffic from an Indian village and two resorts located along its north shore. Nevertheless, its scenic beauty more than compensates for these sounds of civilization. The region south of Lac La Croix, where most of this route lies, receives generally light use, and you will have little or no competition for campsites during all but the busiest summer periods.

Fishing is good for northern pike in most of the lakes on this route. Anglers will also find walleye along the way, particularly in Loon and Agnes lakes and Lac La Croix. Lake trout also inhabit the depths of Oyster Lake and Lac La Croix.

DAY 1: Portage 40 rods, **Little Indian Sioux River,** p. 60 rods, **river, Upper Pauness Lake,** p. 8 rods, **Lower Pauness Lake,** p. 160 rods, **Loon Lake, East Loon Bay.** A great place to eat lunch on your first day is at Devil's Cascade, which plunges 75 feet through a scenic granite gorge from Lower Pauness Lake to Loon Lake. The ½-mile portage around the cascade is mostly downhill, with three portage rests along the way. But there is a fairly steep incline to the second rest, which marks the midpoint of the trail and offers the best view of the gorge below. There are several good campsites on Loon Lake, but those in East Loon Bay may offer a little more peace than those near the motor route to Lac La Croix.

DAY 2: **East Loon Bay, Little Loon Lake,** p. 173 rods, **Slim Lake,** p. 52 rods, **creek, Section 3 pond,** p. 52 rods, **South Lake,** p. 120 rods, **Steep Lake,** p. 45 rods, **Eugene Lake,** p. 50 rods, **Little Bear Track Lake,** p. 30 rods, **Bear Track Lake.** As the crow flies, you are not going far this day, but there's a lot of walking along the way! Your first portage of over half a mile climbs about sixty-five feet from Little Loon Lake to Slim Lake. It is steep in some places and muddy in others, but five canoe rests along the way make portaging a LITTLE easier. The one-third mile portage into Steep Lake climbs an exhausting 125 feet—perhaps the toughest portage during the first half of the route. You'll need all four canoe rests to catch your breath.

DAY 3: **Bear Track Lake,** p. 200 rods, **Thumb Lake,** p. 9 rods, **Finger Lake,** p. 90 rods, **Finger Creek, Pocket Lake,** p. 20 rods, **Pocket Creek,** p. 25 rods, **creek, Lac La Croix.** If you wish, you can probably avoid the 20-rod portage out of Pocket Lake by running, lining or walking the shallow rapids of Pocket Creek. Pocket Creek will lead you into the most scenic part of Lac La Croix, and numerous good campsites are located near the southeast end. Take time to explore the Indian rock paintings and Warrior Hill on the Canadian shoreline. (See comments for Day 6, Route #11.)

DAY 4: **Lac La Croix,** p. 65 rods, **Boulder Bay,** p. 24 rods, **Lake Agnes,** p. 160 rods, **Oyster River,** p. 60 rods, **Oyster Lake.** (See comments for Day 8, Route #13.)

DAY 5: **Oyster Lake,** p. 240 rods, **Hustler Lake,** p. 10 rods, **Ruby Lake,** p. 280 rods, **Lynx Lake,** p. 4 rods, **Little Shell Lake,** p. 15 rods, **Shell Lake.** (See comments for Day 9, Route #13.)

DAY 6: **Shell Lake,** p. 216 rods, **Lower Pauness Lake,** p. 8 rods, **Upper Pauness Lake, Little Indian Sioux River,** p. 60 rods, **river,** p. 40 rods, **Public Access.** Your first portage this day is long, but not too difficult, as it passes over a low ridge between Shell and Lower Pauness Lake. From that point on you will be backtracking on your first day's path.

Route #17: Crooked-Beartrap Loop

9 Days, 84 Miles, 28 Lakes, 4 Rivers, 7 Creeks, 38 Portages
Difficulty: Challenging
Fisher Maps: F-16, F-23, F-17
Travel Zones: 3, 4, 2, 13, 15, 14, 12, 5, 6

Introduction: This Canadian border route actually deserves TWO difficulty ratings: EASY for the first half, RUGGED for the second half. From the parking lot north of the Echo Trail, you will first portage 40 rods to the Little Indian Sioux River and then follow that winding, slow stream north through the Pauness lakes to the international boundary at Loon Lake. Continuing north, you will enter ever-popular Lac La Croix and follow this giant horseshoe first north, then east, and finally south to its most beautiful southeast part. While paddling the length of this 25-mile-lake, you will view two displays of Indian pictographs and a thriving Indian village and climb the legendary Warrior Hill. You will continue paddling southeast along the international boundary through Bottle and Iron lakes, portage around scenic Curtain Falls, and enter the maze of peninsulas and islands in Crooked Lake. From Friday Bay of Crooked Lake, you will then turn south and traverse a series of much smaller lakes and their interconnecting streams to Gun Lake. Turning northwest here, you will follow the Beartrap River down to Sterling Creek and then head west to Stuart Lake. After a brief return to Lac La Croix, at its southernmost bay, you will continue west through a series of lightly traveled lakes and rugged portages back to the Pauness lakes, and then retrace your path up the Little Indian Sioux River to your origin at the Echo Trail.

During the first half of this trip, nearly all your energy will be expended in paddling. From the beginning to the northeasternmost point in this loop, only seven portages are encountered. But you will cross 28 on your return trip, many of which are over ½ mile in length! Wind and large waves are a constant threat on the open expanses of Lac La Croix, and an ever-present menace along much of the Canadian border. Although wind is of little concern along the bottom half of this loop, water level is—particularly on the Beartrap, Dahlgren and Oyster rivers. Be prepared for additional walking during periods of low water.

Fishermen, resort visitors and the residents of a nearby Indian village all operate motorboats on the Canadian side of Lac La Croix. And all the other border lakes, too, are heavily used during most of the summer. But the second half of this loop is through a part of the BWCA that is lightly used throughout most of the summer, and motors are prohibited from all the lakes here.

Anglers will find northern pike and walleye in many of the lakes on this route. And for those who like to WORK for their dinner, you will find lake trout inhabiting the depths of Lac La Croix and Oyster Lake.

DAY 1: P. 40 rods, **Little Indian Sioux River,** p. 60 rods, **river, Upper Pauness Lake,** p. 8 rods, **Lower Pauness Lake,** p. 160 rods, **Loon Lake.** (See comments for Day 1, Route #16.)

DAY 2: **Loon Lake,** p. 50 rods, **Lac La Croix.** (See comments for Day 2, Route #14.)

DAY 3: **Lac La Croix.** (See comments for Day 3, Route #14).

DAY 4: **Lac La Croix,** p. 80 rods, **Bottle Lake, Iron Lake,** p. 140 rods, **Crooked Lake.** (See comments for Day 5, Route #7.)

DAY 5: **Crooked Lake (Friday Bay),** p. 95 rods, **Pappoose Creek, Pappoose Lake, creek, Chippewa Lake, creek,** p. 5 rods, **creek, Niki Lake,** p. 30 rods, **Wagosh Lake,** p. 300 rods, **Gun Lake.** Only during periods of very low water will you have to portage 5 rods around a beaver dam between

Chippewa and Niki lakes. The last two portages this day are exhausting. The 30-rod trail from Niki Lake to Wagosh Lake may be short, but it is steep, gaining 73 feet in elevation before descending 6 feet to Wagosh. The 300-rod path from Wagosh to Gun, in turn, surmounts a 117-foot hill and returns to nearly the same elevation at which it started. It has 6 canoe rests to aid you.

DAY 6: **Gun Lake,** p. 30 rods, **Gull Lake,** p. 40 rods, **Mudhole Lake,** p. 60 rods, **Thunder Lake,** p. 9 rods, **Beartrap Lake,** p. 200 rods, **Beartrap River,** 65 rods, **river,** p. 20 rods, **river, Sunday Lake,** p. 17 rods, **Beartrap River, Sterling Creek,** p. 160 rods, **creek,** p. 8 rods, **Sterling Lake.** After your first short uphill portage, it'll all be downhill to Sterling Creek—over 100 feet down in all. Neither of the two long portages is difficult. The first is downhill, and has four portage rests along the way. The ½-mile carry is mostly level and has three canoe rests.

The Beartrap River is shallow and weedy, and it may be blocked by several beaver dams between the 20-rod portage and Sunday Lake. During dry spells, be prepared to walk more than paddle up Sterling Creek. The two portages along the creek are seldom used by human beings, but moose tracks are common.

DAY 7: **Sterling Lake,** p. 148 rods, **Bibon Lake,** p. 10 rods, **Nibin Lake,** p. 180 rods, **Stuart Lake,** p. 118 rods, **Dahlgren River,** p. 140 rods, **Boulder Bay,** p. 24 rods, **Lake Agnes.** The roughest of the portages this day is the 148-rod carry, which climbs a steep hill separating Sterling and Bibon lakes. Four portage rests will help somewhat. Although most of this day will be spent in an area of light use, you will find yourself camping on a lake receiving heavy use as part of a busy route from the Moose River to Lac La Croix. Many good campsites are located here, but there are also many parties competing for them, as this lake is a popular first stop for those beginning their trips through the Moose River entry point. Be sure to hang your food safely off the ground at night, as bears frequent the area.

DAY 8: **Lake Agnes,** p. 160 rods, **Oyster River,** p. 60 rods, **Oyster Lake,** p. 240 rods, **Hustler Lake,** p. 10 rods,

Ruby Lake, p. 280 rods, **Lynx Lake.** (See comments for Days 8 and 9, Route #13.)

DAY 9: **Lynx Lake,** p. 4 rods, **Little Shell Lake,** p. 15 rods, **Shell Lake,** p. 216 rods, **Lower Pauness Lake,** p. 8 rods, **Upper Pauness Lake, Little Indian Sioux River,** p. 60 rods, **river,** p. 40 rods, **Public Access.** The long portage of this day passes over a low ridge between Shell Lake and Lower Pauness Lake, and it is not difficult. From that point on, you will be backtracking on your first day's path.

Entry Point 16—Moose River-North

Permits: 966

Popularity Rank: 7

Daily Quota: 10

Location: The Moose River begins its course at the northwest corner of Big Moose Lake, 15 miles northwest of Ely, and slowly winds its way north for about 10 miles to Nina-Moose Lake. The Echo Trail crosses the river about 4 miles south of Nina-Moose Lake. To get to the public access, follow the Echo Trail 24½ miles from County Road 88. Just before the road crosses the river, an access road spurs off to the north (right). Follow it for 1 mile to the public parking lot and portage trail to the Moose River. (Note: About a mile before this spur, you will see a sign pointing to the Moose River via Forest Route 464, south of the Echo Trail. Do not turn here; this road leads to the access serving the Moose River-South entry point.)

Description: The Fenske Lake Campground, 16 miles toward Ely on the Echo Trail, offers a good place to spend the night before your trip. There is also a National Forest campground twelve miles farther west on the Echo Trail, at Lake Jeanette. It will cost you to camp at either.

The Moose River is quite narrow and shallow, it meanders considerably, and it is almost choked with vegetation for the first few miles. Since the BWCA Wilderness Act of 1978 took effect, motors are no longer allowed to enter the BWCA here. Even when they were legal, however, over 83% of the travel permits issued in 1977 went to groups using canoes without motors. The Moose is a pretty little river that you are sure to enjoy.

Route #18: The Iron-Duck Loop

5 Days, 43 Miles, 12 Lakes, 4 Rivers, 1 Creek, 27 Portages
Difficulty: Rugged
Fisher Maps: F-16, F-9
Travel Zones: 5, 2, 13, 12, 11

Introduction: This winding route will take you through the entire length of three rivers and the first part of a fourth. In fact, most of your time will be spent on these rivers, with frequent portages thrown in to stretch your muscles, including five carries of over ½ mile in length.

You start right off with one of those portages— 160 rods from the Moose River parking lot to your first "taste" of the Moose River. You will paddle north down this lazy stream to Nina-Moose Lake, and then continue north down the Nina-Moose River to Lake Agnes. After two short portages to the north, you will be on big, beautiful Lac La Croix, which constitutes 25 miles of our international boundary. You will follow the border southeast to Iron Lake and then turn south through a series of tiny lakes to Stuart Lake. Continuing south, you will paddle up the Stuart River, portage nearly 2 miles across the Echo Trail, and find your campsite on Big Lake, situated outside the BWCA. From Big Lake you will paddle and portage your way southwest to Big Moose Lake and then re-enter the Moose River, which will, of course, bring you back to your origin at the Moose River parking lot.

If the water level is low, find another route. This one is best during periods of higher water. Fishing is fairly good for walleye, northern pike and bass in most of the lakes on this route. Lake trout are also found in Lac La Croix.

During your brief visit to the Canadian border, you will have an opportunity to view two scenic waterfalls, a good display of old Indian rock paintings and an outstanding panorama from atop legendary Warrior Hill. All this and more in a five-day flurry that you won't soon forget!

DAY 1: P. 160 rods, **Moose River,** p. 20 rods, **river,** p. 25 rods, **river, Nina-Moose Lake, Nina-Moose River,** p. 70 rods, **river,** p. 96 rods, **river, Lake Agnes.** All these portages are easy, following smooth, sandy pathways that slope gently downhill. Four portage rests along that 160-rod carry will make life easier if you're not in as good shape as you thought. Small beaver dams sometimes pop up on slow streams like these. You may gave an occasional quick liftover in addition to the portages mentioned. On the west shore of Nina-Moose Lake you will see evidence of the 1971 fire that ravaged 25 square miles of woodland between here and the Little Indian Sioux River.

Folks who fear bears might want to avoid camping on Lake Agnes. Bears are traditional pests in this area. Unfortunately, it's a long way to the next cluster of campsites, on Lac La Croix. If you hang your food properly and maintain a clean campsite, you should have nothing to fear.

DAY 2: **Lake Agnes,** p. 24 rods, **Boulder Bay,** p. 65 rods, **Lac La Croix,** p. 80 rods, **Bottle Lake, Iron Lake.** If you prefer a couple of extra miles of paddling to a 65-rod portage, follow the shallow, meandering course of Boulder Bay from the 24-rod portage to Lac La Croix. And, before leaving it to the east you may wish to paddle an extra mile and a half north to two points of historic interest. On the granite cliffs of the Canadian shoreline are the fading red-brown remnants of pictographs long ago painted by the Ojibway Indians who inhabited the area. About a mile to the south is a high, rock-faced hill that was once the testing ground for the bravery and strength of Ojibway braves who ran from the lake's edge to the summit. It is known as Warrior Hill. You will find an outstanding vista after a climb to the top.

Before leaving Iron Lake, be sure to visit two of the most scenic natural attractions in this part of the BWCA—Rebecca Falls, and Curtain Falls. (See comments for Day 5, Route #7.)

DAY 3: **Iron Lake,** p. 72 rods, **Dark Lake,** p. 67 rods, **Rush Lake,** p. 60 rods, **Fox Lake,** p. 320 rods, **Stuart Lake.** The short portages south of Iron Lake require some steep climbing, but they are short enough to cause no major difficulty. The mile trek to Stuart Lake is slightly downhill along most of its course. It follows a good path and has 11 portage rests along the way. Although you should arrive early at Stuart Lake, it is best to go no farther, as there are no Forest Service campsites along the Stuart River.

DAY 4: **Stuart Lake,** p. 74 rods, **Stuart River,** p. 14 rods, **river,** p. 74 rods, **river,** 52 rods, **river,** p. 85 rods, **river,** p. 600 rods, **Big Lake.** (See comments for Day 6, Route #7.)

DAY 5: **Big Lake, creek, Portage River,** p. 150 rods, **Duck Lake,** p. 480 rods, **Big Moose Lake,** p. 60 rods, **Moose River,** p. 160 rods, **river,** p. 17 rods, **river,** p. 40 rods, **river,** p. 40 rods, **river,** p. 77 rods, **river, Moose River parking lot.** This is another rough day of long portages and slow river travel. You could shorten it by having a vehicle waiting at the Moose River access from Forest Route 464. This would eliminate about 4 miles of meandering and four short portages through a portion of the route not contained in the BWCA.

When you reach the point where the small creek draining Big Lake flows into the Portage River, bear left and paddle about 25 rods to the portage landing on the right side of the river.

The first 25 rods of both the 150- and 480-rod carries are across muskeg. The 150-rod portage was nearly impassable with windfalls during the early summer of 1978. The 480-rod trail crosses over several small hills, but there are 10 canoe rests along the way. Both portages are *very* seldom used.

Route #19: The Slim-Indian Sioux Route

8 Days, 85 Miles, 21 Lakes, 4 Rivers, 3 Creeks, 44 Portages
Difficulty: Challenging
Fisher Maps: F-16, F-8, F-9
Travel Zones: 5, 2, 7, 4, 3, 11, 9

Introduction: Like Route #18, this high-quality wilderness route follows rivers for much of its course. From the Moose River parking lot you will paddle down the winding Moose and Nina-Moose rivers, through Lake Agnes to Lac La Croix, an international border lake where fishermen and motorboats are common. But you will soon leave the busy motor route, enter peaceful Pocket Creek and traverse the chain of small lakes and tiny streams west to Slim Lake. Turning south then, you will again touch the Canadian border on popular Loon Lake before continuing south through the

Pauness lakes and up the Little Indian Sioux River to the Echo Trail. You will portage past this popular entry point and continue up the Sioux River, entering a part of the Boundary Waters seldom visited by other canoeists. Along its sluggish, meandering course, you will have an excellent opportunity to view moose, deer, beaver and other forms of wildlife before entering Otter and Cummings lakes. From Cummings Lake you will carry your gear across the longest portage on this route, to Big Moose Lake, and then follow the Moose River again, down its winding course to your origin at the Moose River parking lot.

When finished, you will have seen a good display of Indian rock paintings, an awesome panorama from atop Warrior Hill, the impressive Devil's Cascade, and, most likely, countless forms of North Woods fauna. The part of this route north of the Echo Trail receives moderate-to-heavy use during much of the summer, but the region south of the road has been seen by few other visitors to the Boundary Waters. You will quickly sense the pristine character of the Sioux River, and here you will experience as much solitude and isolation as you could hope to find anywhere in the BWCA.

Northern pike inhabit the waters throughout most of the route. You will also find walleye and bass in Agnes, Nina-Moose and Loon lakes, as well as in Lac La Croix, where lake trout may also be caught.

Water level is a critical factor on this route. The Little Indian Sioux River, in particular, may be too dry for navigation during especially dry years, or during the dry periods of a typical summer. Late spring or early summer, or after the autumn rains, is usually the best time for this trip.

DAY 1: P. 160 rods, **Moose River,** p. 20 rods, **river,** p. 25 rods, **river, Nina-Moose Lake, Nina-Moose River,** p. 70 rods, **river,** p. 96 rods, **river, Lake Agnes.** (See comments for Day 1, Route #18.)

DAY 2: **Lake Agnes,** p. 24 rods, **Boulder Bay,** p. 65 rods, **Lac La Croix.** (See comments for Day 2, Route #18.) You'll find several good campsites in and north of Lady Boot Bay, near the mouth of Pocket Creek, where motors are not allowed.

DAY 3: **Lac La Croix, Pocket Creek,** p. 25 rods, **creek,**

p. 20 rods, **Pocket Lake, Finger Creek,** p. 90 rods, **Finger Lake,** p. 9 rods, **Thumb Lake,** p. 200 rods, **Bear Track Lake,** p. 30 rods, **Little Bear Track Lake,** p. 50 rods, **Eugene Lake.** Your first five portages this day are uphill. The 200-rod trail from Thumb to Bear Track climbs steeply at first, but follows a good path and has eight canoe rests along the way. You may be able to eliminate the 20-rod portage into Pocket Lake by paddling or walking your canoe up the shallow rapids draining Pocket Lake.

DAY 4: **Eugene Lake,** p. 45 rods, **Steep Lake,** p. 120 rods, **South Lake,** p. 52 rods, **Section Three Pond, creek,** p. 52 rods, **Slim Lake,** p. 173 rods, **Little Loon Lake, East Loon Bay, Loon Lake,** p. 160 rods, **Lower Pauness Lake.** The 120-rod path out of Steep Lake is quite steep, but fortunately downhill. The only major uphill trek of the day is the half-mile portage around Devil's Cascade, south of Loon Lake. When you have completed this task, reward yourself by hiking back down into this scenic granite gorge to the second (of three) canoe rests, and viewing the progression of waterfalls and rapids plunging 75 feet from Lower Pauness Lake to Loon Lake. Plan to camp early this evening, as the Pauness lakes are a popular first-night stop for those getting a late start from the Little Indian Sioux River—North entry point.

DAY 5: **Lower Pauness Lake,** p. 8 rods, **Upper Pauness Lake, Little Indian Sioux River,** p. 60 rods, **river,** p. 120 rods, **river,** p. 8 rods, **river,** p. 120 rods, **river, Little Pony River,** p. 60 rods, **river,** p. 60 rods, **Bootleg Lake.** The Little Indian Sioux River is another slow, shallow, meandering stream, fairly wide in its lower reaches, but becoming narrower the farther up stream you get, until it is wide enough only for single-file canoeing as you approach its source. Moose and deer are common sights along its marshy banks. Strong head winds can slow your progress considerably.

When you begin your 120-rod portage across the Echo Trail, follow the less-used trail nearest the river. The more trodden path on the right leads for 40 rods to the Sioux River parking lot. Although you could take this route, it is longer than need be.

DAY 6: **Bootleg Lake,** p. 200 rods, **Little Indian Sioux River,** p. 40 rods, **river,** p. 35 rods, **river,** p. 20 rods, **river,** p.

30 rods, **river,** p. 40 rods, **river,** p. 20 rods, **river,** p. 28 rods, **river,** p. 120 rods, **Otter Lake,** p. 5 rods, **Cummings Lake.** Because of the constant winding and the numerous short portages, travel is deceivingly slow on the upper part of the Sioux River. There are no designated Forest Service camp-sites along the river, and very few places that are even pos-sible for camping along this swampy stream. So it is important that you forge onward to Cummings Lake before dusk, where several good campsites await.

DAY 7: **Cummings Lake,** p. 580 rods, **Big Moose Lake.** As the crow flies, you won't be going far this day, but you'll feel like you have at day's end! Your longest carry of the trip will occupy a good deal of your time, especially if you are unable to transport all your gear in one trip. In spite of its length, the portage is not too difficult. Except for a few small hills at each end, the trail follows a rather level ridge much of the way, and 19 canoe rests are situated at regular intervals along its course. If you can take your mind off the heavy cargo on your shoulders, you will find the scenery to be quite lovely along the trail.

DAY 8: **Big Moose Lake,** p. 60 rods, **Moose River,** p. 160 rods, **river,** p. 17 rods, **river,** p. 40 rods, **river,** p. 40 rods, **river,** p. 77 rods, **river, Moose River parking lot.** What would be a more appropriate end to this meandering trip than another winding little river?

Entry Point 19—Stuart River

Permits: 60

Popularity Rank: 43

Daily Quota: 2

Location: The headwaters of the Stuart River are about 15 miles northwest of Ely, just north of Big Lake. The swampy, little river flows slowly northward for about 6 miles to Stuart Lake, 4 miles south of the Canadian border. Access to the river is across a 513-rod portage from the Echo Trail, 18 miles northwest of County Road 88. This is 8 miles past the point at which the Echo Trail turns to gravel, and one mile past the access road to Whispering Pines Resort. Drive with cau-tion on this narrow, winding, gravel road. Traffic is not heavy, but there is always some headed for either one of the two resorts on Big Lake or one of the busier entry points farther up the road.

A small parking area adjacent to the 513-rod portage serves the Stuart River entry point.

Description: A National Forest campground at Fenske Lake, 10 miles closer to Ely on the Echo Trail, is a good place to spend the night before your trip. This enables you to get an early start the following morning—and you'll need it. There is a fee to camp there.

The long access portage to the river is mostly downhill, but it's a rugged way to start any trip. Beyond it, you will find no designated campsites along the tiny, shallow river—not until persistent paddling and six more portages have taken you into Stuart Lake. Motors are not allowed on this river, and few canoes utilize it. Consequently, this BWCA access point offers a quick entrance into the kind of pristine wilderness that might take several days to find from many other entry points.

During a very dry year you may want to avoid the river. It may be too shallow in the final stretch leading into Stuart Lake, even when it appears fine in the upper stretches. Consult with the Forest Service and/or the local outfitter before heading out.

Route #20: Five Rivers Route

4 Days, 35 Miles, 7 Lakes, 5 Rivers, 1 Creek, 24 Portages
Difficulty: Rugged
Fisher Maps: F-9, F-16
Travel Zones: 12, 5, 11

Introduction: After the first grueling portage from the Echo Trail, this river-running route will take you north down the lazy Stuart River to Stuart Lake. You will then portage onto the Dahlgren River and follow it northwest to Boulder Bay on Lac La Croix. Then you will head south into Lake Agnes and up the Nina-Moose River to Nina-Moose Lake. Continuing south, you will paddle up your fourth winding stream, the Moose River, under the Echo Trail to Big Moose Lake. From the east side of this beautiful, large lake, you will portage 1½ miles into Duck Lake and another ⅓ mile to the

Portage River, which carries you into Big Lake, a short portage away from your origin at the Echo Trail. Although you will be camping only on lakes, you'll be paddling almost exclusively on rivers for the first three days of this trip. Accordingly, water level is an important consideration. The Stuart River and the upper portion of the Moose River, in particular, could provide difficult passage during dry periods. Normally, therefore, spring and early summer, as well as after the fall rains, are the best times to take this trip.

Motors are prohibited from most of the route. Only in the stretch from the Moose River Parking Lot south to just north of Big Moose Lake and on Big Lake are they allowed.

For anglers, walleye, northern pike and smallmouth bass prevail throughout much of the route.

DAY 1: P. 513 rods, **Stuart River,** p. 85 rods, **river,** p. 52 rods, **river,** p. 74 rods, **river,** p. 14 rods, **river,** p. 74 rods, **Stuart Lake.** That first long portage from the Echo Trail follows a good path over several small hills to the third canoe rest. It then drops steadily downhill to a creek that crosses the trail near its end. There are a total of six canoe rests.

Beaver dams are scattered throughout the course of the shallow, winding, weedy Stuart River. Thanks to Nature's "corps of engineers" you may find the water level a bit too low during the latter part of the summer as you approach your final portage. If so, plan on wet feet.

If you should get a late start and Stuart Lake is too far for the first night, there is a campsite on White Feather Lake, accessible through a short stream that connects to the Stuart River just south of the 52-rod portage.

DAY 2: **Stuart Lake,** p. 118 rods, **Dahlgren River,** p. 140 rods, **Boulder Bay,** p. 24 rods, **Lake Agnes, Nina-Moose River,** p. 96 rods, **river,** p. 70 rods, **river, Nina-Moose Lake.** You will probably see the most people this day, as you travel up the popular route from the Moose River entry point. So try to find a campsite early on busy Nina-Moose Lake. Along the west shore of this lake you will see scars of the great fire of 1971 that ravaged nearly 25 square miles of woodland between here and the Little Indian Sioux River.

DAY 3: **Nina-Moose Lake, Moose River,** p. 25 rods,

river, p. 20 rods, **river,** p. 160 rods, **river,** p. 77 rods, **river,** p. 40 rods, **river,** p. 40 rods, **river,** p. 17 rods, **river,** p. 160 rods, **river,** p. 60 rods, **Big Moose Lake.** (See comments for Day 8, Route #11.)

DAY 4: **Big Moose Lake,** p. 480 rods, **Duck Lake,** p. 150 rods, **Portage River, creek, Big Lake,** p. 73 rods. Few if any other people will share your route in spite of the location of two resorts on Big Lake. The two portages between Big Moose and Big lakes are seldom used by canoeists. The 480-rod trail passes over several small hills before ending across 25 rods of muskeg, adjacent to Duck Lake. From the end of the 150-rod carry, paddle left onto the Portage River and follow it northeast for about 25 rods. From that point, a small meandering creek leads eastward to Big Lake.

Your final portage leads almost due north from a parking area at the north end of Big Lake. Don't follow the road, or you will find yourself at the Echo Trail about 0.1 mile east of your origin.

Route #21: The Beartrap-Range Rivers Route

7 Days, 55 Miles, 30 Lakes, 5 Rivers, 1 Creek, 45 Portages
Difficulty: Rugged
Fisher Maps: F-9, F-16, F-17, F-10
Travel Zones: 12, 14, 15, 11

Introduction: This is another loop through a part of the BWCA that receives light-to-moderate use most of the summer. From the Echo Trail, you will portage 513 rods to the Stuart River and then follow it north to the portage into Nibin Lake. After paddling through Nibin and Bibon lakes and down Sterling Creek, you will soon meet the Beartrap River and follow it southeast to its headwaters at Beartrap Lake. Continuing southeast, you will paddle and portage your way through a chain of popular fishing lakes to the Range River. This shallow, marshy creek will lead you southwest to the Grassy River and on to Grassy Lake. From Grassy Lake you will pass through a chain of small, picturesque lakes, cross the Echo Trail and eventually go onto the North Arm of big Burntside Lake, a populated lake just outside the BWCA.

After portaging across County Road 644, you will re-enter the Boundary Waters and travel through one of the least used portions in the BWCA, between Slim and Big lakes. At the north end of Big Lake you will find the portage that takes you back to your origin at the Echo Trail.

Motors are prohibited on most of this route, except on those lakes outside of the Boundary Waters. Elsewhere, you will surely find a high-quality wilderness setting, with lovely scenery and plentiful wildlife. Nearly all the route will be on narrow rivers, winding creeks and small lakes. Walleye, northern pike and pan fish prevail.

Because rivers are a major portion of the loop, water level plays an important role in the suitability of this route. During especially dry periods, the Stuart and Range rivers, in particular, may be too low for navigation.

DAY 1: P. 513 rods, **Stuart River,** p. 85 rods, **river,** p. 52 rods, **river,** p. 74 rods, **river,** p. 14 rods, **river,** p. 100 rods, **Nibin Lake.** (See comments for Day 1, Route #20.) If the campsite on Nibin Lake is taken, you should consider a side trip to Stuart Lake, where sites are more plentiful, rather than continuing east, where sites continue to be scarce. But, then, this means over a mile of additional portaging.

DAY 2: **Nibin Lake,** p. 10 rods, **Bibon Lake,** p. 148 rods, **Sterling Lake,** p. 8 rods, **Sterling Creek,** p. 160 rods, **creek, Beartrap River,** p. 17 rods, **Sunday Lake, Beartrap River,** p. 20 rods, **river,** p. 65 rods, **river,** p. 200 rods, **Beartrap Lake,** p. 9 rods, **Thunder Lake.** If you thought the first day was tough, you may find this day downright miserable. But I call it the price one must pay to find an isolated part of the earth. All of the portages between Bibon Lake and the Beartrap River are very seldom used, and the pathways are sometimes hard to see. The 148-rod carry may be the toughest, as it surmounts a steep hill separating Bibon and Sterling lakes. It has four canoe rests to help you out a bit.

Beaver dams across the Beartrap River, just south of Sunday Lake, may require quick liftovers. After crossing the 65-rod portage, continue paddling south for about 15 to 20 minutes, and then watch *very* carefully for the junction of the Beartrap River and Spring Creek. The widest and deepest channel of water continues straight south, into the mouth of Spring Creek. The much narrower Beartrap River drains from a tiny inlet on your left (east) and is partly hidden by an old, broken beaver dam. It would be very easy to miss the confluence of these two streams if you were not paying careful attention.

You will climb nearly 80 feet on that last long portage to Beartrap Lake. But it follows a more well-beaten path than the earlier long walks, and there are four canoe rests along the way.

DAY 3: **Thunder Lake,** p. 60 rods, **Mudhole Lake,** p. 40 rods, **Gull Lake,** p. 30 rods, **Gun Lake,** p. 50 rods, **Fairy Lake,** p. 15 rods, **Boot Lake,** p. 35 rods, **Fourtown Lake,** p. 1–3 rods, **Fourtown Lake,** p. 10 rods, **pond,** p. 70 rods, **Horse Lake.** Fourtown Lake was once a popular "fly-in" point of departure for fishermen. Since the BWCA Wilderness Act of 1978, however, motors are no longer allowed on Fourtown Lake. This will be one of your easiest days, but make camp early. It is a popular area and good fishing awaits you in both Fourtown and Horse lakes.

DAY 4: **Horse Lake,** p. 90 rods, **Tin Can Lake,** p. 117 rods, **Sandpit Lake,** p. 109 rods, **Range Lake, Range River,** p. 10 rods, **river,** p. 23 rods, **river,** p. 1 rod, **river, Grassy River,** p. 24 rods, **Beaver Pond, Grassy Lake.** The portages between Tin Can and Range lakes follow an old railroad bed that once served logging operations in the area. Don't be surprised to see a couple of beaver dams obstructing the Range River. The 1-rod portage is merely a liftover, where the Cloquet Road crosses the river. If the water level is low, there may be another short portage between the beaver pond and Grassy Lake. (See detailed sketch of Range River region in Route #9.)

DAY 5: **Grassy Lake,** p. 48 rods, **Tee Lake,** p. 120 rods, **Sletten Lake,** p. 70 rods, **Little Sletten Lake,** p. 10 rods, **Fenske Lake,** p. 120 rods, **Everett Lake,** p. 14 rods, **East Twin Lake, West Twin Lake.** Take your time this day, and enjoy the scenic appeal of the tiny lakes on which you are traveling—as lovely as any portion of the route in the BWCA. Your first two portages are entirely uphill, and the third is over a small hill. But from there on, it is easy going all the way to West Twin Lake. You will cross the Echo Trail near the end of the 120-rod portage from Fenske to Everett Lake.

DAY 6: **West Twin Lake,** p. 250 rods, **North Arm of Burntside Lake,** p. 140 rods, **Slim Lake,** p. 77 rods, **Rice Lake,** p. 130 rods, **Hook Lake.** If the time is right, you will have a good opportunity to pick enough blueberries this day for a pie, pancakes, muffins, and other concoctions. At the end of the portage to Slim Lake is a trail off to the right that leads up to a rock cliff that abounds with berry bushes. If high, scenic lookouts thrill you, take the time to paddle out of your way to the south end of Slim Lake and hike to Old Baldy. (See comments for Day 1, Route #8.)

DAY 7: **Hook Lake,** p. 540 rods, **Big Rice Lake,** p. 8 rods, **Portage River, Lapond Lake,** p. 150 rods, **Big Lake,** p. 73 rods. This part of the BWCA is seldom visited, except for the immediate vicinity of Big Lake. Your first portage is *very* seldom used, and may be difficult to follow. But there are many canoe rests. You will find two resorts on the north shore of Big Lake, should you wish to satisfy any cravings for "civilized" food or drink.

Entry Point 20—Angleworm Lake

Permits: 49

Popularity Rank: 49

Daily Quota: 2

Location: As the crow flies, Angleworm Lake lies about 12 miles northwest of Ely. The signed trailhead ("Angleworm Trail") and small parking lot are on the right (east) side of the Echo Trail, 13 miles north of County Road 88.

Description: The Fenske Lake Campground is a good place to spend the night before your trip. It's located along the Echo Trail, 5 miles closer to Ely. There are 16 campsites, well water, and a small swimming beach. A fee is charged to campers.

It doesn't take a long study of the map to understand why Angleworm Lake is ranked 49th in popularity. On the other hand, the fact that 49 groups braved the 2¼-mile portage to the lake in 1986 is a tribute to Angleworm's unparalleled beauty.

No doubt, if Angleworm Lake were easily accessible to canoeists, it would be one of the most popular entry points along the Echo Trail.

As it is, however, the lake is seen more often by hikers than by canoeists. A 10-mile foot path encircles Angleworm, Home and Whisky Jack lakes and intersects the long portage from the Echo Trail at a point ¼ mile south of Angleworm Lake. Considered by many to be one of the best hiking trails in the Ely area, the Angleworm Trail follows high rock ridges with scenic overlooks, passes through impressive stands of large red and white pines, and frequently drops down to touch the shore of Angleworm Lake. At those points, canoeists also have access to the trail. It provides a good opportunity to stretch your legs and gain a unique perspective of the long lake on which you're paddling.

To further discourage canoeists from using this lovely entry point, there is also no easy exit. The only outlets are by way of either a 1½-mile portage south to Trease Lake or a ⅔-mile portage north to Gull Lake (after a 40-rod portage into Home Lake). The conclusion? Angleworm Lake is not for the weak or timid!

If you don't mind the hard work, though, it is a wonderful way to quickly escape from the summer crowds. And it's seldom necessary to make a reservation in advance of arrival. Only on 13 nights during the Visitor Distribution period in 1986 did Angleworm Lake fill up its quota of two groups.

Route #22: The Angleworm-Stuart Lakes Loop

4 Days, 32 Miles, 11 Lakes, 2 Rivers, 1 Creek, 21 Portages
Difficulty: Rugged
Fisher Maps: F-9, F-17, F-16
Travel Zones: 14, 12

Introduction: This is by far one of the most difficult routes in this guide. It leads north from Angleworm Lake to Home, Gull and Thunder lakes and then veers northwest to follow the Beartrap River and Sterling Creek to Stuart Lake.

From there the Stuart River will carry your canoe south to the Echo Trail. Several long, seldom-used portages will test your strength and stamina. The reward? Peaceful seclusion in a region that receives very little canoeing traffic at any time of the summer.

This is *not* a complete loop. Unless you are willing to hike five miles back to the Angleworm trailhead, plan to have a car waiting at the Stuart River parking lot.

WARNING: When water levels are low, two of the streams on this route may be too shallow for the navigation of a loaded canoe. Sterling Creek and the lower (northernmost) stretch of the Stuart River are capable of nearly drying up.

DAY 1: P. 720 rods, **Angleworm Lake.** During the first mile of the long portage from the parking lot, the trail first crosses nearly level to gently rolling terrain, then gradually descends and finally plunges into the valley of Spring Creek— a total descent of more than 150 feet. After crossing the small creek on a log bridge, the trail climbs abruptly from the creek and ascends 100 feet to a high rocky ridge overlooking the valley. Parts of the trail follow the route of an old roadway, while other parts utilize more recently cut hiking trails (more scenic for hikers, but more difficult for those who must carry a canoe). At the 2-mile point, there is a junction of three trails. A portage to Trease Lake leads south. The east branch of the Angleworm Trail heads east, while the portage continues in a northeast direction toward the south end of Angleworm Lake. Just ¼ mile farther, watch for a short spur trail branching off to the right from the hiking trail that leads down to the lake.

Do yourself a favor: plan to go no farther than Angleworm Lake this day. You won't be traveling far, but it will seem as though you did. There are four campsites along the west shore of the lake for backpackers. The nicest sites, however, are on the east shore of the lake, easily accessible to canoeists. Find your home for the night, and then take time to explore this beautiful lake. Anglers will find walleyes and northern pike in its shallow depths.

DAY 2: **Angleworm Lake,** p. 40 rods, **Home Lake,** p. 240 rods, **Gull Lake,** p. 40 rods, **Mudhole Lake,** p. 60 rods, **Thunder Lake.** Compared to the previous day, this one will be a "piece of cake." But there is a good reason to go no farther than Thunder Lake. There are only two campsites between Thunder and Sterling lakes (on Beartrap and Sunday lakes); and, if they are occupied, you'll be in for a LONG day—too long for most mortals. The only long portage of this day follows a good path, climbing gently from Home Lake and then descending 130 feet to Gull Lake. Four canoe rests are there if you need them. With plenty of spare time in the evening, anglers may want to fish for the walleyes and northern pike that inhabit Thunder and Beartrap lakes.

Strong canoeists in good shape with only three days to spare, could easily make the 8-mile journey to Thunder Lake in just one day. But that would leave little time to enjoy this beautiful route. And if you must two-trip your portages, you'll be walking nearly seven miles! That's too much for an "average" canoe-camper.

DAY 3: **Thunder Lake,** p. 9 rods, **Beartrap Lake,** p. 200 rods, **Beartrap River,** p. 65 rods, **river,** p. 20 rods, **river, Sunday Lake,** p. 17 rods, **Beartrap River, Sterling Creek,** p. 160 rods, **creek,** p. 8 rods, **Sterling Lake,** p. 148 rods, **Bibon Lake,** p. 10 rods, **Nibin Lake,** p. 180 rods, **Stuart Lake.** (See comments for Day 5, Route # 9.)

DAY 4: **Stuart Lake,** p. 74 rods, **Stuart River,** p. 14 rods, **river,** p. 74 rods, **river,** p. 52 rods, **river,** p. 85 rods, **river,** p. 513 rods, **Echo Trail.** (See comments for Day 6, Route # 9, paragraphs 1–3.)

Entry Point 77—South Hegman Lake

Permits: 103

Popularity Rank: 38

Daily Quota: 2

Location: South Hegman Lake is located ten miles almost due north of Ely. To drive there, follow the Echo Trail north from County Road 88 for 11 miles, a mile beyond the point at which the blacktop ends and gravel begins.

Description: A small parking area on the east side of the road will accommodate 5 or 6 vehicles. From the parking lot a 76-rod portage leads gently downhill to South Hegman Lake.

The Hegman lakes have been included in the BWCA

Wilderness only since January 1, 1979. But they have long been favorites among weekend campers and dayhikers, as well as amateur historians in search of the best display of Indian rock paintings in all of the Quetico-Superior region. This is one entry point for which a reservation is nearly always necessary. It ranks among the top three entry points in the BWCA with quotas filled the highest percent of the time. During the summer of 1986 its quota was filled on 85 days. That means, without a reservation, your chances of getting a permit at the last minute on weekends, holidays or during the months of June and August are slim at best. Motors are not allowed here.

Although picnic facilities are available at the base of the portage to South Hegman, camping is prohibited there. The closest public campground is at Fenske Lake, located along the Echo Trail, four miles closer to Ely. That is a good place to spend the night prior to your canoe trip. There is a campsite fee at Fenske.

Route #23: The Pictograph Route

2 Days, 4 Miles, 3 Lakes, 4 Portages

Difficulty: Easy

Fisher Map: F-9

Travel Zone: 14

Introduction: This brief but fascinating route will take you through South Hegman, North Hegman and Trease lakes. Then you will backtrack to your origin at the Echo Trail.

This is by far the shortest and easiest of all the suggested routes in this guide. Normally a jaunt of this nature would not be included because: 1) it backtracks to its origin, and 2) it is scarcely long enough to even be considered as a "trip." Nevertheless, I have included it because 1) South Hegman is one of the loveliest entry lakes in all of the BWCA, 2) to go beyond Trease Lake involves some rugged portaging that might discourage would-be trippers from trying this point of entry, and 3) there is plenty for the weekend sojourner to do right here, without paddling for miles and miles. This route offers an excellent opportunity for the wilderness greenhorn to get a fulfilling taste of the Boundary Waters Canoe Area—with very little effort needed.

DAY 1: P. 76 rods, **South Hegman Lake.** Side trip: p. 15 rods, **North Hegman Lake, Trease Lake.** Even if you have never carried a canoe before, that first ¼-mile portage should pose no problem. It follows an excellent path and has one canoe rest midway down the sloping trail. The final 2 rods, however, are down a set of stair steps, so watch it!

Find a nice campsite on South Hegman Lake immediately after completing the portage. Then hang your food pack properly and prepare for an afternoon of exploration. Your side trip to Trease Lake will lead you past a vivid display of ancient Indian pictographs—in fact, the best art gallery in all the BWCA. They are found on the steep cliffs between North Hegman and Trease lakes, about 8 feet above the waterline.

DAY 2: **South Hegman Lake,** p. 76 rods. If hiking appeals to you, paddle back to the north end of Trease Lake this morning and you'll find a trail there that leads north to the Angleworm Trail. Since 1979, this is part of a trail system that extends from the Echo Trail to Angleworm Lake and then encircles Angleworm and Home lakes—a total of nearly 15 miles of trails. Get up early if you intend to make it all of the way around the lakes!

Entry Point 21—Mudro Lake

Permits: 911 (Range and Mudro combined)

Popularity Rank: 8

Daily Quota: 5

Location: Mudro Lake is accessible from Nels Lake, located almost 9 miles straight north of Ely. To get there, follow County Road 116 (Echo Trail) north and west from County Road 88 for 10 miles, ¾ mile past the intersection with County Road 644. As the Echo Trail bends to the left, a one-lane primitive road branches to the right (east). Follow this narrow, winding path for ¾ mile to Nels Lake, where a small parking lot is adjacent to the public landing. During the muddy spring months, a 4-wheel-drive vehicle might be required—at least when you try to *leave* Nels Lake.

Description: Camping is prohibited at the landing, but a Forest Service campsite is located nearby on the lake, with a path leading to it from the landing. If it is occupied or inconvenient, you may wish to spend the night before your trip at Fenske Lake Campground, 2 miles closer to Ely on the Echo Trail. A camping fee will be assessed.

Before the BWCA Wilderness Act of 1978, Entry Point 21 was at Fourtown Lake, two miles north of Mudro Lake. Fourtown was a motor-designated lake and a popular fly-in point of departure for fisherman who could afford such luxury, rather than endure the six portages between Fourtown and Nels lakes.

All motorized use of this entry point ended on January 1, 1979, however, when the BWCA border was moved south to Mudro Lake. What was once a haven for motor-toting anglers is now an easy target for paddlers. Now the area is devoid of most noise pollution, but the lakes are still loaded with fish.

The two lakes and two creeks leading to Mudro Lake are outside the Boundary Waters, but receive only moderate use. You may eliminate all but the final creek to Mudro by driving to the east end of Picket Lake. The gravel road leading to Mudro Lake intersects the Echo Trail 8.4 miles north of County Road 88. Turn right there and proceed on this narrow, rough gravel road 4.3 miles to its "T" intersection with Forest Route 457. Turn left and drive 1.3 miles to Picket Creek. Logging operations may be underway in this region, so beware of truck traffic on the road. Just across the old, wood bridge is a private parking lot and access to the Picket-Mudro portage. Visitors can buy pop there, and there are plans by the owners of this parcel to construct a small campground on the site. A daily fee is charged to park there, as well as a fee to launch your canoe.

For those who don't want to pay for parking and boat access, the Forest Service has constructed a "drop-off landing" 0.2 mile south of the creek. A small loop road spurs off Forest Route 457, and there is a 5-rod portage from the loop down to Picket Lake. No parking is allowed here, however. Nor is it permitted along the road near the access.

This is one entry point for which a reservation is nearly always necessary. It ranks among the top three entry points in the BWCA with quotas filled the highest percent of the time. During the summer of 1986 its quota was filled on 82 days. That means, without a reservation, your chances of getting a permit at the last minute on weekends, holidays or during the months of June and August are slim at best.

Route #24: Three Falls Loop

3 Days, 37 Miles, 7 Lakes, 3 Rivers, 3 Creeks, 21 Portages
Difficulty: Challenging
Fisher Maps: F-9, F-10
Travel Zones: 15, 16, 17

Introduction: This interesting loop will lead you through tiny creeks, small lakes, three rivers and a portion of the largest lake in the BWCA. From the public landing on Nels Lake, you will paddle east through Picket to Mudro and north to Fourtown Lake. Continuing east, you will cross Horse Lake, and glide down the Horse River to the Basswood River on the Canadian border. Going up this beautiful river, you will view three scenic waterfalls before crossing a 340-rod portage into enormous Basswood Lake. Turning southwest, you will paddle through Jackfish Bay and into the Range River, through Sandpit Lake and back into the chain of lakes connecting Mudro with Nels Lake.

Portages are evenly spaced throughout this route, the longest marking the midpoint of the loop. Three full days are required for the "average group"; four days would be more pleasant, but no doubt some rugged voyagers could do it in two. If the wind is strong out of the south or west, you may wish to reverse the route to avoid getting wind-bound on Jackfish Bay.

Anglers will find walleye inhabiting most of the lakes along this route. Northern pike and bluegill are also present in Fourtown and Horse lakes. You'll find lake trout, walleye, northern pike, bass and whitefish occupying the depths of Basswood Lake.

DAY 1: **Nels Lake,** p. 185 rods, **Picket Creek,** p. 30 rods, **Picket Lake,** p. 30 rods, **Mudro Creek, Mudro Lake,** p. 30 rods, **Fourtown Creek,** p. 110 rods, **Fourtown Creek,** p. 10

rods, **Fourtown Lake,** p. 1–3 rods, **Fourtown Lake,** p. 10 rods, **pond,** p. 70 rods, **Horse Lake.** Your first portage is well over ½ mile, but mostly level, with three rests along the way. A new beaver dam sprang up in 1980 just before the portage. It either requires a liftover or extends the portage by 6 rods. A log bridge midway through the carry is slippery when wet, so watch your step. In periods of low water, the creeks between Nels and Fourtown Lake may be too dry to transport a loaded canoe. If so, you may be walking much of the day. On the other hand, if the water level is high, you may find it unnecessary to portage between Picket and Mudro; simply paddle under Forest Route 457 and through the narrow, shallow creek beyond. Several nice campsites are located on Horse Lake, one of the best walleye lakes in the area.

DAY 2: **Horse Lake, rapids, Horse River, rapids, river,** p. 50 rods, **river, rapids, river,** p. 50 rods, **river,** p. 70 rods, **river, Basswood River,** p. 32 rods, **river,** p. 30 rods, **river,** p. 340 rods, **Basswood Lake.** This day is full of strenuous activity and beautiful scenery. In addition to the three sets of rapids on the Horse River around which portages are necessary, you will encounter at least three small rapids through which you can shoot, line or walk your canoe, depending on the water level and your ambition. Take time to contemplate the splendor of Lower Basswood Falls, Wheelbarrow Falls and Basswood Falls. That portion of the Basswood River in the vicinity of Basswood Falls is considered "dangerous waters". The safest route, therefore, is the 340-rod portage around it. It has six rests and follows a good, well-worn path over a gentle uphill grade. If you prefer, however, you may take shorter portages instead. Use your own discretion, based on the water conditions and your own skill. Numerous good campsites are located in the narrows between Jackfish Bay and the main body of Basswood Lake.

DAY 3: **Jackfish Bay, Range River,** p. 20 rods, **river,** p. 27 rods, **Sandpit Lake,** p. 80 rods, **Mudro Lake, Mudro Creek,** p. 30 rods, **Picket Lake,** p. 30 rods, **Picket Creek,** p. 185 rods, **Nels Lake.** The 80-rod portage between Sandpit and Mudro Lakes looks innocent on the map; but it is not. The trail climbs steeply to 90 feet above Sandpit Lake before descending about 47 feet to Mudro Lake.

Route #25: The Crooked Border Route

7 Days, 78 Miles, 19 Lakes, 3 Rivers, 2 Creeks, 32 Portages
Difficulty: Challenging
Fisher Maps: F-9, F-17, F-16, F-10
Travel Zones: 15, 14, 12, 13, 16

Introduction: The Crooked Border route will take you through a well-balanced variety of small rivers and creeks, large lakes and small ones. From Mudro Lake you'll paddle north and west through the chain of lakes leading to the Beartrap River and then down the river itself to Iron Lake. A side trip from Iron Lake will take you further northwest to the beautiful southeast end of Lac La Croix, where you may view old Indian pictographs and climb the legendary Warrior Hill. Turning east now, you'll have an opportunity to visit two of the spectacular falls bordering Iron Lake—Curtain and Rebecca—before challenging long and winding Crooked Lake. You will continue along the international border southeast up the Basswood River to splendid Lower Basswood Falls. From there you'll leave the historic Voyageurs' Highway and paddle southwest up the Horse River to Horse Lake and the chain of lakes that lead you back to your origin at Nels Lake.

Fishing is fairly good along this route. Walleye and/or northern pike, in particular, may be found in Nels, Mudro, Fourtown, Iron, Crooked and Horse lakes. Bluegill are abundant in Tin Can, Horse and Fourtown lakes.

Without the side trip to Lac La Croix, this scenic trip could easily be completed in six days by the average group of canoeists. But it would be a shame to be so close to the beauty of Lac La Croix without seeing it for yourself. Nearly one third of your time will be spent on small rivers and creeks, and there you should have ample opportunity to see various forms of wildlife. Although the international border lakes and the immediate vicinity of Fourtown Lake may be well-traveled, you should feel a degree of isolation throughout much of the rest of the route. Four beautiful waterfalls, numerous rapids and a host of attractive lakes all add up to a most delightful trip.

DAY 1: **Nels Lake,** p. 185 rods, **Picket Creek,** p. 30 rods, **Picket Lake,** p. 30 rods, **Mudro Creek, Mudro Lake,** p. 30

rods, **Fourtown Creek,** p. 110 rods, **creek,** p. 10 rods, **Fourtown Lake.** (See Comment for Day 1, Route #24.)

DAY 2: **Fourtown Lake,** p. 35 rods, **Boot Lake,** p. 15 rods, **Fairy Lake,** p. 50 rods, **Gun Lake,** p. 30 rods, **Gull Lake,** p. 40 rods, **Mudhole Lake,** p. 60 rods, **Thunder Lake.** Beyond Fourtown Lake, travel is relatively light. You'll encounter no difficulty on the portages, most of them being nearly level or downhill. The only significant climb is along the 30-rod trail from Gun to Gull Lake, which gains 24 feet—nothing to worry about.

DAY 3: **Thunder Lake,** p. 9 rods, **Beartrap Lake,** p. 200 rods, **Beartrap River,** p. 65 rods, **river,** p. 20 rods, **river, Sunday Lake,** p. 17 rods, **Beartrap River,** p. 10 rods, **river,** p. 35 rods, **river,** p. 110 rods, **Iron Lake.** All of your portages this day are basically downhill, as you follow the Beartrap River down to its mouth at Iron Lake. In fact, you'll descend over 140 feet in all. The Beartrap is a shallow, weedy river. You may encounter several beaver dams along its course. During dry spells, you might find paddling a bit of a drag, so to speak. Find a good campsite on Iron Lake and plan to stay two nights.

DAY 4: **Iron Lake, Bottle Lake,** p. 80 rods, **Lac La Croix,** p. 80 rods, **Bottle Lake, Iron Lake.** Leave your tents and gear on Iron Lake this morning. Pack your lunch, first-aid kit, rain coat and camera, and paddle northwest for a pleasant outing on beautiful Lac La Croix. (See comments for Day 4, Route #7.) Before returning to your campsite on Iron Lake, take time to paddle to Rebecca Falls at the outlet into McAree Lake. (See comments for Day 5, Route #7.) Don't forget to hang up your food pack in camp while you take this side trip. Blueberries are good, but you probably don't want to survive on them for the next three days.

DAY 5: **Iron Lake,** p. 140 rods, **Crooked Lake.** A beautiful 29-foot drop in the water level between Iron and Crooked lakes is called Curtain Falls. Take time to enjoy it. Your portage (US side) will be uphill, but not difficult. You may put in at the top of the falls, the very brink of the falls, or about 100 feet farther into Crooked Lake. The choice is yours, but I prefer the second during normal water conditions as the safest for a group that may not be strong enough to fight the swift current at the top of the falls. Use your own judgment and be careful. Many good campsites are scattered throughout Crooked Lake, including one at historic Table Rock, where many a Voyageur rested en route from Lake Superior to Lake Athabasca. An eagle's nest is located on an island near the east end of this long lake. A compass may be useful this day, as portions of Crooked Lake can be confusing even to an experienced guide.

DAY 6: **Crooked Lake, Basswood River,** p. 32 rods, **Basswood River, Horse River,** p. 70 rods, **river,** p. 50 rods, **river, rapids, river,** p. 50 rods, **river, rapids, river, rapids, Horse Lake,** p. 90 rods, **Tin Can Lake.** Lower Basswood Falls is a scenic 12-foot drop around which the first 12-rod portage passes. Although this route takes you up the Horse River, the mouth of which is just beyond this falls, you may wish to paddle beyond this confluence to another scenic cascade first—Wheelbarrow Falls, about ¾ mile up the Basswood River. While traveling up the Horse River, you will encounter at least three short, shallow rapids up which you will have to pull your canoe. These are located near the source of this pretty little river. A very nice campsite on Tin Can Lake is at the northwest corner of the lake, with ample space for more tents than you need. If time permits, cast your line for some of the many pan fish that inhabit the depths of this scenic lake.

DAY 7: **Tin Can Lake,** p. 117 rods, **Sandpit Lake,** p. 80 rods, **Mudro Lake, Mudro Creek,** p. 30 rods, **Picket Lake,** p. 30 rods, **Picket Creek,** p. 185 rods, **Nels Lake.** The two longest portages look threatening on the map (117 r. and 185 r.) but they are virtually level and not difficult. The 80-rod portage, however, climbs steeply to 90 feet above Sandpit Lake before descending about 47 feet to Mudro Lake.

Entry Point 22—Range Lake

Permits: 911 (Range and Mudro combined)

Popularity Rank: 8

Daily Quota: 4

Location: Range Lake is 8 miles northeast of Ely, and is accessible from either Fenske Lake or Bass Lake along the

Echo Trail, or from the Cloquet Road. I recommend starting at Fenske Lake, located adjacent to the Echo Trail, 8 miles north and west of County Road 88. The public landing is 0.1 mile past the Fenske Lake Campground, which is a good place to spend the night before your trip's departure. A camping fee is charged there.

Description: Range Lake is a full day's paddling northeast of Fenske Lake. Since this route is outside the BWCA, motorboats are legal all the way up to Range Lake. Since the BWCA Wilderness Act of 1978 took effect, however, motorized craft cannot continue through Range Lake into the Boundary Waters. And, as a result, you are not likely to hear many motors (if any) east of Fenske Lake, which has a small resort at its west end and several private cabins along its shoreline. With lots of good scenery and even more variety, this is a delightful way to begin a wilderness trip.

Nevertheless, if you would rather eliminate this first day of paddling outside the BWCA, you can drive via the primitive Cloquet Road most of the way to Range Lake. From County Road 88, one mile north of Highway 169, turn right onto County Road 781 and drive 0.5 mile to township road TM-4575. One-half mile farther, this gravel road makes a sharp right bend and then joins the Cloquet Road (0.2 mile). Bear left and then continue on the old Cloquet Road (formerly a railroad line) 10 miles to its end. The road gets narrower and rougher the farther you go, and it may be under water in places. It doesn't require 4-wheel-drive, but high clearance is useful. A USFS gate blocks the road at the boundary of the BWCA Wilderness.

A 200-rod portage leads from the small parking lot next to the gate (room for half-a-dozen vehicles). Beyond the gate, the road continues into the Wilderness, and the portage trail uses it for the first 125 rods. (The old roadway continues all the way to Sandpit Lake!) A foot trail then veers away from the road toward the west and leads 75 rods to Range Lake, dropping downhill over the final 40 rods. (Note: this eliminates Route #26 entirely!)

During dry periods, water levels could be a problem on the Range and Grassy rivers. Persistent beavers will do their best to stop the water from flowing past their dams. Consequently, you may be periodically slowed down at various points along the rivers.

Whether for a weekend or for a full nine days, this entry point offers a good deal to the canoeist in search of true high adventure! Like Mudro and South Hegman lakes, this is an entry point for which a reservation is nearly always necessary. It ranks among the top three entry points in the BWCA with quotas filled the highest percent of the time. During the summer of 1986 its quota was filled on 82 days. That means, without a reservation, your chances of getting a permit at the last minute on weekends, holidays or during the months of June and August are slim at best.

Route #26: The Range River Route

2 Days, 15 Miles, 10 Lakes, 2 Rivers, 2 Creeks, 13 Portages
Difficulty: Challenging
Fisher Map: F-9
Travel Zone: 15

Introduction: This little loop will first take you northeast from Fenske Lake through a chain of scenic small lakes and tranquil streams to Sandpit Lake. After one night in the Boundary Waters, you'll turn westward and follow another chain of lakes and streams past the Mudro Lake entry point to Nels Lake. A 2½-mile hike west and south, then, will return you to your origin.

The only part of the route contained in the BWCA is from Range Lake to Mudro Lake. But that fact should not discourage you. The lakes excluded from the BWCA are every bit as beautiful as those within it. And this route offers you an excellent taste of the variety that can be found in the North Woods—tiny creeks, placid rivers laced with beaver dams, scenic lakes and relatively easy portages—all squeezed into one short weekend.

Note: This route can be reversed by entering the BWCA at Mudro Lake (Entry Point 21).

DAY 1: **Fenske Lake,** p. 10 rods, **Little Sletten Lake,** p. 70 rods, **Sletten Lake,** p. 120 rods, **Tee Lake,** p. 48 rods, **Grassy Lake, beaver pond,** p. 24 rods, **Grassy River, Range**

River, p. 1 rod, **river,** p. 23 rods, **river,** p. 10 rods, **river, Range Lake.** (See comments for Day 1, Route #27.) If the campsite on Range Lake is occupied, continue on to Sandpit Lake or Jackfish Bay of Basswood Lake.

DAY 2: **Range Lake,** p. 109 rods, **Sandpit Lake,** p. 80 rods, **Mudro Lake, Mudro Creek,** p. 30 rods, **Picket Lake,** p. 30 rods, **Picket Creek,** p. 185 rods, **Nels Lake.** When the water level is high, you may find the portage between Mudro and Picket lakes avoidable by paddling up the narrow, shallow creek and under the Cloquet Road. On the other hand, when the water level is low, Picket and Mudro creeks may be unnavigable with loaded canoes. Watch your step on that last ½-mile portage when crossing a log bridge midway through the carry. It is slippery when wet!

Unless you arrange to have a car waiting for you at the Nels Lake landing, you'll have to walk nearly a mile out to the Echo Trail and another 1½ miles south to Fenske Lake.

Route #27: The Canadian Border Route

9 Days, 114 Miles, 24 Lakes, 7 Rivers, 1 Creek, 41 Portages
Difficulty: Challenging
Fisher Maps: F-9, F-10, F-17, F-16, F-23, F-8
Travel Zones: 15, 16, 13, 2, 4, 3, 11, 9

Introduction: This route will take you north from Fenske Lake through a chain of beautiful small lakes and streams to Horse Lake. After paddling down the Horse River to the Basswood River at lovely Lower Basswood Falls, you will then head north and west along the international border, through the entire length of Lac La Croix to Loon Lake. Here you will depart from the land of the maple leaf and paddle south into the Pauness Lakes and up into the winding wilderness of the Little Indian Sioux River to its source at Otter Lake. From Cummings Lake you will turn south, leave the Boundary Waters at Crab Lake, and go into ever-popular and populated Burntside Lake. After crossing most of this beautiful, island-studded lake you will turn northeast again through the Dead River and into Twin, Everett and Fenske lakes.

This challenging route will require nine full days for the

average group of canoeists, without a layover day. Strong winds, however, could slow travel considerably on parts of Burntside Lake, the Little Indian Sioux River, Lac La Croix and Crooked Lake. The Little Indian Sioux River offers a fine opportunity to view moose, deer, beaver and other forms of wildlife, for it flows through a region in the BWCA seldom visited by tourists. Early summer is usually the best time to make this journey, since the Sioux and Range rivers may be too dry for navigation later in the summer, or during an especially dry year. Although there are numerous portages along the route, few are longer than 100 rods. Most of the route is well traveled, with the exception of the Sioux River south of the Echo Trail, where portage trails may be difficult to follow. In addition to the abundant wildlife and generally good fishing, voyagers will also find two good displays of prehistoric Indian pictographs adorning the sheer granite cliffs of Lac La Croix and the Basswood River. Splendid waterfalls, treacherous rapids, beautiful big lakes and quaint little ones all interconnect to create a fascinating variety of canoeing terrain.

DAY 1: **Fenske Lake,** p. 10 rods, **Little Sletten Lake,** p. 70 rods, **Sletten Lake,** p. 120 rods, **Tee Lake,** p. 48 rods, **Grassy Lake, beaver pond,** p. 24 rods, **Grassy River, Range River,** p. 1 rod, **river,** p. 23 rods, **river,** p. 10 rods, **river, Range Lake,** p. 109 rods, **Sandpit Lake,** p. 117 rods, **Tin Can Lake.** Most of your first day is not in the BWCA. Nevertheless, although a resort and several private cabins are situated at the west end of Fenske Lake, it won't take you long on this route to feel the essence of true wilderness. In fact, I rate this first day as one of the most interesting first days of any route in the BWCA. Of the five portages that greet you immediately, all but one are downhill. The only one to watch out for is the 70-rod trek between Little Sletten and Sletten lakes, which rather steeply crosses over the hill between. There may be a beaver dam between Grassy Lake and the pond thereafter, as well as on the upper part of the Grassy River and the lower stretches of the slow, winding, marshy Range River, near Range Lake. You will have two options for reaching Tin Can Lake from Range Lake. If portaging doesn't get you down, you can walk the entire distance, skirting Sandpit Lake along its east shore, a total distance of 301 rods. Or you can portage 109 rods from Range to Sandpit, and another 117 rods from Sandpit to Tin Can (see detailed sketch of Range River region in Route #9). You will find a nice campsite near the north end of Tin Can Lake, with ample space for a large group.

DAY 2: **Tin Can Lake,** p. 90 rods, **Horse Lake, Horse River, rapids, river, rapids, river,** p. 50 rods, **river, rapids, river,** p. 50 rods, **river,** p. 70 rods, **river, Basswood River,** p. 32 rods, **Basswood River, Crooked Lake.** A short side trip up the Basswood River from its confluence with the Horse River will take you to scenic Wheelbarrow Falls. About ¾ mile downstream is Lower Basswood Falls, the last significant drop (12 feet) in the Basswood River before it enters Crooked Lake. Along the Horse River you will encounter at least three short, shallow rapids near the source, in addition to those farther down that require portaging. You should be able to shoot, line or walk your canoe through these, depending on the water level. A display of Indian paintings can be seen along the west shore of the Basswood River, about a mile downstream from Lower Basswood Falls. Several nice campsites are located between Lower Basswood Falls and Wednesday Bay of Crooked Lake, including Table Rock, long ago used by Voyageurs carrying furs from the Northwest to outposts on Lake Superior.

DAY 3: **Crooked Lake,** p. 140 rods, **Iron Lake.** There are many confusing bays, islands and peninsulas in Crooked Lake. (The eastern stretch may be confusing to even the most experienced Northwoods canoeist.) At least one eagle's nest is located near the east end, and it is not unusual to see eagles soaring overhead. Curtain Falls, with a total drop of 29 feet, separates Crooked and Iron lakes. Use caution and stay close to the left shoreline as you approach the misty brink of this beautiful falls. You'll see two possible portage landings on the US shoreline, one a hundred feet away from the falls and one at the very edge. It appears from the portage trails that a good many people prefer the safer landing, several rods from the falls' edge. Use your best judgment. Several campsites are within a mile of Curtain Falls on Iron Lake.

DAY 4: **Iron Lake, Bottle Lake,** p. 80 rods, **Lac La Croix.** Two points of historical interest await you on Lac La

Croix: Warrior Hill and Indian pictographs. (See comments for Day 6, Route #11.) There are several outstanding campsites in the vicinity of the pictographs, but this part of the border is usually heavily traveled by Canadian motor boats and canoeists alike. Since the BWCA Wilderness Act of 1978, motorboats have been banned from the US side of most of Lac La Croix (east of Snow Bay). So the quietest (and perhaps the most beautiful) part of the lake is south of Coleman Island, in or near Lady Boot Bay. Find your campsite there.

DAY 5: **Lac La Croix.** No portages today! Just a lot of paddling across the expanse of this 25-mile long, potentially confusing lake. An Indian village is located at the source of the Namakan River, in the Neguaguon Lake Indian Reservation, adjacent to Quetico Provincial Park. Farther west along the Canadian shoreline are two resorts to break the monotony of paddling and to allow replenishment of any needed provisions.

DAY 6: **Lac La Croix,** p. 50 rods, **Loon Lake,** p. 160 rods, **Lower Pauness Lake,** p. 8 rods, **Upper Pauness Lake.** Don't miss the third set of Indian pictographs along the American shore just north of the 50-rod portage into Loon Lake. And take time during your steep uphill 160-rod climb to view the scenic granite gorge through which Devil's Cascade plunges 75 feet from Lower Pauness Lake to Loon Lake. The best view is at the second (of three) portage rests, where a spacious campsite accommodates hikers using the Sioux Hustler Trail. Upper Pauness Lake is on a well-traveled route, so grab a campsite as early as possible.

DAY 7: **Upper Pauness Lake, Little Indian Sioux River,** p. 60 rods, **river,** p. 120 rods, **river,** p. 8 rods, **river,** p. 120 rods, **river, Little Pony River,** p. 60 rods, **river,** p. 60 rods, **Bootleg Lake.** Watch out for traffic as you cross the Echo Trail at the 120-rod portage. You'll find two portages from which to choose. Paddle about 5 rods beyond the first and best landing (which leads to a parking lot) to the second, more obscure alternative. This trail is seldom used and may be nearly choked with vegetation, but it offers the most direct route for those canoeists who are continuing south on the river. There are no portage rests, but a scenic lunch spot next to a cascading rapids marks the midpoint. From that point on, the number of canoes you see will greatly decrease. Campsites are few and far between on the swampy, winding Little Indian Sioux River. In fact, you will find no designated Forest Service campsites, unless you divert your route up the Little Pony River to Bootleg Lake.

DAY 8: **Bootleg Lake,** p. 200 rods, **Little Indian Sioux River,** p. 40 rods, **river,** p. 25 rods, **river,** p. 20 rods, **river,** p. 30 rods, **river,** p. 40 rods, **river,** p. 20 rods, **river,** p. 28 rods, **river,** p. 120 rods, **Otter Lake,** p. 5 rods, **Cummings Lake.** The nine short portages and considerable meandering make travel deceivingly slow this day, as the Sioux becomes narrower and shallower. Between portages it is virtually impossible to know EXACTLY where you are. Use the portages as landmarks, and alert yourself to the GENERAL direction of travel. Moose and deer are not uncommon sights along the river.

DAY 9: **Cummings Lake,** p. 35 rods, **Korb Creek, Korb Lake, Korb Creek,** p. 1–3 rods, **creek, Little Crab Lake,** p. 20 rods, **Crab Lake,** p. 320 rods, **Burntside Lake, Dead River, East Twin Lake,** p. 14 rods, **Everett Lake,** p. 120 rods, **Fenske Lake.** You will encounter the longest portage of the route this day, but it is a gently sloping downhill trek that passes through a wet area flooded by beaver dams. Burntside Lake, with well over 100 picturesque islands, could be confusing to even an experienced map reader. Keep constant count of the islands and bays as you weave through them to the outlet into Twin Lakes. You'll see many cabins and motor boats on popular Burntside Lake. If you wish to avoid the last 120-rod portage into Fenske Lake, you can simply walk along the Echo Trail (left) to your vehicle parked at the access to Fenske Lake, less than a mile from the Everett Lake portage.

Ch. 5
Entry from the Fernberg Road

The North-Central Area

The Fernberg Road is probably known by more visitors to the BWCA than any other highway. Three of the 6 most popular entry points are served by this road, including Moose Lake, the most heavily used entry point in all the BWCA. Three other entry points included in this guide are also served by the Fernberg Road.

To get there, simply follow State Highway 169 northeast from the Chamber of Commerce building in Ely (see paragraphs 2 and 3 in the introduction to Chapter 4), past the small town of Winton, and across the Lake County line. This highway becomes the Fernberg Road, an extension of Highway 169 into Lake County.

The road surface is blacktop all the way to its end at the Lake One landing. Generally, it is a good road, with relatively few sharp curves. Locals who are familiar with the road drive it quite fast, so beware . . .

Entry Point 24—Fall Lake

Permits: 1233
Popularity Rank: 6
Daily Quota: 32 (with Four Mile Portage #63)
Location: Fall Lake is located about three miles northeast of Ely. Follow the Fernberg Road 5½ miles from the Ely Chamber of Commerce building to Forest Route 551, the Fall

Lake Road. Turn left and follow this good, paved road slightly more than 1 mile to the public access and parking lot on the left side of the road.

Description: Farther down the Fall Lake Road you will find a Forest Service campground, a good place to spend the night before your trip. A fee is charged to camp there.

Fall Lake is by far the most convenient entry point into the Boundary Waters, being located so close to Ely and accessible by such good paved roads. At its northeast end is the 4-Mile Truck Portage, on which heavy motor boats are easily transported to popular Basswood Lake, on the international boundary. Along with several resorts and many private cabins, local outfitters also have bases on this lake. Consequently, traffic into the BWCA is heavy, and less than half of it is canoes without motors. Motorboats are limited to 25 h.p.

Although Fall Lake itself has little appeal to the wilderness canoeist, it does provide easy access into big, beautiful Basswood Lake, the enticing Basswood River, and a degree of wilderness solitude beyond. If you can tolerate the wakes of passing motor boats and the frustrating winds on Basswood, you'll surely find a worthwhile trip from a Fall Lake origin. See Entry Point 26-Wood Lake for other route ideas in this area.

Route #28: The Four Falls Route

4 Days, 46 Miles, 6 Lakes, 3 Rivers, 14 Portages
Difficulty: Challenging
Fisher Map: F-10
Travel Zones: 17, 16, 15

Introduction: This short loop will lead you north to the Canadian border, via Fall, Newton and Basswood lakes, and around Pipestone Falls. Then you will paddle down the beautiful Basswood River, where you will view three more attractive waterfalls. Turning south from Lower Basswood Falls, you will paddle up the tranquil Horse River to Horse Lake before returning to Basswood Lake via the Range River. Then you will backtrack through familiar waters as you return south to your origin at Fall Lake.

If the wind is strong, you should probably consider another entry point that does not lead to Basswood Lake, which is both frustrating and dangerous at such times. In fact, if the weather is merely threatening, avoid wide open stretches on this lake. Similarly, beware of dangerous waters on the Basswood River, which has tempted and destroyed many a foolish voyager over the years.

Motors are permitted on much of this route. Between upper Basswood Falls and the Range River, however, you will find the going much quieter than elsewhere. You will surely find the Basswood and Horse Rivers rewarding. But you may find the paddling to be tedious on the first and last days of this challenging route.

Northern pike and walleye inhabit much of the water along this route. You will also find smallmouth bass and lake trout in Basswood Lake, and bluegill in Horse and Tin Can lakes. I have found parts of the lower Basswood River, in particular, to be tastily rewarding.

DAY 1: **Fall. Lake,** p. 80 rods, **Newton Lake,** p. 40 rods, **Pipestone Bay of Basswood Lake.** Again, beware of wind and the wakes of motor boats. Campsites are plentiful at the north end of Pipestone Bay. Portages are very easy, and downhill.

DAY 2: **Jackfish Bay, Basswood Lake,** p. 340 rods, **Basswood River,** p. 30 rods, **river,** p. 32 rods, **river.** You will see three scenic waterfalls this day: Basswood Falls, Wheelbarrow Falls, and Lower Basswood Falls. That portion of the Basswood River near its source is considered "dangerous waters." The safest route, therefore, is the 340-rod portage around it that I recommend. It has six rests and follows a good, downsloping path. If you prefer, however, you can take shorter portages instead. Use your own discretion, based on the water conditions and your own skill. If the campsites are not available (or suitable) between Wheelbarrow and Lower Basswood Falls, you may wish to portage an easy 12 rods around Lower Basswood Falls to Crooked Lake, on which several nice campsites are located near the base of the falls. You may wish to paddle another mile downstream to view a display of Indian rock paintings decorating the sheer granite cliffs along the west shoreline.

DAY 3: **Basswood River, Horse River,** p. 70 rods, **river,** p. 50 rods, **river, rapids, river,** p. 50 rods, **river, rapids, river, rapids, Horse Lake,** p. 90 rods, **Tin Can Lake,** p. 117 rods, **Sandpit Lake,** p. 27 rods, **Range River,** p. 20 rods, **river, Jackfish Bay of Basswood Lake.** In addition to the three sets of rapids on the Horse River around which portages are necessary, you will encounter at least three small rapids up which you will have to pull your canoe. (See detailed sketch of the Range River region in Route #9.)

DAY 4: **Jackfish Bay, Pipestone Bay,** p. 40 rods, **Newton Lake,** p. 80 rods, **Fall Lake.** If wind discourages paddling on Jackfish Bay, you may wish to take a short-cut by portaging 60 rods into a small bay between Jackfish and Pipestone Bays.

Route #29: The Basswood Lake Loop

5 Days, 62 Miles, 7 Lakes, 8 Portages

Difficulty: Easy

Fisher Map: F-10

Travel Zones: 17, 18, 19

Introduction: This heavily traveled route will take you north from Fall Lake to the international boundary, via Newton and Basswood lakes. You will follow enormous Basswood Lake east along the Canadian border to Sucker Lake, where you will turn southwest and follow the busy Moose Chain to the south edge of the BWCA on Moose Lake. You'll then cross back to Basswood Lake through Wind Lake, and follow the southern bays of this mighty lake back to your origin at Fall Lake.

At trip's end you will have crossed only eight portages, only two of which are challenging. The vast majority of your time will be spent paddling across the largest lake in the BWCA, Basswood, where motor traffic is heavy and strong winds a constant threat. As mentioned for Route #28, if menacing winds prevail, consider a different route through a different entry point. Basswood Lake is not a good place to be in the middle of a gale.

Throughout most of the route you will find smallmouth bass, northern pike and walleye beneath you. Lake trout are also present in parts of Basswood Lake. Since motors are permitted throughout the route, except on Wind Lake, you will see many fishermen everywhere.

DAY 1: **Fall Lake,** p. 80 rods, **Newton Lake,** p. 40 rods, **Pipestone Bay of Basswood Lake.** (See comments for Day 1, Route #28.)

DAY 2: **Pipestone Bay, Jackfish Bay, Basswood Lake, Bayley Bay.** Since January of 1984, motors have been prohibited in the part of Basswood Lake that lies northeast of Jackfish Bay and north of Washington Island. Be alert to possible storms and gales while crossing big Basswood. Do as the Indians always did: paddle close to the shore. Not only is it safer; it's also much more interesting.

DAY 3: **Bayley Bay,** p. 20 rods, **Sucker Lake, New Found Lake, Moose Lake,** p. 170 rods, **Wind Lake.** This last portage into Wind Lake is, no doubt, the most challenging trek on this route, climbing nearly 80 feet and extending over ½ mile. Because of it, however, Wind Lake is much more peaceful than the rest of the route. Several campsites are available around the lake.

DAY 4: **Wind Lake,** p. 170 rods, **Wind Bay, Basswood Lake, Hoist Bay, Back Bay,** p. 70 rods, **Pipestone Bay.** The half-mile path leading out of Wind Lake is downhill, and not as difficult as the one leading into the lake at the other end.

DAY 5: **Pipestone Bay,** p. 40 rods, **Newton Lake,** p. 80 rods, **Fall Lake.** This will be the reverse of your first day. Portages are still not difficult, but uphill this time.

Entry Point 25—Moose Lake

Permits: 3361

Popularity Rank: 1

Daily Quota: 35

Location: Moose Lake is located 16 miles northeast of Ely, a scant 4 miles south of the Canadian border. To get there, follow the Fernberg Road 16½ miles from the Ely Chamber of Commerce building to Forest Route 438 (Moose Lake Road). Turn left and follow the gravel road north for nearly 3 miles to the Public Landing and large parking area.

Description: A good public campground is at Fall Lake,

just off the Fernberg Road, about 14 miles toward Ely. This offers a good place to spend the night prior to your canoe trip. There is a fee charged to camp there.

Moose Lake is by far the busiest of all entry points into the Boundary Waters Canoe Area. On more than one occasion I have passed well over 100 canoes on the Moose chain of lakes, and that includes neither those paddling in my direction nor the many motor boats used by fishermen in the area! Of the 3361 permits issued in 1986, 17% were issued to groups using motors. This was due in large part to the fact that the Moose chain is one of two major routes to the ever-popular Basswood Lake (the other is from Fall Lake). Motorboats are limited to 25 h.p. It is also the quickest link to Canada's Quetico Provincial Park, and that accounts for many of the paddlers using this busy entry point—the quickest access to Canadian Customs at Prairie Portage.

Many resorts, outfitters and private cabins are located at the southwest end of the lake, and most of the once-good campsites on the chain are now closed due to overuse. The scenery is not especially attractive from Moose to the Canadian border, and signs of wildlife during the busy summer months are virtually nonexistent.

Nevertheless, if all of these facts do not drive you away, you will find that the busy Moose Chain does *lead* you to some of the most beautiful, interesting and peaceful lakes and streams in all the BWCA. Don't expect to experience total solitude anywhere on either of the routes suggested below between Memorial Day and Labor Day, but, if sharing "your" lakes with other nature lovers doesn't bother you, you'll surely find these routes delightful. See Entry Point 27-Snowbank Lake for other route ideas in this area.

Route #30: The Knife River-Disappointment Loop

4 Days, 34 Miles, 19 Lakes, 1 River, 18 Portages
Difficulty: Challenging
Fisher Maps: F-10, F-11
Travel Zones: 19, 30, 20, 21

Introduction: This short loop should probably be classified with two difficulty ratings: the first half EASY, and the last half RUGGED. Your first day should bring you to no more than one portage as you paddle your way northeast along the busy Moose chain of lakes to the Canadian border. Following the border farther northeast, you'll walk your canoe up the series of Knife River rapids to big Knife Lake. From Knife, you'll depart from the international boundary and turn back to the southwest through Vera, Ensign and a series of small lakes to island-studded Disappointment Lake. Then westward, you will slip through Parent Lake and across giant Snowbank Lake to Flash Lake and your origin at the Moose Lake public landing. Most of the loop is along a motor route.

If the winds are westerly (as they usually are) you will make good time, but if they swoop down from the north, beware of Snowbank Lake! All along the route, campsites are at a premium, so don't wait too late each day to find yours. Throughout most of the loop, you'll find northern pike, walleye and bass inhabiting the depths, as well as lake trout in Knife and Snowbank lakes.

Although deer and moose are seldom seen along the route, the same is not true for bears, unfortunately. Be sure to tie your food pack up in the air at night, and during the day when you are away from camp. This is particularly important between the Knife River and Ensign Lake.

DAY 1: **Moose Lake, New Found Lake, Sucker Lake, Birch Lake.** This day is short for no other reason than the lack of available Forest Service campsites between Birch and Knife lakes. Although much of the traffic from Moose Lake heads east to Ensign Lake or northwest to Basswood Lake, a good deal of it continues along the border to Knife Lake. On a busy weekend and in August, it is not unusual to find all the "legal" campsites from Birch through the southwest end of Knife Lake taken. You have two alternatives: 1) stop early, or 2) stop at Canada customs for the necessary permits that will enable you to camp on the Canadian side of these busy lakes. Regulations restrict campers to only one night at campsites between Moose Lake and Knife Lake.

DAY 2: **Birch Lake,** p. 48 rods, **Carp Lake,** p. 16 rods, **Knife River,** p. 15 rods, **Seed Lake,** p. 15 rods, **Knife River,**

p. 75 rods, **Knife Lake,** p. 200 rods, **Vera Lake.** If the water level is high enough (but not too high) you can eliminate all of the portages on the Knife River by walking your canoe up the series of gentle rapids around which the portages pass. Only on one occasion will you have to lift your canoe and gear—around a low falls.

During the summer of 1987 high water caused the old logging dam at the southwest end of Knife Lake, built in the early 1900s, to wash out. Consequently, the water level on Knife Lake has returned to its natural level, about three feet lower than it has been during this century. For the next few years, the exposed rocky shoreline may look strange to returning visitors.

Not far from the old dam, in a cluster of three small islands in Knife Lake, is the homesite of the BWCA's last permanent resident. Dorothy Molter, who sold home-made root beer to canoeing passersby for nearly half a century passed away in December 1986. Two of her log cabins were then moved, log by log, to Ely and reconstructed as a memorial to her next to the Chamber of Commerce building.

The 200-rod portage from Knife to Vera Lake is a tough one, climbing steeply to an elevation of 80 feet above Knife. But, thanks to it, canoe traffic on Vera is much lighter than on either Knife or Ensign Lake. A nice campsite is found along the north shore soon after the portage. Bears are common in the area, so prepare for visitors.

DAY 3: **Vera Lake,** p. 180 rods, **Ensign Lake,** p. 53 rods, **Ashigan Lake,** p. 105 rods, **Gibson Lake,** p. 25 rods, **Cattyman Lake,** p. 10 rods, **Adventure Lake,** p. 40 rods, **Jitterbug Lake,** p. 15 rods, **Ahsub Lake,** p. 25 rods, **Disappointment Lake.** Very low water could cause some difficulty between Gibson and Ahsub lakes, and rocks and stumps may present a hazard at the northwest end of Cattyman Lake. Jitterbug, which is always shallow, may be too low for navigation near the portage into Ahsub Lake, requiring an extended portage through marshy terrain. You may see a lot of daytime traffic on Disappointment Lake, coming from two resorts on Snowbank Lake.

DAY 4: **Disappointment Lake,** p. 85 rods, **Parent Lake,** p. 80 rods, **Snowbank Lake,** p. 140 rods, **Flash Lake,** p. 250

rods to the **Moose Lake Road.** Numerous motor boats and wind are potential hazards on Snowbank Lake, a long-time favorite among fishermen in search of lake trout. Flash Lake is a delightfully peaceful change from Snowbank. Unfortunately, however, your trip must end with its longest portage—a nearly level trek from Flash Lake to the Moose Lake Road. You will find the parking lot a short distance down the road (turn right off the portage trail).

Route #31: The Silver Falls-Kekekabic Route

8 Days, 94 Miles, 31 Lakes, 1 River, 1 Creek, 37 Portages
Difficulty: Challenging
Fisher Maps: F-10, F-11, F-19
Travel Zones: 19, 30, 39, 38, 32, 29, 28, 21

Introduction: This popular route will take you northeast along the Canadian border to mighty Saganaga Lake, less than three miles from the Gunflint Trail. You will spend two nights on this beautiful lake to accommodate a side trip to magnificent Silver Falls, northwest of Cache Bay. From Saganaga Lake, you will turn southwest and follow a lovely chain of lakes to impressive Kekekabic Lake. South to Fraser and Thomas lakes, you will then turn northwest through Ima, Jordan and a group of tiny lakes to popular Ensign Lake. Finally, you will retrace your path through New Found and Moose lakes to the Public Landing.

Virtually every inch of this route is very popular in summertime, most of the first half of it being designed for motors. Portages are neither long nor difficult, though some are rather steep, particularly between Kekekabic and Fraser lakes. Seldom if ever will you feel isolated, and at times you may even feel crowded. Nevertheless, the route offers many scenic attractions, and enticing opportunities for the avid angler. Lake trout inhabit the depths under much of the route, including Knife, Ottertrack, Saganaga, Alpine, Kekekabic and Thomas lakes. Northern pike, walleye and bass are also found in most of these waters, as well as in the Moose chain of lakes and Red Rock, Fraser, Ima and Ensign lakes, among others.

If winds are out of the south or west, you should make

excellent time traveling along the Canadian border to Saganaga Lake. The water level should make little difference to your plans, except as regards your ability to walk several rapids and thus to eliminate portages.

DAY 1: **Moose Lake, New Found Lake, Sucker Lake, Birch Lake.** (See comments for Day 1, Route #30.)

DAY 2: **Birch Lake,** p. 48 rods, **Carp Lake,** p. 16 rods, **Knife River,** p. 15 rods, **Seed Lake,** p. 15 rods, **Knife River,** p. 75 rods, **Knife Lake.** (See comments for Day 2, Route #30.) Although the southwest end of Knife Lake is often crowded with campers, vacant campsites should appear as you get closer to Little Knife Portage into Ottertrack Lake. Where the South Arm joins the main part of Knife Lake is Thunder Point. Take time to climb the ¼-mile trail to the overlook, where you will be treated to a fabulous panorama of the Canadian border from over 150 feet above the lake.

DAY 3: **Knife Lake,** p. 5 rods, **Ottertrack Lake,** p. 80 rods, **Swamp Lake,** p. 5 rods, **Saganaga Lake.** Ottertrack Lake is long, narrow and lined with high bluffs and a rocky shoreline. It is one of my favorites. Along the north shore of the lake, you may see a clearing where once stood the cabins of Benny Ambrose. Benny was a prospector who sought gold for more than 60 years, until his death in 1982 at age 84. Saganaga is a big, beautiful lake that is heavily traveled because of its easy access from the Gunflint Trail. 25 horsepower motor boats are permitted on most of the lake. Several nice campsites are in the vicinity of American Point, west of which motors are not allowed.

DAY 4: **Side trip through Cache Bay to Silver Falls.** Silver Falls are by far the highest and most spectacular falls in this guide. Although you may not need a permit from Canadian Customs to visit the falls, you will have to stop at the Canadian Ranger Station on the southernmost of the three islands near the entrance to Cache Bay to get permission to enter Quetico Provincial Park. The extra paddling across gusty Cache Bay is well worth it. (Bears are reported in the area, so don't leave your food packs on the ground while you are away from camp.)

Once you've returned to U.S. waters, the anglers in your group may want to explore Saganaga Lake for some of the lake trout, walleyes, northern pike and smallmouth bass that dwell there. Saganaga is considered one of the best lakes in Minnesota in which to catch a trophy walleye. In fact, the state record (17.5 pounds) was pulled from the Seagull River, which feeds the lake.

DAY 5: **Saganaga Lake, Red Rock Bay,** p. 10 rods, **Red Rock Lake,** p. 50 rods, **Alpine Lake,** p. 45 rods, **Jasper Lake,** p. 25 rods, **King Fisher Lake,** p. 38 rods, **Ogishkemuncie Lake.** Motors are not allowed beyond Red Rock Bay. If the water level permits, you may wish to walk your canoe up the rapids between King Fisher and Ogishkemuncie lakes, and eliminate the 38-rod portage. Watch for eagles on Saganaga Lake: at least one nest is nearby. Along the southeast shore of Red Rock Bay you'll witness the charred remains of a 1976 fire that ravaged the area. Ogishkemuncie is a long and pretty lake, with many small islands and numerous good campsites. Because of its great popularity, you should look for a campsite early.

DAY 6: **Ogishkemuncie Lake,** p. 15 rods, **Annie Lake,** p. 15 rods, **Jean Lake,** p. 15 rods, **Eddy Lake,** five portages through "**Kekekabic Ponds,**" **Kekekabic Lake,** p. 85 rods, **Strup Lake,** p. 10 rods, **Wisini Lake,** p. 90 rods, **Ahmakose Lake** p. 30 rods, **Gerund Lake,** p. 15 rods, **Fraser Lake.** With 13 portages, this day should prove to be the toughest one of the trip. On the other hand, it is also your only full day on lakes where motors are prohibited. The first eight portages leading into Kekekabic Lake are short and easy, providing more of a nuisance than a challenge, and your entrance to Kekekabic makes it all worth while anyway. The narrow entrance to this magnificent lake gradually widens as it winds to the west and the high-rising bluffs that encircle it come into view. In the distance, you'll see hills rising as high as 400 feet above the lake.

The next three portages provide some challenge. The 85-rod portage out of Kekekabic climbs more than 100 feet before descending 21 feet to Strup Lake. The next short portage ascends 17 feet in 10 rods. And, although Wisini and Ahmakose lakes lie at nearly the same elevation, the 90-rod path between them climbs 54 feet above their level.

DAY 7: **Fraser Lake, Thomas Lake,** p. 5 rods, **pond,**

p. 10 rods, **Thomas Creek,** p. 10 rods, **creek,** p. 10 rods, **Hatchet Lake,** p. 50 rods, **Ima Lake,** p. 5 rods, **Jordan Lake,** p. 55 rods,**Cattyman Lake,** p. 25 rods, **Gibson Lake,** p. 105 rods, **Ashigan Lake.** If the water level is high enough, you can walk, line or shoot your canoe down the narrow rapids around which two of the 10-rod portages pass between Thomas and Hatchet lakes. The first 10-rod portage crosses the famed Kekekabic Trail. A short hike off the 25-rod portage into Gibson Lake will lead you to a waterfall, where the water drops 37 feet from the stump-filled pond.

DAY 8: **Ashigan Lake,** p. 53 rods, **Ensign Lake, Splash Lake,** p. 35 rods, **New Found Lake, Moose Lake.** A shallow and narrow rapids separates Ensign and Splash lakes, but under normal water conditions you should be able to shoot through it easily. After Splash Lake, you'll be back on the busy motor route from which you earlier departed.

Entry Point 26—Wood Lake

Permits: 104
Popularity Rank: 37
Daily Quota: 3

Location: The portage to Wood Lake is located on the north (left) side of the Fernberg Road, 13 miles from the Chamber of Commerce building in Ely, near a small parking lot. The campground at Fall Lake is a good place to spend the night before your trip, and the only public campground along the Fernberg Road. Follow the Fall Lake Road north from its junction with the Fernberg Road, 7½ miles closer to Ely. There is a fee charged to camp there.

Description: Since January 1, 1979, Wood Lake is completely within the BWCA, and motors are not allowed on it. It provides the wilderness canoeist with a much more pleasant access to Basswood Lake than does either the Moose Lake or Fall Lake entry route. The only draw-back is the initial half-mile-plus portage from the Fernberg Road. (See Entry Point 24-Fall Lake for other route ideas in this vicinity.)

Route #32: The Basswood Bays Loop

3 Days, 34 Miles, 4 Lakes, 1 Creek, 9 Portages
Difficulty: Easy
Fisher Map: F-10
Travel Zones: 18, 17

Introduction: This easy loop takes you straight north from Wood Lake to the Canadian border on big Basswood Lake. You'll follow the international boundary north and west for several miles, before looping back to the south and east through portions of four of Basswood's bays. You will then backtrack through Good, Hula and Wood lakes to your origin at the Fernberg Road.

The only challenging part of this route is at the beginning and the end, where you encounter the same 196-rod portage. It follows a very good path, however, with four portage rests, sloping gently downhill to Wood Lake. If winds are strong or the weather is ominous, you should probably avoid potentially dangerous Basswood Lake, where waves can quickly swell to a height of three feet or more.

The only lakes in this route on which motors are not allowed are Wood, Hula and Good. Much of Basswood is open to 25 horsepower motor boats, and it is extremely popular with fishermen. There you will find walleye, northern pike, small-mouth bass and lake trout.

DAY 1: P. 196 rods, **Wood Lake,** p. 72 rods, **Hula Lake,** p. 110 rods, **Good Lake,** p. 2 rods, **Good Creek, Hoist Bay, Basswood Lake.** Between Wood Lake and Hoist Bay the portages are seldom used and may be fairly overgrown during the latter part of the summer. Fortunately, though, they are generally downhill toward Basswood Lake and not too long. During dry spells, you may have difficulty crossing shallow Hula Lake and navigating Good Creek. During the dry summer of 1980, I found the creek to be so shallow and so choked with lily pads, reeds and other vegetation that navigation was nearly impossible. You will have no trouble finding campsites on or in the vicinity of Washington Island. Be certain that you are camped in the US. Motorboats are banned from the part of Basswood that lies north of Washington Island.

DAY 2: **Basswood Lake, Jackfish Bay, Pipestone Bay,** p. 70 rods, **Back Bay.** Beware the wakes from motor boats throughout this huge lake. High, treacherous waves caused by gale-force winds, too, are not uncommon on Basswood Lake. Regardless of the direction of the wind, at least some portion of the lake will feel the effects. Even if the lake is calm when you start across, be alert for threatening changes in the weather and stay close to the lee shoreline. For the sake of variety on this long day of paddling, you may wish to visit Basswood Falls, at the outlet of the Basswood River from the northwest corner of Basswood Lake.

Compared to the rest of Basswood Lake, you may find a degree of solitude in Back Bay.

DAY 3: **Back Bay, Hoist Bay, Good Creek,** p. 2 rods, **Good Lake,** p. 110 rods, **Hula Lake,** p. 72 rods, **Wood Lake,** p. 196 rods. You will see civilization at the south end of Hoist Bay, which is the northeast end of the busy 4-Mile Truck Portage from Fall Lake. Many of the large motorboats seen on Basswood Lake come this way. The entrance to Good Creek is just east of there. From that point on, you will be retracing your first day.

Route #33: The Triangle Loop

4 Days, 48 Miles, 13 Lakes, 1 Creek, 15 Portages
Difficulty: Challenging
Fisher Maps: F-10, F-11
Travel Zones: 18, 19, 20

Introduction: This not-too-difficult route will take you north to Basswood Lake, and then east along the Canadian border to Birch Lake. From the east end of Birch you will portage into two seldom-visited lakes before entering Ensign Lake and turning your course back west. From Moose Lake you will portage into Wind Lake and then into Basswood Lake, where you begin to retrace your path back to Wood Lake.

You will be paddling on large lakes most of the time, with a few delightful exceptions. Motors are permitted on all of the border lakes and on Moose and New Found, and most of the route is very heavily traveled.

DAY 1: P. 196 rods, **Wood Lake,** p. 72 rods, **Hula Lake,** p. 110 rods, **Good Lake,** p. 2 rods, **Good Creek, Hoist Bay, Basswood Lake.** Campsites are plentiful along the south shore of Basswood. Don't camp north of the international border unless you have received clearance from Canadian Customs.

DAY 2: **Basswood Lake, Bayley Bay,** p. 20 rods, **Sucker Lake, Birch Lake,** p. 100 rods, **Frog Lake,** p. 70 rods, **Trident Lake.** You'll pass Canadian Customs at the 20-rod portage from Bayley Bay into Sucker Lake. Stay close to the left shore of Sucker, so you don't miss the narrow channel into Birch Lake. The two portages between Birch and Trident lakes are not well-used, and you will find Frog and Trident lakes to be a peacefully pleasant change from the busy lakes on either side. Motors are not allowed here.

DAY 3: **Trident Lake,** p. 120 rods, **Ensign Lake, Splash Lake,** p. 35 rods, **New Found Lake, Moose Lake,** p. 170 rods, **Wind Lake.** The portage into Wind Lake is certainly the most difficult trek of the entire trip. It climbs nearly 80 feet and is over ½ mile long. Because of it, however, Wind Lake is considerably more peaceful than either Moose or Basswood Lake. Motors are not allowed on Wind Lake.

DAY 4: **Wind Lake,** p. 170 rods, **Wind Bay, Basswood Lake, Hoist Bay, Good Creek,** p. 2 rods, **Good Lake,** p. 110 rods, **Hula Lake,** p. 72 rods, **Wood Lake,** p. 196 rods. The half-mile path leading out of Wind Lake is downhill, and not as difficult as the one leading into the lake at the other end. You'll find the entrance to Good Creek just east of the busy 4-Mile Truck Portage station on the south shore of Hoist Bay. From that point on, the route should look familiar to you.

Entry Point 27—Snowbank Lake

Permits: 671

Popularity Rank: 10

Daily Quota: 8

Location: Snowbank Lake is located about 20 miles northeast of Ely, 3 miles south of the Canadian border. To get there, follow the Fernberg Road for 18½ miles from the Ely

Chamber of Commerce building to the Snowbank Lake Road. Turn left here and drive carefully on this narrow, winding gravel road for about 4 miles to the public landing, providing access to the southeast end of Snowbank Lake. En route, you'll pass four private roads, two leading to resorts. At each of these intersections bear to the right, and stay on the county road to its end.

Description: A public campground at Fall Lake, 17 miles closer to Ely, just north of the Fernberg Road via Forest Route 551, provides a good place to spend the night before your trip. A fee is charged to camp there.

Snowbank Lake has two active resorts along its southern shoreline. Fishermen base themselves at these resorts and fish during the days in Snowbank and its neighbors. Barely more than half of the travel permits for this entry point are issued to groups using canoes without motors, so you will not find much peace and quiet in the immediate vicinity of this beautiful big lake. Motors are limited to 25 h.p. on that portion of the lake contained in the BWCA. The southwestern part of the lake, however, has no horsepower limits.

A long time favorite among anglers, Snowbank contains lake trout, walleye, northern pike and bass. You will probably have better luck in the neighboring lakes, however.

Route #34: The Disappointment Loop

3 Days, 19 Miles, 11 Lakes, 12 Portages

Difficulty: Easy

Fisher Map: F-11

Travel Zones: 21, 20

Introduction: This little loop will take you through the chain of Snowbank's eastern neighbor lakes. From the public landing, you will paddle across the protected southern part of Snowbank to the portage into Parent Lake. From Parent, you will set a course to the northeast and wind your way through Disappointment Lake, into the chain of tiny lakes to the north, and on to popular Ensign Lake. You will travel west on this long lake for 1½ miles and then portage south to Boot Lake. After two more portages and a small pond, you will once again find yourself on Snowbank Lake. A 4-mile paddle to the southwest will return you to your origin at the public landing.

Although portages are frequent, only the one to Boot Lake is long enough to provide a challenge. Motors are permitted only on Snowbank Lake. A group of strong canoeists could complete this route in one day.

Popular among fishermen, Ensign Lake contains northern pike, walleye and bass. Not as common in this part of the country are the rainbow trout and brook trout that have been stocked in Ahsub Lake, just north of Disappointment.

Although this route is not long, you will surely find a good deal of variety here, from tiny, shallow lakes like Jitterbug to the wide open expanse of Snowbank Lake, as deep as 140 feet.

The water level will not present a serious problem on this route, but low water can alter the complexion of the smaller lakes between Disappointment and Ensign. When it does, stumps and rocks protrude from the bottom of Cattyman Lake, and the landing for the portage from Jitterbug to Ahsub extends for several more rods out into the marshy lake. At such times, in fact, Jitterbug is scarcely more than a foot deep at any point.

DAY 1: **Snowbank Lake,** p. 80 rods, **Parent Lake,** p. 85 rods, **Disappointment Lake.** Take your time paddling across Parent Lake and fish for one of the walleye that are known to inhabit it. The two portages are easy.

DAY 2: **Disappointment Lake,** p. 25 rods, **Ahsub Lake,** p. 15 rods, **Jitterbug Lake,** p. 40 rods, **Adventure Lake,** p. 10 rods, **Cattyman Lake,** p. 25 rods, **Gibson Lake,** p. 105 rods, **Ashigan Lake,** p. 53 rods, **Ensign Lake.** When the water level is high enough, you may be able to paddle through the channel connecting Adventure and Cattyman lakes, eliminating the 10-rod portage. Your first two portages this day are uphill, but the rest are downhill.

DAY 3: **Ensign Lake,** p. 220 rods, **Boot Lake,** p. 30 rods, **pond,** p. 50 rods, **Snowbank Lake.** On this day you will be portaging uphill, gaining 80 feet from Ensign to Snowbank Lake. If the wind is strong out of the west, good luck! If so, you may want to settle down in the campsite just south of the portage in the northeast corner of Snowbank, and wait until the winds subside later in the evening.

Route #35: The Lake Trout Route

7 Days, 60 Miles, 39 Lakes, 1 Creek, 48 Portages
Difficulty: Challenging
Fisher Maps: F-11, F-12
Travel Zones: 21, 28, 29, 33, 37, 32, 30, 20

Introduction: This wilderness route first follows the route from Snowbank Lake east and north through Disappointment Lake to Ima Lake. You will paddle southeast through Hatchet and into Thomas Lake. From Fraser Lake you will continue east and enter into an interior portion of the BWCA that is seldom visited by other canoeists. A series of tiny lakes and long portages will lead you eventually to popular Little Saganaga Lake. From Little Sag you will point your course northwest and paddle through beautiful big Gabimichigami Lake and across a lovely series of pools and rapids that drain into another popular lake, Ogishkemuncie. Through a chain of small lakes and even tinier ponds, you will continue moving west, into impressive, cliff-lined Kekekabic Lake and then north through Pickle, Spoon and Bonnie lakes to Knife Lake, on the international border. You will follow this long, clear border lake southwest to its end, and beyond to Vera and Ensign lakes. After three more portages to the south, you will find yourself back on familiar Snowbank Lake. Four miles of paddling across this big lake will return you to your origin at the public landing on the south shore.

Although this route starts and ends on a busy motor-designated lake, motors are prohibited from most of the loop. Your third day will take you through the most remote interior portion of all the BWCA, where you will see only dedicated wilderness canoeists like yourself. Attractive scenery exists all along the way, but the part of the route between Little Saganaga Lake and Kekekabic Lake is truly exceptional. Nowhere will you find scenery more beautiful!

If you are an angler in search of lake trout, you will have a golden opportunity to catch them on this trip. This species is known to inhabit Snowbank, Thomas, Little Saganaga, Gabimichigami, Kekekabic and Knife lakes. And you will also find northern pike and walleye in Ima, Fraser, Vera, Ensign and other lakes en route.

DAY 1: **Snowbank Lake,** p. 80 rods, **Parent Lake,** p. 85 rods, **Disappointment Lake,** p. 25 rods, **Ahsub Lake,** p. 15 rods, **Jitterbug Lake,** p. 40 rods, **Adventure Lake,** p. 10 rods, **Cattyman Lake,** p. 55 rods, **Jordan Lake,** p. 5 rods, **Ima Lake.** Although five of these portages are uphill, none is difficult. When the water level is high enough, you may be able to paddle through the channel connecting Adventure and Cattyman lakes, eliminating the 10-rod portage.

DAY 2: **Ima Lake,** p. 50 rods, **Hatchet Lake,** p. 10 rods, **Thomas Creek,** p. 10 rods, **creek,** p. 10 rods, **pond,** p. 5 rods, **Thomas Lake, Fraser Lake,** p. 65 rods, **Sagus Lake.** Under normal water conditions, you can probably pull your canoe up through the first two rapids in the creek between Thomas and Hatchet lakes, eliminating two 10-rod portages. The third short carry crosses the famed Kekekabic Trail.

DAY 3: **Sagus Lake,** p. 42 rods, **Roe Lake,** p. 60 rods, **Cap Lake,** p. 190 rods, **Ledge Lake,** p. 160 rods, **Vee Lake,** p. 80 rods, **Fee Lake,** p. 40 rods, **Hoe Lake,** p. 100 rods, **Makwa Lake,** p. 45 rods, **Elton Lake,** p. 19 rods, **pond,** p. 19 rods, **Little Saganaga Lake.** You will surely look back at this day as your roughest of the whole trip. Few people penetrate this remote portion of the BWCA, and for the first time along this route you will sense a feeling of true wilderness solitude.

DAY 4: **Little Saganaga Lake,** p. 30 rods, **Rattle Lake,** p. 25 rods, **Gabimichigami Lake,** p. 15 rods, **Agamok Lake,** 3 portages, **Mueller Lake,** p. 80 rods, **Ogishkemuncie Lake.** This area must rank as one of the most beautiful in the North Woods, from island-studded Little Saganaga, to wide-open Gabimichigami, to the sheltered little pools and rapids between Mueller and Agamok lakes. It is possible to portage directly from Agamok to Mueller via a 100-rod trail, but in doing so you would miss the lovely series of pools, rapids and a scenic waterfall. Instead, I recommend the three short, rocky portages, which are steep in places but not longer than 20 rods. The final portage of the day is steep, but mostly downhill, from

Mueller to Ogishkemuncie*Lake. This is a very popular lake, so find your campsite early! Campers are limited to a one-night stay on Ogishkemuncie.

DAY 5: **Ogishkemuncie Lake,** p. 15 rods, **Annie Lake,** p. 15 rods, **Lake Jean,** p. 15 rods, **Eddy Lake,** 5 portages, **Kekekabic Lake,** p. 80 rods, **Pickle Lake,** p. 25 rods, **Spoon Lake.** The five portages between Eddy and Kekekabic lakes join a series of tiny pools, known as the Kekekabic Ponds. All the carries are short and quite easy, but they may slow your progress considerably. Kekekabic Lake is nothing less than spectacular when you enter it from the ponds. As you emerge from the narrow east end, scenic bluffs tower above your canoe, and along the distant southern shoreline hills rise to 400 feet above the lake. Ahead of you lie over four miles of scenic lake shore—most impressive after the chain of little ponds from which you came.

DAY 6: **Spoon Lake,** p. 25 rods, **Bonnie Lake,** p. 33 rods, **Knife Lake,** p. 200 rods, **Vera Lake.** (See comments for Day 2, Route #30.)

DAY 7: **Vera Lake,** p. 180 rods, **Ensign Lake,** p. 220 rods, **Boot Lake,** p. 30 rods, **pond,** p. 50 rods, **Snowbank Lake.** (See comments for Day 3, Route #34.)

Entry Point 30—Lake One

Permits: 2209

Popularity Rank: 2

Daily Quota: 22

Location: Lake One is seventeen miles straight east of Ely. To get there, follow the Fernberg Road for 19½ miles from the Ely Chamber of Commerce building to its end. A large parking lot is adjacent to the nice public landing.

Description: Camping is prohibited at the landing. A National Forest Campground is located next to Fall Lake, 14 miles closer to Ely on the Fernberg Road, a good place to spend the night before your trip. A fee is charged to camp there.

Before the BWCA Wilderness Act of 1978, Lake One served as access to an extensive (and popular) motor route that extended as far east as Alice Lake and looped north through Thomas and Ima lakes to Snowbank Lake. Motorboats, though, are no longer allowed on the Lake One chain, and all of the lake is contained within the BWCA.

That was unfortunate for aquatic motorists, but it was a delightful turn of events for wilderness canoeists. Lake One may be confusing to even an experienced map reader, so don't leave home without your compass. And bring along plenty of film! You'll encounter beautiful scenery regardless of which route you choose. Moose are abundant in this region, too.

Route #36: The Clearwater-Kawishiwi Loop

3 Days, 28 Miles, 8 Lakes, 1 River, 14 Portages

Difficulty: Challenging

Fisher Maps: F-10, F-4, F-3

Travel Zones: 22, 29, 25, 24

Introduction: This little loop will take you southeast through Lake One and into Lake Two. Then you will leave this busy route and paddle south into a part of the BWCA that receives lighter use, from Rock Island Lake to Turtle Lake. From Turtle, you will portage into the southernmost route through the Boundary Waters, and follow it northwest from Bald Eagle Lake to the South Kawishiwi River. You will walk your canoe up the shallow rapids and paddle through the quiet pools of the Kawishiwi, following its course northeast to the public landing on Lake One.

Although the beginning of this route receives heavy use, the remainder receives only light to moderate travel. Motors are prohibited throughout the route.

Fishermen will find walleye, northern pike, bass and pan fish throughout much of the route.

DAY 1: **Lake One,** p. 30 rods, **pond,** p. 45 rods, **Lake Two,** p. 45 rods, **creek, Rock Island Lake,** p. 242 rods, **Clearwater Lake.** This last, long portage is relatively level most of the way, but downhill at the end, where a nice sandy beach greets you. Clearwater Lake is aptly named, and you will find several nice campsites along its north shore. Try fishing for walleye here.

You may find this trip's route confusing from the beginning. Lake One, with its many islands and meandering bays, offers a sporty challenge to the map reader. From the landing, first bear to the left and then to the right, as you pass through a very narrow channel en route to the main body of the lake. If confused by the many islands in the lake, use your compass and common sense, and don't treat the map as "gospel." Things won't look the way you think they should!

DAY 2: **Clearwater Lake,** p. 252 rods, **Turtle Lake,** p. 186 rods, **Bald Eagle Lake, rapids, Gabbro Lake, Little Gabbro Lake,** p. 122 rods, **South Kawishiwi River.** Your first long portage is nearly level and nothing to worry about. The second, on the other hand, climbs steeply uphill from Turtle Lake before descending to Bald Eagle Lake. The short, swift rapids between Bald Eagle and Gabbro lakes can be easily shot in your canoe.

DAY 3: **South Kawishiwi River,** p. 28 rods, **river,** p. 18 rods, **river,** p. 12 rods, **river,** p. 8 rods, **river,** p. 40 rods, **river,** p. 20 rods, **river,** p. 19 rods, **Lake One.** With normal water conditions, you may eliminate four of the portages along the Kawishiwi River by walking your canoe up the shallow rapids. The only two that must be portaged around are at the 8-rod and the 40-rod trails. Make certain that your last carry is the 19-rod path to Lake One. It is an easy mistake to take the 25-rod trail to Confusion Lake instead. Continue past the first portage that you pass on the right around a small island to the portage at the east end of the tiny bay.

Route #37: The Alice-Thomas Route

5 Days, 55 Miles, 26 Lakes, 1 River, 2 Creeks, 32 Portages
Difficulty: Challenging
Fisher Maps: F-10, F-4, F-11
Travel Zones: 22, 28, 33, 29, 21

Introduction: This interesting loop penetrates the remote interior portion of the Boundary Waters where motors are not allowed and where few canoeists travel. From Lake One, you will paddle southeast through Lakes Two, Three and Four to the island-studded bays of beautiful Lake Insula. From the north end of Insula, you will continue northeast up the Kawishiwi River, then north through Elbow and Adams lakes, and camp on isolated Boulder Lake, your farthest point east. Turning back to the west, you will paddle through Fraser and Thomas lakes, portage across the Kekekabic Trail, and float down the shallow stream to Ima Lake. From Ima, you will travel southwest through the tiny lakes leading to Disappointment, Parent and Snowbank lakes. Your canoe trip will end at the public landing on Snowbank Lake, five miles by road from your origin at the Lake One Landing. Unless you have made arrangements to have a vehicle waiting, your trip will end with a five-mile hike.

All along this route, fishing is good for northern pike and walleye. Lake trout are also found in Thomas and Snowbank lakes. The largest fish I have caught was pulled from the Kawishiwi River east of Lake Insula—a northern pike that stole three lures before he finally met his match.

DAY 1: **Lake One,** p. 30 rods, **pond,** p. 45 rods, **Lake Two, Lake Three, Lake Four,** p. 20 rods, **Kawishiwi River,** p. 25 rods, **river,** p. 10 rods, **river, Hudson Lake.** (See comments for Day 1, Route #36.) You will see many other travelers this day, but most of them go no farther than the numbered lakes. In spite of the traffic, moose are commonly seen throughout the area.

DAY 2: **Hudson Lake,** p. 105 rods, **Lake Insula,** p. 18 rods, **Kawishiwi River, Alice Lake,** p. 20 rods, **Kawishiwi River,** p. 90 rods, **river.** The southwest end of Lake Insula may be confusing to even an experienced map reader. Use your compass, if necessary, and follow a general heading, instead of trying to account for every little island you see. You will find a display of Indian rock paintings south of your last portage this day, on the west shore of the Kawishiwi River. Several good campsites are nearby.

DAY 3: **Kawishiwi River,** p. 15 rods, **river,** p. 15 rods, **Trapline Lake,** p. 30 rods, **Beaver Lake,** p. 90 rods, **Adams Lake, Boulder Creek,** p. 15 rods, **creek, Boulder Lake.** You will see few, if any, other people after you veer north from the Kawishiwi river. Between Adams and Boulder lakes, there may be a couple of liftovers, in addition to the 15-rod portage.

DAY 4: **Boulder Lake,** p. 220 rods, **Cap Lake,** p. 60 rods, **Roe Lake,** p. 42 rods, **Sagus Lake,** p. 65 rods, **Fraser Lake, Thomas Lake,** p. 5 rods, **pond,** p. 10 rods, **Thomas Creek,** p. 10 rods, **creek,** p. 10 rods, **Hatchet Lake,** p. 50 rods, **Ima Lake.** Your first long portage will split after 135 rods of hiking. The right trail leads to Ledge Lake, so bear to the left for 85 more rods, to Cap Lake. When you enter Thomas Lake, traffic will increase. If the water level is not too low, the second and third 10-rod portages between Thomas and Hatchet lakes may be eliminated by walking or lining your canoe down the shallow rapids. Ima Lake is a popular one, so find a campsite as early as possible.

DAY 5: **Ima Lake,** p. 5 rods, **Jordan Lake,** p. 55 rods, **Cattyman Lake,** p. 10 rods, **Adventure Lake,** p. 40 rods, **Jitterbug Lake,** p. 15 rods, **Ahsub Lake,** p. 25 rods, **Disappointment Lake,** p. 85 rods, **Parent Lake,** p. 80 rods, **Snowbank Lake.** If the water level is high enough, you may be able to eliminate the 10-rod portage between Cattyman and Adventure lakes by paddling through the interconnecting channel. Rainbow trout and brook trout are stocked in Ahsub Lake, and Parent Lake is known for its good walleye fishing.

Entry Point 31—Farm Lake

Permits: 236

Popularity Rank: 27

Daily Quota: 3

Location: Farm Lake is located about 5 miles straight east of Ely. To get there, follow State Highway 169 1½ miles from the Ely Chamber of Commerce building to its intersection with County Road 58. Turn right and follow St. Louis Co. Rd. 58, which soon becomes Lake Co. Rd. 16. Continue driving east on Co. Rd. 16 for a total of 4.3 miles from Highway 169. An access road leads north (turn left) 0.2 mile to the small landing and parking lot. Co. Rd. 16 is hard-surfaced, but rough, for the first 3½ miles. The last mile is on gravel.

Description: A public campground at nearby Fall Lake is a good place to spend the night before your trip. It is reached via the Fall Lake Road, which meets the Fernberg Road 5½ miles east of the Chamber of Commerce building. There is a camping fee at Fall Lake.

Farm Lake, located entirely outside the BWCA, is decorated with resorts and private cabins along the southern and western shorelines. It is not a heavily used entry point, and a good deal of solitude and relative isolation can be had at several lakes within easy reach.

40% of the travel permits written in 1979 went to those with motorboats or motorized canoes. Since motors are no longer allowed on the North Kawishiwi River, it is evident that at *least* 40% of the groups that enter the BWCA from Farm Lake head for South Farm Lake, where motors *are* allowed. You'll be heading for the North Kawishiwi River, so don't let all the traffic on Farm Lake get you down!

Route #38: The North-South Kawishiwi Rivers Loop

2 Days, 25 Miles, 2 Lakes, 2 Rivers, 10 Portages
Difficulty: Challenging
Fisher Maps: F-3, F-4
Travel Zones: 24, 25

Introduction: This fun-filled weekend loop will first take you east, up the North Kawishiwi River to its junction with the South Kawishiwi River. At that point, you will turn to the southwest and paddle down a short segment of the South Kawishiwi River. Then you will portage north, through Clear Lake, and back to the North Kawishiwi. An hour of westward paddling will return you to your origin at the Farm Lake landing.

Until January 1, 1979, the entire route was open to motorboat traffic. Since then, however, the only part of the loop where motors are permitted is on Farm Lake, which is outside the BWCA. You'll find this pretty route to be lightly used during all but the very busiest parts of the summer. If the water level is appropriate, you will have an opportunity to eliminate several portages by shooting, lining or walking your canoe through small rapids on both rivers.

If you prefer an easy 3-day route to a challenging 2-day

loop, camp your second night on Clear Lake and take your time. If you have no intention of shooting those short rapids, you might consider reversing the route. That will make all your short portages along the South Kawishiwi River uphill, but the challenging 210-rod trek along the north branch will be mostly *down*hill. Regardless of the direction you take or the number of days you allow, you are bound to enjoy this very lovely loop.

DAY 1: **Farm Lake, North Kawishiwi River,** p. 10 rods, **river,** p. 10 rods, **river,** p. 18 rods, **river,** p. 210 rods, **river.** (See comments for Day 1, Route #39.)

DAY 2: **North Kawishiwi River, South Kawishiwi River,** p. 12 rods, **river,** p. 18 rods, **river,** 28 rods, **river, rapids, river,** p. 70 rods, **Clear Lake,** p. 144 rods, **North Kawishiwi River,** p. 10 rods, **river, Farm Lake.** If the water level is right, and your enthusiasm and whitewater skill are sufficient, you can eliminate the first three portages and the last one by running (or walking) these rapids.

Route #39: The Clearwater-Turtle Loop

4 Days, 40 Miles, 11 Lakes, 2 Rivers, 19 Portages

Difficulty: Challenging

Fisher maps: F-3, F-10, F-4

Travel Zones: 24, 22, 29, 25

Introduction: This interesting route will take you through some of the busiest and also some of the least traveled lakes in the BWCA, as well as through portions of the mellow Kawishiwi river. From Farm Lake you will paddle east into the North Kawishiwi River, along the border of the Boundary Waters to Lakes One and Two. Leaving these heavily used lakes, you will then turn south and portage into more peaceful lakes. Then you will return to a busier route at Bald Eagle Lake and journey northwest through Gabbro and Little Gabbro lakes to the South Kawishiwi River. After paddling through Clear Lake you will return to the North Kawishiwi River and retrace your strokes to the public landing at Farm Lake.

Although most of the route has fairly heavy traffic, the

only place where it may be a disturbance is in the vicinity of Lake One, the second busiest entry point in the BWCA. Not far away, however, you will experience true wilderness solitude during your night on Clearwater Lake. Gentle rapids and quiet pools, large open lakes and generally good fishing all combine to make this route a great one. Walleye and northern pike are prevalent throughout. Farm is the only lake where motors are allowed.

DAY 1: **Farm Lake, North Kawishiwi River,** p. 10 rods, **river,** p. 10 rods, **river,** p. 18 rods, **river,** 210 rods, **river.** The first 10-rod portage is necessary only during periods of very low water; normally you can paddle right up the channel. The other two short rapids can be easily walked up or lined. But psych up for the 210-rods portage—it's rough! The path is not well-used and it is nearly all uphill, gaining almost 100 feet in elevation. You'll find two splendid campsites just before the junction of the North and South Kawishiwi rivers, both with ample space for large groups.

DAY 2: **Kawishiwi River,** p. 8 rods, **river,** p. 40 rods, **river,** p. 20 rods, **river,** p. 25 rods, **Confusion Lake,** p. 41 rods, **Lake One,** p. 30 rods, **pond,** p. 45 rods, **Lake Two,** p. 45 rods, **creek, Rock Island Lake,** p. 242 rods, **Clearwater Lake.** If you prefer walking up rapids to carrying all your gear overland, the 20-rod portage along the Kawishiwi River is usually no problem. But resist the temptation to walk up the two rapids before it. The 8-rod portage bypasses a small waterfall, and the 40-rod path goes around what appears from the bottom to be "just another pretty rapids" but becomes swifter and deeper the farther up you get, and at the top you are greeted by a small dam. I once pulled through it with empty canoes—just barely—but I would never attempt it with a loaded craft. Don't worry about the 242-rod portage. It is the second longest carry of the trip, but mostly level.

DAY 3: **Clearwater Lake,** p. 252 rods, **Turtle Lake,** p. 186 rods, **Bald Eagle Lake, rapids, Gabbro Lake, Little Gabbro Lake,** p. 122 rods, **South Kawishiwi River, rapids, river,** p. 70 rods, **Clear Lake.** Your first two portages are long and not very well-traveled, but not very difficult either. The 252-rod path from Clearwater to Turtle is virtually level. The 186-rod trail into Bald Eagle, on the other hand, begins rather steeply uphill, but then descends most of the way. You will have no trouble shooting through the small rapids between Bald Eagle and Gabbro lakes and on the South Kawishiwi River. Clear Lake is a serene and pretty little lake that offers good northern pike fishing.

DAY 4: **Clear Lake,** p. 144 rods, **North Kawishiwi River,** p. 10 rods, **river, Farm Lake.** As on the first day, the 10-rod portage on the North Kawishiwi River may not be necessary unless the water level is extremely low.

Ch. 6
Entry from State Highway 1

The South-Central Area

Eight entry points are accessible from State Highway 1 southeast of Ely, but only one—South Kawishiwi River—is easily accessible. Four of the points require extensive backwoods driving on county roads and forest routes—gravel for many miles. Three are not quite as far from Highway 1. I would venture to say that the entry points in this part of the Boundary Waters Canoe Area are probably the least familiar to paddlers from outside the Ely area. The prevailing attitude among BWCA visitors seems to be, "Head north toward Canada." Consequently, these southernmost routes are often overlooked. Perhaps that is why I like these eight best!

Ely is still the closest commercial center to these entry points (see paragraphs 2 and 3 in Chapter 4). You'll probably find the most accurate information about canoe routes originating at entry points #32 and #33 at the Ely Chamber of Commerce building, where Kawishiwi Ranger District officials are stationed. For more information about entry points #34, #35, #75 and #84, your best bet is at the Isabella Ranger Station (one mile west of "downtown" Isabella, 35 miles southeast of Ely). Finally, the best source for accurate information about entry points #36 and #37 is the Tofte Ranger Station (on Highway 61, 25 miles north of its junction with Highway 1).

To get to these entry points, simply follow Highway 1 south from Ely. The South Kawishiwi River entry point is just off the highway. Two are reached via the "Tomahawk Road," which spurs off of Hwy 1 19 miles southeast of Ely. The other four are reached from the little town of Isabella, located about halfway between Ely and Lake Superior on Highway 1.

The highway is usually quite good, but it does wind considerably and is rather hilly at times. Drive carefully! Logging trucks are abundant in this area.

Entry Point 32—South Kawishiwi River

Permits: 250
Popularity Rank: 26
Daily Quota: 3

Location: Public access to the Kawishiwi River is located 8 miles southeast of Ely. To drive there, follow State Highway 1 for 11 miles southeast of its intersection with Hwy 169 in Ely, 100 yards past the river bridge.

An alternative access is located off the Spruce Road (Lake County Road 16) which intersects Highway 1 ¼ mile beyond the Kawishiwi Campground. Turn left onto the the gravel road and follow it northeast four miles. There you will find the beginning of a portage trail on the left (north) side of the road, adjacent to a small parking area that will accommodate half a dozen vehicles. The 140-rod portage is rough and rocky in places, rooty in others, and could be muddy in spring or after rains. There is one portage rest at the midway point. A 5-rod board-walk will make passage much easier near the end of the trail. By using this access, you will eliminate three miles of paddling and four shorter portages; but you will also bypass a lovely section of the river. So I suggest putting in at the Campground, unless time is of the essence.

Description: The Forest Service Kawishiwi Campground, with public swimming beach and parking lot, is adjacent to the boat access. It is an excellent place to spend the night before your journey into the Boundary Waters Canoe Area. A fee is charged to camp there.

The Kawishiwi is a shallow, wide, rocky-bottomed series of pools and rapids. Red pine, balsam, cedar and spruce populate its shore, and walleye and northern pike inhabit its depths. Good campsites are found all along its course, wherever a rocky outcropping exists. Under normal water conditions, many of the portages en route may be avoided by walking, lining or running your canoe through the accompanying white-water. The portages may be more desirable, however, when the water is low or the day is cool.

Motors are no longer allowed through this entry point. They are permitted only in the section of the river which is outside the BWCA, to the fourth portage, about 3 miles upstream.

Route #40: The Split River Route

3 Days, 30 Miles, 1 Lake, 2 Rivers, 18 Portages
Difficulty: Challenging
Fisher Map: F-3
Travel Zones: 25, 24

Introduction: This short loop will take you up the South Kawishiwi River to its junction with the North Kawishiwi River. You will then paddle to the west down this scenic river until you reach the portage to Clear Lake. Beyond Clear Lake, you'll re-enter the South Kawishiwi River and follow it back to your origin at Highway 1.

All but the first (and last) three miles of the route are closed to motor traffic. If the water level is appropriate, you will have an excellent opportunity to shoot through several small rapids, as well as to walk your canoe up many more. A good group of competent paddlers could easily complete this route in two days. But stretch it to three days and take time to appreciate the natural beauty that surrounds you.

DAY 1: **South Kawishiwi River,** p. 33 rods, **river,** p 26 rods, **river,** p. 25 rods, **river,** p. 62 rods, **river,** p. 7 rods, **river.** You can probably avoid all of the portages this day by walking your canoe up the accompanying rapids.

On the opposite shore from the first portage is the Voyageur Outward Bound School, which uses this set of rapids to train its students. You may see several canoes lined up on the river, awaiting turns to negotiate these Class II rapids.

The second portage could be very muddy if the water level had been high, or after rains. The 62-rod trail could be split into two shorter portages around two short rapids. The first would then be 13 rods and the second 23 rods, with about 26 rods of paddling between them.

DAY 2: **South Kawishiwi River, rapids, river,** p. 28 rods, **river,** p. 18 rods, **river,** p. 12 rods, **North Kawishiwi River,** p. 210 rods, **river,** 18 rods, **river,** p. 10 rods, **river,** p. 144 rods, **Clear Lake.** Again you will be able to walk your canoe up all the rapids on the South Kawishiwi River this day. Unfortunately, the 210-rod portage must be taken, because the river drops 60 feet in ½ mile. The trail is not heavily used, but it is primarily downhill, so it should not cause you too much difficulty.

DAY 3: **Clear Lake,** p. 70 rods, **South Kawishiwi River,** p. 7 rods, **river,** p. 62 rods, **river,** p. 25 rods, **river,** p. 26 rods, **river,** p. 33 rods, **river.** After the initial 70-rod portage, you can eliminate all of the other portages by walking, lining or running the shallow rapids, depending on the water conditions and your whitewater skills. Be cautious, though, and scout ahead before attempting any rapids.

Route #41: The Bald Eagle-Gull Route

5 Days, 46 Miles, 11 Lakes, 1 River, 1 Creek, 29 Portages
Difficulty: Challenging
Fisher Maps: F-3, F-4, F-10
Travel Zones: 25, 23, 22, 24

Introduction: This interesting route will take you through some of the busiest and some of the *least* traveled lakes in the BWCA as well as through all of the south branch of the Kawishiwi River. You will paddle northeast up the South Kawishiwi River to the portage into Little Gabbro Lake, then southeast through Gabbro and Bald Eagle lakes. Then you'll head north into a chain of lakes that sees far fewer people and requires considerably more portaging. At Lake Two you'll point west and make your return trip through Lake One and down the Kawishiwi River, then into the south branch from which you came. Motorboats are prohibited from all of the route except the first and last 3-mile segment, which is outside the BWCA. The only place where you may encounter heavy canoe traffic is in the vicinity of Lake One, the fourth busiest entry point in the BWCA. The region between Lake Two and Bald Eagle is very lightly traveled and here you will experience the essence of wilderness solitude. Gentle rapids and quiet pools, large open lakes and generally good fishing all combine to make this route a great one. Walleye and northern pike are prevalent throughout.

DAY 1: **South Kawishiwi River,** p. 33 rods, **river,** p. 26 rods, **river,** p. 25 rods, **river,** p. 62 rods, **river,** p. 7 rods, **river.** You can avoid all the portages this day by walking your canoe up the accompanying rapids.

DAY 2: **South Kawishiwi River, rapids, river,** p. 122 rods, **Little Gabbro Lake, Gabbro Lake,** p. 2–5 rods, **Bald Eagle Lake,** p. 189 rods, **Gull Creek,** p. 41 rods, **Gull Lake.** The true adventurer with time to kill can avoid the 122-rod portage from the South Kawishiwi River to Little Gabbro Lake by walking up two sets of gentle rapids, and portaging around a small falls and an old logging dam. The map won't show this, so here is what to look for: just beyond the north end of the 122-rod portage you'll encounter a short stretch of rapids that must be walked up (no portage). Bearing to the left shoreline, you'll soon come to a picturesque little waterfall that must be passed on the left by a steep, overgrown 10-rod portage that appears to have been used only once or twice since the last Chippewa Indians moved out of the region. Soon after, you will again have to walk up a somewhat longer stretch of rapids, until you arrive at the old dam, which can be passed on the right via an even less traveled path. *Voila:* the back door to Little Gabbro Lake. It is kind of fun, but takes much longer than the 122-rod portage.

Beware the 189-rod portage out of Bald Eagle Lake. It is mostly uphill, climbing to 90 feet above the lake. Several campsites await you on Gull Lake, but most are out of the way.

DAY 3: **Gull Lake,** p. 50 rods, **Pietro Lake,** p. 64 rods, **Camdre Lake,** p. 125 rods, **Clearwater Lake,** p. 242 rods, **Rock Island Lake, creek,** p. 45 rods, **Lake Two.** The only notably uphill trek of this day is the 64-rod portage from Pietro to Camdre Lake. The long 242-rod trail out of Clearwater

Lake has a steep uphill portion at the beginning, but it soon levels off and does not present a major challenge.

DAY 4: **Lake Two,** p. 45 rods, **pond,** p. 30 rods, **Lake One,** p. 41 rods, **Confusion Lake,** p. 25 rods, **Kawishiwi River,** p. 20 rods, **river,** p. 40 rods, **river,** p. 8 rods, **river, South Kawishiwi River,** p. 12 rods, **river,** p. 18 rods, **river,** 28 rods, **river, rapids, river.** For those who prefer a little whitewater to the drugery of portaging, four of the six portages on the Kawishiwi River this day may be avoided (20, 12, 18 and 28 rods) by shooting, lining or walking the respective rapids, depending on the water depth. Be sure to check them out first, because, although the rapids are not considered dangerous, sharp rocks could damage your canoe.

DAY 5: **South Kawishiwi River,** p. 7 rods, **river,** p. 62 rods, **river,** p. 25 rods, **river,** p. 26 rods, **river,** p. 33 rods, **river.** Again, you can eliminate all of the portages this day by walking, lining, or running the shallow rapids, if the water level is right.

Entry Point 33—Little Gabbro Lake

Permits: 231

Popularity Rank: 28

Daily Quota: 3

Location: Little Gabbro Lake lies near the southwest corner of the central part of the Boundary Waters, 10 miles southeast of Ely as the goose flies. From the Chamber of Commerce building, drive south on Highway 1 11¼ miles to the Spruce Road (Lake County Road 16), about one-half mile beyond the Kawishiwi River bridge. Turn left and drive 4 miles to the end of the gravel County Road. At that point, continue driving northeast on Forest Route 181 (the *right* fork of the "Y") for 1.8 additional miles to the junction of Forest Route 158 on the left. Turn there and drive 0.6 mile to the road's end at the beginning of the Little Gabbro Lake portage. You'll find County Road 16 to be an excellent gravel road, but the final 2.4 miles of forest routes are rough, sometimes under water, and very slow going. Four-wheel-drive is not necessary, but a vehicle with high clearance is recommended.

Description: At the trailhead there is space on a large, flat rock to accommodate parking for at least a dozen vehicles (and there are frequently that many vehicles present). The 265-rod-portage trail leads north from the parking area and gradually descends much of the way to Little Gabbro Lake. It is rocky in places, and wet and muddy in other spots, but generally a good, wide, well-used path that sometimes follows the route of an old road bed. There are two canoe rests along the way.

The South Kawishiwi Campground, which you pass 6 miles before reaching this entry point (just south of the bridge on Highway 1), is a fine USFS campground at which to spend the night before your trip. There are 32 campsites, well water, and a small swimming beach. A fee is charged to camp there.

Discussion of this entry point was omitted from the first edition of this book becauseNat that time, Little Gabbro Lake was grouped with Entry Point #32 for the purpose of quota restrictions. The South Kawishiwi River was an easier and considerably more popular entry point. Since then, the popularity of Entry Point #33 has grown so much that it is used almost as often as its river neighbor. In fact, if you're planning to begin your trip on Saturday, Sunday or Monday, it would be a good idea to make a reservation early. Little Gabbro Lake's quota was filled 45 days in 1986 (ranking 18th among all entry points).

Nearly half of those days were in the last half of May and in June, when fishing is usually at its best. That's due to the fact that Little Gabbro provides quick access to two lakes with excellent reputations among anglers. Gabbro Lake, just east of Little Gabbro, is known for its good walleye population, and Bald Eagle Lake, beyond Gabbro, is a good source of northern pike.

It's a lovely region with some nice campsites, rocky shorelines, and ample wildlife and seldom any human congestion. Motorboats are prohibited in the area. For other route ideas using Entry Point #33, refer to Entry Point #32. Both of those routes could be modified to start at Little Gabbro Lake.

Route #42: The Clear-Eskwagama Lakes Loop

2 Days, 10 Miles, 3 Lakes, 1 River, 7 Portages
Difficulty: Easy
Fisher Map: F-3
Travel Zones: 25, 24

Introduction: This short loop is stretched over three days to accommodate anglers who like to explore every nook and cranny along the way. From Little Gabbro Lake you'll head north into the most isolated part of the South Kawishiwi River and then portage to a small, peaceful lake that's off the beaten path. From Clear Lake, you'll portage into Eskwagama Lake and then return to the South Kawishiwi River and retrace your route back to Little Gabbro Lake. Although the first portage is a challenge to most folks, it's the only major carry of this loop. With two full days to travel only ten miles, the route should still be considered "easy" by most canoeists—unless you're packing an ice chest and a keg of beer!

Walleyes are found along most of the loop, and northern pike are everywhere. Serious anglers may want to add another day for the route, enabling them to spend a night at Gabbro Lake—considered one of the best spots in the area for catching walleyes. Canoeists with little interest in fishing, on the other hand, could easily complete the entire loop in just one day.

DAY 1: P. 265 rods, **Little Gabbro Lake,** p. 122 rods, **South Kawishiwi River, rapids, river,** p. 70 rods, **Clear Lake.** Anglers will no doubt want to explore the depths of Little Gabbro Lake for the walleyes that live there before continuing on to the second portage. The 120-rod portage begins just upstream (west bank) from the site of an old, now nearly indistinguishable dam. It is a good, well-beaten trail that descends to the river below. Less than a mile beyond the end of the portage, you'll encounter a small rapids that you should easily glide through. Walleyes and northern pike inhabit the South Kawishiwi River.

There are five campsites on Clear Lake. If you prefer to spend the night alone, continue on to Eskwagama, where there is only one site, on the east shore of the lake. Both lakes contain northern pike. The midpoint of the loop is the portage connecting the two lakes.

DAY 2: **Clear Lake,** p. 100 rods, **Eskwagama Lake,** p. 85 rods, **South Kawishiwi River, rapids, river,** p. 122 rods, **Little Gabbro Lake,** p. 265 rods. When you return to that little rapids on the South Kawishiwi River, you may have to line your canoe up through the swift current. The true adventurer with time to spare can avoid the 122-rod portage from the South Kawishiwi River to Little Gabbro Lake by walking up the two sets of gentle rapids and portaging around a small waterfall (10 rods) and an old dam (8 rods). It's longer and more time-consuming, but an interesting change of pace.

Entry Point 84—Snake River

Permits: 46

Popularity Rank: 50

Daily Quota: 1

Location: The Snake River enters the Boundary Waters about 17 miles southeast of Ely and about 15 miles northwest of Isabella. To get there from Ely, drive southeast on State Highway 1 for 19 miles from its intersection with Highway 169. Turn left onto Forest Route 173, the Tomahawk Road. Continue east on the Tomahawk road for 6 miles to Forest Route 381, the North Kelly Road. Turn left at this intersection and drive north for 1½ miles to a "Y" intersection. From the "Y" drive northwest on the *left* fork 1½ miles to a deadend barrier of boulders across the road. The final three miles of forest roads north of the Tomahawk Road are quite rough and narrow—barely accessible to "normal" vehicles. A heavily loaded car with low clearance may "bottom out" frequently, if the driver is not very careful.

Description: Currently there is no designated parking space for this access. With few other people using it, however, you will have no problem finding a spot along the road near the barrier.

The South Kawishiwi River Campground is the closest place to camp on the night before your trip. It is located 11 miles southeast of Ely, along Highway 1. A fee is charged to camp there.

From the road's end a 180-rod portage continues along the same old logging road on which you were driving. It gradually descends during the first 125 rods to a narrow log bridge that crosses the Snake River at a rapids. Beyond the bridge, the trail climbs for 10 rods to the site of an abandoned 1960's logging camp in a large clearing. At that point large rock cairns mark the trail across the clearing, as the portage trail veers north, away from the old logging road, and begins its final 32-rod descent to the Snake River. Three canoe rests are located along the entire portage.

The habitat along the Snake River is unique, where plants such as blood root, calypso orchids and elm trees are found. The marshy lower part of the river is good habitat for the American Bittern, the Great Blue Heron, and the Common Snipe, as well as many other species of birds.

This is the quickest way to get to Bald Eagle, which is one of the best lakes in the area for catching northern pike. For another route idea, see Entry Point 75—North Kelly Road.

Route #43: The Snake and Turtle Loop

2 Days, 22 Miles, 6 Lakes, 1 River, 1 Creek, 13 Portages
Difficulty: Challenging
Fisher Map: F-4
Travel Zones: 25, 23

Introduction: This weekend route will first take you north, down the Snake River, to Bald Eagle Lake. You will continue paddling northward, through Gull, Pietro and Camdre lakes to Clearwater Lake. The next morning you will point southwestward and return to Bald Eagle via Turtle Lake, and then backtrack up the Snake River to your origin.

If you are not in the greatest shape, you may find this trek a bit too demanding for just two short days. If so, stretch it to three days and take more time to fish.

Except for Bald Eagle Lake, the route is very lightly traveled. Only during the busiest part of the summer will you have much competition for campsites on Clearwater Lake.

Bald Eagle Lake has long been popular among anglers. Persistence should yield walleyes and northern pike, and maybe a few pan fish too. You'll also find walleyes in the other lakes along this route.

DAY 1: P. 180 rods, **Snake River,** p. 20 rods, **river,** p. 10 rods, **river, Bald Eagle Lake,** p. 189 rods, **Gull Creek,** p. 41 rods, **Gull Lake,** p. 50 rods, **Pietro Lake,** p. 64 rods, **Camdre Lake,** p. 125 rods, **Clearwater Lake.** Beware the 189-rod portage out of Bald Eagle Lake. It is mostly uphill, climbing to 90 feet above the lake. The 64-rod carry from Pietro to Camdre Lake is also uphill.

Clearwater Lake is aptly named. You will find several nice campsites along its north shore and a nice, sandy beach at the portage leading to Rock Island Lake. Try fishing for walleye in this crystalline lake.

DAY 2: **Clearwater Lake,** p. 252 rods, **Turtle Lake,** p. 186 rods, **Bald Eagle Lake, Snake River,** p. 10 rods, **river,** p. 20 rods, **river,** p. 180 rods. Yes, three long portages await you this day. But none is too rough. The first is virtually level. The second, on the other hand, begins rather steeply uphill, but then it descends most of the way to Bald Eagle Lake. Of course, you know what awaits you at the end of the Snake River.

Entry Point 75—North Kelly Road

Permits: 30

Popularity Rank: 54

Daily Quota: 2

Location: The North Kelly Road leads to the Little Isabella River, which enters the Boundary Waters about 20 miles southeast of Ely and about 13 miles northwest of Isabella. To get there from Ely, drive southeast on State Highway 1 for 19 miles from its intersection with Hwy 169. (From the Isabella Ranger Station, drive 19 miles northwest via Hwy 1 to Forest Route 173.) Turn left onto Forest Route 173, the "Tomahawk Road." Continue driving east on the Tomahawk Road for 6 miles to Forest Route 381, the North Kelly Road. Turn left at this intersection and drive north for 1.8 miles to a "Y" intersection. Continue driving northeast via the *right* fork for nearly a mile to a deadend at the Little

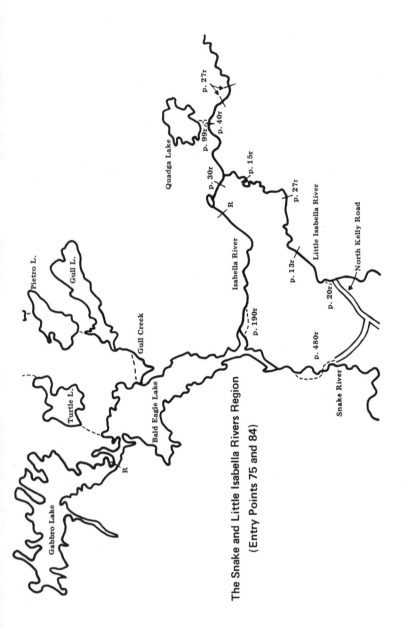

The Snake and Little Isabella Rivers Region
(Entry Points 75 and 84)

Isabella River. This last stretch of road is frequently under water, but it is not as bad as it looks. A 4-wheel-drive vehicle is *not* necessary.

Description: There is a small parking area that should be sufficient for the few people who use this isolated entry point.

The South Kawishiwi River Campground is the closest public facility for camping the night before your canoe trip's departure. It is located adjacent to Hwy 1, 11 miles southeast of Ely. There is a campsite use fee.

A 20-rod portage begins at the road's end and leads north, bypassing a set of rapids, to the narrow river. This is a slow, meandering river that is bordered by alder brush, black spruce and jack pine. There are no campsites along the 3-mile segment leading south to the Isabella River. When the water level is high, the current will be swift in the upper stretches of this little river. During drier periods, the current won't be as swift, but the river's level will never (or very seldom) be too low for canoe navigation. Motors are prohibited.

Route #44: The Little Isabella-Snake Loop

3 Days, 27 Miles, 2 Lakes, 3 Rivers, 9 Portages

Difficulty: Easy

Fisher Map: F-4 (see sketch with Route #43)

Travel Zones: 26, 25

Introduction: This river-running loop will first take you northeast, down the primitive Little Isabella River to its big sister, the Isabella River. You'll then paddle east a short distance up the Isabella to camp at Quadga Lake. The next morning you'll return to the Isabella River and follow it west, this time *down*stream to Bald Eagle Lake, where you will sleep the second night. On the final day of this brief trip, you will paddle to the south end of Bald Eagle and then up the Snake River to a branch of the North Kelly Road, nearly 2½ miles from your origin.

Motors are banned from all of this route. Except for Bald Eagle Lake, the entire loop is very lightly traveled. Only 76 permits were issued in 1986 to users of both the North Kelly and the Snake River entry points. Except during the busiest part of the summer, the chances are good that you will see nobody else on any part of the loop, except Bald Eagle Lake.

This is a good area to view wildlife, including beaver, deer and moose, so keep a watchful eye! NOTE: This loop can be reversed by entering the BWCA at Entry Point 84—Snake River.

DAY 1: P. 20 rods, **Little Isabella River,** p. 13 rods, **river,** p. 27 rods, **river,** p. 15 rods, **river, Isabella River, rapids, river,** p. 99 rods, **Quadga Lake.** During mid- and late summer, the mouth of the Little Isabella River may be nearly choked with reeds. A narrow passage, however, parallels the right shoreline. Because of the reeds, it would be very easy to miss the river's outlet, should you reverse this route.

Soon thereafter, just after pulling through a small set of rapids, you will see a 40-rod portage on the right (south) side of the Isabella River. On the opposite shoreline (left side) is the beginning of the 99-rod portage to Quadga Lake. There you will find four campsites from which to choose. Then cast your line for one of the walleyes or northern pike that reside in Quadga.

DAY 2: **Quadga Lake,** p. 99 rods, **Isabella River, rapids, river,** p. 33 rods, **river, rapids, river,** p. 190 rods, **Bald Eagle Lake.** A 190-rod carry—and I call this route easy!?! Don't worry. It is mostly downhill and follows a good path, with five canoe rests along the way. Don't try to avoid the portage by running the adjacent rapids; it's a long walk back to your car! The better campsites are at the north end of Bald Eagle Lake. But, then, that's where the other people will be, too. The lake's south end is less desirable (and may be confusing) because of all the aquatic vegetation—reeds, cattails, lilypads, etc. It looks more like land than water at a glance! This is one of the best lakes in the area for catching northern pike. You may also find walleyes and crappies.

DAY 3: **Bald Eagle Lake, Snake River,** p. 10 rods, **river,** p. 20 rods, **river,** p. 180 rods. The habitat along the Snake River is unique, where plants such as blood root, calypso orchids and elm trees are found. The marshy lower part of the river is good habitat for the American Bittern, the Great Blue Heron, and the Common Snipe, as well as many other species of birds. At the beginning of that long, final portage, you'll climb 32 rods up from the boggy shore of the Snake River to a large, open clearing where a logging camp once stood. At that point the trail joins the path of an old logging road, then drops 10 rods down to cross the Snake River on a log bridge, and continues the final 125 rods on a good, smooth path leading to road's end at the edge of the BWCA Wilderness. There are three canoe rests along the entire portage.

Entry Point 34—Island River

Permits: 110

Popularity Rank: 36

Daily Quota: 5

Location: The Island River entry point is located 28 miles southeast of Ely. From Isabella on State Highway 1, follow Forest Route 172 one mile east to Forest Route 369. Turn left and follow 369 north for 7 miles to Forest Route 373 and follow it another 5½ miles northwest to Forest Route 377. Turn right and follow 377 4½ miles to the Island River bridge.

Description: Several National Forest Campgrounds are located along State Highway 1, providing places to spend the night before your trip. Coming from Ely, you will pass campgrounds at the South Kawishiwi River, McDougal Lakes and Little Isabella River. All require a camping fee. The closest to the entry point (and the smallest) is the Little Isabella River Campground.

High-quality wilderness canoe trips can be taken from the Island River entry point. The Island and Isabella river valleys teem with wildlife, including moose and bald eagles. Both are scenic rivers with occasional white water and little canoe traffic. You will be well-rewarded for the extra driving time it takes to get there.

Route #45: The Isabella-South Kawishiwi Rivers Loop

5 Days, 57 Miles, 12 Lakes, 3 Rivers, 1 Creek, 37 Portages
Difficulty: Challenging
Fisher Maps: F-4, F-10, F-3
Travel Zones: 26, 25, 23, 22, 24

Introduction: This fascinating route will take you on three of the prettiest rivers in the BWCA. You will also visit several lakes that are seldom visited by others, as well as two of the most heavily used lakes in the Boundary Waters. From Forest Route 377, you will paddle for only a couple of miles down the Island River before entering the Isabella River. You'll continue on down this placid, forest-lined stream to Bald Eagle Lake. From this popular lake you will head north through Gull to Clearwater and on to popular Lakes One and Two. From near the busy Lake One landing you will turn west and paddle down the scenic Kawishiwi River, and then follow the south branch to Little Gabbro Lake. Beyond Gabbro and Bald Eagle lakes, you will then retrace your path up the Isabella and Island rivers to your origin at Forest Route 377. Motors are not allowed on any part of this route (since January 1, 1979). You may encounter heavy canoe traffic near the Lake One landing, however, which is the 2nd busiest entry point in all the BWCA. Although this route requires that you paddle through the Isabella and Island rivers twice, I'm sure its attractiveness will make it worthwhile.

Fishing for walleye is possible throughout most of the route. You will also find northern pike, bass and pan fish in Lakes One and Two, Gabbro, Bald Eagle and the south Kawishiwi and Isabella rivers. It will take five full days to complete this challenging route. If fishing is your main purpose, you may wish to stretch it into six days. Strong trippers, however, could make it in four.

DAY 1: **Island River,** 11 rods, **river,** p. 10 rods, **river, Isabella River,** p. 130 rods, **river, Rice Lake, Isabella River,** p. 10 rods, **river,** p. 27 rods, **river,** p. 27 rods, **river,** p. 40 rods, **river, rapids, river,** p. 33 rods, **river, rapids, river,** p. 190 rods, **Bald Eagle Lake.** Your first day will be a long one, but you should make fairly good time paddling down the two rivers. Though not extremely swift, the current is noticeable. And two or three of the shorter rapids may be safely shot if the water level is sufficiently high. ALWAYS check them out first! I found an abandoned fiberglass canoe at the base of one of the longer rapids, overturned on a large rock with a fist-sized hole punched out of the bottom. Chances are, the owner didn't look first. . . . On the same trip, I also saw three moose along the Isabella River. This is a good route for seeing wildlife. Your last, long portage follows a good path, mostly downhill, and has five rests along the way.

DAY 2: **Bald Eagle Lake,** p. 189 rods, **Gull Creek,** p. 41 rods, **Gull Lake,** p. 50 rods, **Pietro Lake,** p. 64 rods, **Camdre Lake,** p. 125 rods, **Clearwater Lake.** This day will be much easier than the first, so as to end at Clearwater. If you prefer to spend your nights on peaceful, isolated lakes, you will surely enjoy Clearwater Lake much more than Lake Two. There is a campsite on Rock Island Lake, but only one, and after you cross the 242-rod portage from Clearwater Lake, you are committed to continue on. The only major portage of the day is your first, a 189-rod uphill trek that climbs over a 90-foot hill. The only other uphill path is the 64-rod trail from Pietro to Camdre Lake. You'll find a nice sandy beach for swimming at the portage leading to Rock Island Lake. A good campsite is close by on the northeast shore.

DAY 3: **Clearwater Lake,** p. 242 rods, **Rock Island Lake, creek,** p. 45 rods, **Lake Two,** p. 45 rods, **pond,** p. 30 rods, **Lake One,** p. 41 rods, **Confusion Lake,** p. 25 rods, **Kawishiwi River,** p. 20 rods, **river,** p. 40 rods, **river,** p. 8 rods, **river.** The 242-rod portage out of Clearwater Lake has a steep uphill portion at the beginning, but it soon levels off and does not present a major challenge. You will probably see many canoes on the busy route through lakes One and Two. The Kawishiwi River will be much more peaceful. You should be able to walk, line or shoot your canoe down the first set of rapids on the river, eliminating the 20-rod portage. Two very nice campsites are found just beyond the entrance into the North Kawishiwi River, with plenty of space for the largest of groups. Should you need additional supplies or have a craving for pop and candy bars, you may wish to paddle to Kawishiwi

Lodge at the north end of Lake One, on the edge of the Boundary Waters and less than a mile from the Lake One Landing. If you go this way, you will portage 19 rods directly from Lake One into Kawishiwi River and bypass Confusion Lake altogether. The choice is yours.

DAY 4: **Kawishiwi River, South Kawishiwi River,** p. 12 rods, **river,** p. 18 rods, **river,** p. 28 rods, **river,** p. 122 rods, **Little Gabbro Lake, Gabbro Lake,** p. 2–5 rods, **Bald Eagle Lake.** If desired you can eliminate the three portages on the Kawishiwi River by shooting, lining or walking your canoe down the white water. But be sure to check them out first, because, although the rapids are not considered dangerous, sharp rocks could damage your canoe. A small, swift rapids separates Gabbro and Bald Eagle. Your canoe could be pulled through if you prefer to avoid the short but tricky portage on the right.

DAY 5: **Bald Eagle Lake,** p. 190 rods, **Isabella River, rapids, river,** p. 33 rods, **river, rapids, river,** p. 40 rods, **river,** p. 27 rods, **river,** p. 27 rods, **river,** p. 10 rods, **river, Rice Lake, Isabella River,** p. 130 rods, **river, Island River,** p. 10 rods, **river,** p. 11 rods, **river.** Your last day is merely the reverse of the first, but you can count on its taking longer. Not only will you be paddling against the current but you will also have to portage around several short rapids through which you may have shot or lined your canoe going down. You may even wish to spend the night at a campsite at the junction of the island and Isabella rivers, and then paddle the short distance to your car early the next morning.

Route #46: The Four Rivers Route

7 Days, 94 Miles, 20 Lakes, 4 Rivers, 1 Creek, 54 Portages
Difficulty: Challenging
Fisher Maps: F-4, F-3, F-10, F-11, F-5
Travel Zones: 26, 25, 24, 22, 28, 33, 34, 27

Introduction: This fascinating route will lead you west down the lovely Island and Isabella rivers to the base of Bald Eagle Lake. From here you will point northwest and navigate the open waters of Bald Eagle and Gabbro lakes until you intersect the South Kawishiwi River. You will paddle, pull and carry your canoe through the scenic pools and up the foaming white water of the Kawishiwi River, across the popular "numbered lakes" and into island-studded Lake Insula. On up the Kawishiwi River you will pause to view a display of old Indian rock paintings decorating the vertical cliffs along its shore. At Malberg Lake you will turn south and continue on up the system of lakes, ponds, and creeks that compose the upper reaches of the Kawishiwi River, until you reach its source at Kawishiwi Lake. From there, a 2.4 mile trek on Forest Route 354 will take you to the winding wilderness of Hog Creek and Perent Lake beyond. Across Perent Lake you will enter the pristine wilderness of the Perent River, along whose shores moose abound. Then into Isabella Lake you will paddle, and at the other side you will re-enter the Isabella River and follow it to the familiar waters of the Island River from which you emerged a week earlier.

Wildlife is plentiful along this scenic route. Countless beaver homes decorate the scenic banks of the Kawishiwi River. In addition, a high-density moose population exists in the southeast part of this trip. In the early summer of 1977, my wife and I saw eight moose along the way, and fresh tracks were frequently seen on portage trails beside the Perent River.

Fishing is generally excellent throughout the loop. Walleye and northern pike, in particular, are plentiful in Perent and Isabella lakes, in all parts of the Kawishiwi River and in such lakes as Malberg, Koma and Polly. Crappies and bass may also be found in several of the lakes. Motorboats are not permitted on any part of this route, since the BWCA Wilderness Act of 1978 took effect. But the region around Lake One is very heavily used during much of the summer, and the Kawishiwi-Polly-Malberg chain of lakes is also very popular. But the variety of beautiful scenery that exists along the "Four Rivers Route" more than compensates for the number of people encountered along the way. A good blend of large and small lakes with rivers and tiny creeks eliminates any chance of boredom. Although portages are frequent, most are quite short and easily traversed; the longest is 2 miles.

Allow seven full days to complete this challenging route.

Eight would permit more time to fish. An experienced crew of strong paddlers could complete the route in six days, or even less. Low water and occasional beaver dams may slow travel considerably, especially on the Perent River and Hog Creek, as well as eliminate the possibility of running rapids on the Isabella River.

DAY 1: **Island River,** p. 11 rods, **river,** p. 10 rods, **river, Isabella River,** p. 130 rods, **river, Rice Lake, Isabella River,** p. 10 rods, **river,** p. 27 rods, **river,** p. 27 rods, **river,** p. 40 rods, **river, rapids, river,** p. 33 rods, **river, rapids, river,** p. 190 rods, **Bald Eagle Lake.** (See comments for Day 1, Route #45.)

DAY 2: **Bald Eagle Lake, rapids, Gabbro Lake, Little Gabbro Lake,** p. 122 rods, **South Kawishiwi River,** p. 28 rods, **river,** p. 18 rods, **river,** p. 12 rods, **Kawishiwi River,** p. 8 rods, **river,** p. 40 rods, **river,** p. 20 rods, **river,** p. 19 rods, **Lake One.** A short swift rapids in the narrows between Bald Eagle and Gabbro lakes can be easily and safely run. And if the sun is bright and the air is warm, you may wish to eliminate all but two of the portages on the South Kawishiwi River. The first three rapids that you encounter (28, 18 and 12 rods) can be walked up with little difficulty in normal to low water. So can the last rapids (20 rods) before the portage into Lake One. You had better resist the temptation to walk up the white water bypassed by the 8-rod and 40-rod portages, however. The first one is a small waterfall. The longer one begins innocently enough, but becomes progressively more difficult as the gradient increases and the rocky banks become steeper, climaxed by an old log dam at the top.

After the final portage of 19 rods into Lake One, you will soon see the public landing serving one of the busiest entry points for the BWCA. Less than a mile farther into the narrow corridor leading to the main body of Lake One, you will paddle past Kawishiwi Lodge, your only direct contact with civilization on this route.

If you wish not to blemish your wilderness experience by this direct contact, you may avoid the more popular entry route into Lake One by portaging 25 rods into Confusion Lake, followed by 41 rods into Lake One. This eliminates about three miles of paddling, but increases portaging by 47 rods.

DAY 3: **Lake One,** p. 30 rods, **pond,** p. 45 rods, **Lake Two, Lake Three, Lake Four,** p. 20 rods, **Kawishiwi River,** p. 25 rods, **river,** p. 10 rods, **river, Hudson Lake,** p. 105 rods, **Lake Insula.** You will be traveling the entire day on a heavily used route as you leave the second most popular entry point for the BWCA. If this day is Saturday, Sunday or Monday, when campsites are at a premium, you would be wise to stop early for the night.

DAY 4: **Lake Insula,** p. 18 rods, **Kawishiwi River, Alice Lake,** p. 20 rods, **Kawishiwi River,** p. 90 rods, **river,** p. 15 rods, **river,** p. 60 rods, **Malberg Lake.** Island-studded Lake Insula may provide a challenge to the novice map reader. Watch the landmarks carefully, or you may spend most of the day on this beautiful lake. If you are tired of freeze-dried and dehydrated foods by now, this day should provide an excellent opportunity to catch walleye and northern pike. Take time out for a short side trip to the Indian pictographs, located just south of the 90-rod portage after Alice Lake. A careful examination of the vertical cliffs bordering the river on the west side will yield reminders of a civilization that once flourished in this water wilderness.

DAY 5: **Malberg Lake,** p. 24 rods, **Koma Lake,** p. 127 rods, **Kawishiwi River,** p. 48 rods, **river,** p. 19 rods, **Lake Polly,** p. 91 rods, **Townline Lake,** p. 181 rods, **Kawasaschong Lake.** Canoe traffic from the Kawishiwi Lake entry point is often heavy. Nevertheless, there are plenty of campsites along the way to accommodate the traffic. Fishing is very good in all of these lakes.

DAY 6: **Kawasaschong Lake, Kawishiwi River,** p. 11 rods, **river,** p. 20 rods, **Square Lake, Kawishiwi River, Kawishiwi Lake,** p. 768 rods, **Hog Creek,** p. 15 rods, **Hog Creek, Perent Lake.** When the water level is low, the 20-rod portage could extend to 25 or 30 rods, and Hog Creek could be a problem. Your 768-rod trek from Kawishiwi Lake to Hog Creek follows a good gravel road; but then, 2½ miles is a long portage on any path! Watch for moose in this area; they abound, in spite of the summer influx of canoeists. A road sign marks the Hog Creek access, and a small parking lot is located on the east side of the road just north of the creek. Hog Creek is barely wide enough for a canoe to slip between its brush

banks. In addition to the 15-rod portage near the road, small
beaver dams may spring up occasionally and require quick
liftovers.

DAY 7: **Perent Lake,** p. 61 rods, **Perent River,** p. 31
rods, **river,** p. 25 rods, **river,** p. 33 rods, **river, rapids, river,** p.
17 rods, **river,** p. 39 rods, **river, rapids, river,** p. 22 rods,
river, p. 16 rods, **river,** p. 40 rods, **river,** p. 22 rods, **river,** p.
16 rods, **river, Boga Lake,** p. 26 rods, **Isabella Lake,** p. 28
rods, **Isabella River,** p. 15 rods, **river, Island River,** p. 10
rods, **river,** p. 11 rods, **river.** Both Perent and Isabella lakes
are easily accessible to canoeists, but it seems that few travel
between them on the Perent River. Consequently, this final day
of your trip will take you through one of the most exciting
wilderness experiences in the BWCA, where you will portage
between towering virgin pine, stepping on terrain only recently
vacated by moose, and over which bald eagles are frequently
sighted. (See sketch of the Perent River region below). Most of
the portages in the Perent-Isabella region were built by the
Civilian Conservation Corps in the late 1930's and the 1940's.
These extremely well-made portages have survived the years
with very little maintenance. They were built to a standard that
would be very expensive, labor-intensive, and probably not
possible today. If you prefer, you may eliminate the final three
portages and about three miles of paddling by walking 1½
miles from the public landing on Isabella Lake to your vehicle
at the Island River access.

Entry Point 35—Isabella Lake

Permits: 277

Popularity Rank: 23

Daily Quota: 5

Location: Isabella Lake is located 28 miles southeast of
Ely. To get there, follow Forest Route 172 one mile east from
State Highway 1 at Isabella to Forest Route 369. Turn left and
follow 369 north for 7 miles to Forest Route 373, then follow
373 another 5½ miles northwest to Forest Route 377. Turn
right and follow 377 5½ miles to Forest Center landing near
the south shore of Isabella Lake. You'll be driving on good

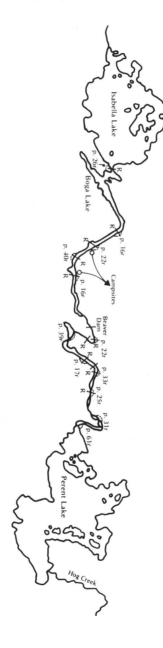

Isabella Lake

p. 26r R

Boga Lake

R p. 16r
R
R p. 22r
p. 40r R
R p. 16r

Campsites

Beaver p. 22r
Dam R
p. 39r R
R p. 33r
p. 17r R
R p. 25r
R
p. 31r
p. 61r

Perent Lake

Hog Creek

The Perent River

gravel roads all the way. The final 2½ miles, however, are on a rather narrow road, considered "one lane."

Description: Several Forest Service campgrounds are located along State Highway 1, providing a place to spend the night before your trip. Coming from Ely, you will pass campgrounds at the South Kawishiwi River, McDougal Lakes and Little Isabella River. The closest is at the Little Isabella River. All require a camping fee.

From 1949 to 1964, 250 people called Forest Center their home. In addition to a sawmill, there were 53 homes, a 2-room school house, a recreation center and a restaurant. There were also barracks and a mess hall for the lumbermen. Timber was hauled away by railroad. Forest Center Landing is now covered with a young growth of pine, but explorers may still find evidence of the logging era near the parking lot. Currently, Forest Center is the site of three BWCA entry points, including two for hikers using the Powwow Lake Trails—a 50-mile network of trails that extends north of Isabella Lake. The parking lot is shared by hikers and canoeists, but most of the vehicles will belong to canoeists headed for Isabella Lake.

You will note that, because of their closeness, the Isabella Lake and Island River entry points both provide good access to canoe routes following the Isabella River. Both routes suggested for the Island River entry point (#34), therefore, could also begin at Isabella Lake. This is good to remember, in case the entry point you wish to use is "filled up" on the day of your scheduled trip.

Route #47: The Isabella-South Kawishiwi Rivers Loop

5 Days, 57 Miles, 13 Lakes, 2 Rivers, 1 Creek, 39 Portages
Difficulty: Challenging
Fisher Maps: F-4, F-10, F-3
Travel Zones: 26, 25, 23, 22, 24

Introduction: After the first two short portages, this is exactly the same trip as outlined in Route #45. *The only difference is this:*

The Cloquet Road crosses the Range River, requiring a 1-rod portage ("liftover")

A mammoth beaver house in the Loon Lake Narrows

Beginning the portage from Sandpit Lake to Tin Can Lake

The Little Indian Sioux River leads south from the Echo Trail to a region seldom visited by modern Voyageurs

Some of the best Indian pictographs in the BWCA are at the north end of North Hegman Lake

Smallmouth bass like this one abound in many lakes throughout the BWCA

A deteriorated bridge abutment adjacent to Horse Lake serves as a reminder of the logging industry that once thrived in this area

It's peanut butter and jelly time along the Range River

A log stairway begins the portage up to the Echo Trail from
South Hegman Lake

The public access to Fenske Lake

Paddling on North Hegman Lake

The author writing notes after measuring the portage connecting Range and Tin Can Lakes

DAY 1: DELETE: **Island River,** p. 11 rods, **River,** p. 10 rods, **river,**

ADD: P. 35 rods, **Isabella Lake,** p. 28 rods, **Isabella River,** p. 15 rods. The remainder of the route is identical, until you return to the junction of the Island and Isabella rivers. Obviously, you will return to Isabella Lake instead of turning south into the Island River.

Route #48: The Knife Border Route

12 Days, 125 Miles, 46 Lakes, 3 Rivers, 3 Creeks, 80 Portages

Difficulty: Challenging

Fisher Maps: F-4, F-5, F-11, F-12

Travel Zones: 26, 27, 34, 33, 37, 32, 29, 30, 20, 21, 28, 22, 23, 25

Introduction: You'll begin this long route by paddling east across Isabella Lake, through Boga Lake and into one of the most interesting and wildest regions within the BWCA— the Perent River—where you will see virgin pine, bald eagles, and a preponderance of moose. Across Perent Lake and into meandering Little Hog Creek, you will then encounter the longest portage of the route—a 2-12-mile trek on Forest Route 354 to Kawishiwi Lake. From popular Kawishiwi Lake, you will travel north via the scenic lakes and interconnecting creeks that compose the upper reaches of the Kawishiwi River system to Malberg Lake. From Malberg you will angle to the northeast through a less traveled interior part of the BWCA to another popular lake, Little Saganaga, and then north to breathtaking Gabimichigami Lake. You will paddle northwest from Gabi through one of the most beautiful parts of all the Boundary Waters to ever-popular Ogishkemuncie Lake, and then on to the international border at Knife Lake. From the southwest end of sparkling Knife Lake you will portage a weary ⅔ mile to Vera Lake and another ½ mile to Ensign Lake. Your course will then take you southeast through a series of small lakes and short carries to Thomas Lake, and then south to sprawling Lake Insula. Paddling west again, you'll navigate the busy route from the southwest end of Lake Insula to the numbered lakes as you return to the Kawishiwi River system. At the southwest end of Lake Two you will portage south into a much less traveled part of the BWCA, from Rock Island Lake to Bald Eagle Lake. Finally, you will paddle east up the lovely Isabella River to your origin at Isabella Lake.

Fishing is usually excellent throughout most of this loop. Walleye and northern pike, in particular, are plentiful in Isabella, Perent, Polly, Koma, Malberg, Kivaniva and Fraser lakes, as well as in most parts of the Kawishiwi River system. Lake trout may also be caught in Little Saganaga, Gabimichigami, Eddy, Knife and Thomas lakes. In addition, crappies and bass may be found in several of the lakes en route.

The region from Knife Lake south and east to Lake Two is quite heavily traveled much of the summer. The Kawishiwi-Polly-Malberg chain of lakes is also very popular.

The astute wildlife observer will see evidence of beaver throughout the trip. Moose are common in the regions between Kawishiwi Lake and Little Saganaga, along the Isabella and Perent rivers, and near the "numbered lakes."

A good blend of lakes with rivers and small creeks eliminates any chance of boredom along this beautiful route. Although portages are frequent, most are quite short and easily traversed. The longest, however, is 2.4 miles.

Allow 12 full days to complete this challenging route. 13 would permit more time to fish, however, and 14 would be better for an easy-going crew. Low water and occasional beaver dams could slow travel on the Perent River and Hog Creek.

DAY 1: P. 35 rods, **Isabella Lake,** p. 26 rods, **Boga Lake,** p. 16 rods, **Perent River,** p. 22 rods, **river,** p. 40 rods, **river,** p. 16 rods, **river,** p. 22 rods, **river, rapids, river,** p. 39 rods, **river,** p. 17 rods, **river, rapids, river,** p. 33 rods, **river,** p. 25 rods, **river,** p. 31 rods, **river,** p. 61 rods, **Perent Lake.** This day will find you in one of the wildest portions of the Boundary Waters, an area containing a very high density moose population. Although both Isabella and Perent lakes are easily accessible to canoeists, it seems that few navigate the winding little river between. (See detailed sketch of the Perent River region in Route #46.)

DAY 2: **Perent Lake, Hog Creek,** p. 15 rods, **creek,** p. 768 rods, **Kawishiwi Lake, Kawishiwi River, Square Lake,** p. 20 rods, **Kawishiwi River,** p. 11 rods, **river, Kawasaschong Lake.** Although the southeast end of Perent Lake is not shown on Fisher map #113, you will have no trouble finding the mouth of Hog Creek. (See detailed sketch of the Perent River region in Route #46.) Because of considerable meandering and an opposing current, travel up Hog Creek is slow. In addition to the portage near the creek's junction with Forest Route 354, there may also be occasional beaver dams that require liftovers. Your 2.4-mile trek is along a good gravel road, but is a burden, nevertheless. When the water level is low, you may run into difficulty in Hog Creek and in the upper reaches of the Kawishiwi River between Kawishiwi Lake and Kawasaschong. In fact, the 20-rod portage could be closer to 25 or 30 rods and muddy at the east end.

DAY 3: **Kawasaschong Lake,** p. 181 rods, **Townline Lake,** p. 91 rods, **Lake Polly,** p. 19 rods, **Kawishiwi River,** p. 48 rods, **river,** p. 127 rods, **river, Koma Lake,** p. 24 rods, **Malberg Lake.** Don't worry about the 181-rod portage between Kawasaschong and Townline lakes; it is an easy, slightly downhill trek. You may find fishing for walleye and northern pike to be excellent in Malberg Lake. Since Malberg is the apparent destination of many fishermen using this popular route, you should get a campsite as soon as possible. There are several very nice ones from which to choose.

DAY 4: **Malberg Lake,** p. 48 rods, **Kawishiwi River,** p. 40 rods, **Kivaniva Lake,** p. 14–35 rods, **Anit Lake,** p. 25 rods, **pond,** p. 19 rods, **Pan Lake,** p. 55 rods, **Panhandle Lake,** p. 89 rods, **pond,** p. 65 rods, **Makwa Lake,** p. 45 rods, **Elton Lake,** p. 19 rods, **pond,** p. 19 rods, **Little Saganaga Lake.** None of the portages this day is difficult, but their frequency will slow travel somewhat. You will not see as many people between Malberg and Little Saganaga as on either side of this section of the route. Little Saganaga Lake itself, however, is quite popular and many of the campsites there may be taken if you arrive late in the day. If time permits, you may wish to proceed to one of the pleasant campsites on the south-east shore of awesome Gabimichigami Lake. Most of these sites are outstanding for any size of group, and the view is breathtaking from those that border the main body of the lake.

DAY 5: **Little Saganaga Lake,** p. 30 rods, **Rattle Lake,** p. 25 rods, **Gabimichigami Lake,** p. 15 rods, **Agamok Lake,** 3 portages, **Mueller Lake,** p. 80 rods, **Ogishkemuncie Lake,** p. 15 rods, **Annie Lake,** p. 15 rods, **Jean Lake,** p. 15 rods, **Eddy Lake,** p. 25 rods, **Knife Lake.** On this day you will find yourself canoeing through some of the most scenic terrain in all the BWCA. Each part of the route offers a unique form of beauty, from island-studded Little Saganaga and Ogishkemuncie lakes to the large, open expanses on Gabimichigami and Knife lakes to the scenic series of serene little pools and rapids between Gabi and Ogishkemuncie lakes. At the northwest end of Agamok Lake you will have a choice of portages: either three short portages around three sets of rapids, or one continuous portage of about 100 rods from Agamok directly to Mueller Lake. If time is of the essence, choose the latter, but you would not regret taking the time for the other alternative. All three portages are rocky and somewhat steep in places; but none exceeds 25 rods. The second portage crosses the Kekekabic Trail, which utilizes a wooden bridge to pass over a picturesque waterfall flowing parallel to the portage. Those who bypass the area via the longer portage are missing a real treat!

The 80-rod portage from Mueller into Ogishkemuncie Lake looks innocent on the map, but it's not. It begins with a steep uphill climb, before descending to the lower Ogishkemuncie Lake. Several portage rests along the way will be a welcome relief if you find yourself out of shape.

Ogishkemuncie is a pretty lake and, consequently, quite popular among canoeists originating their trips from both the Gunflint Trail and the Fernberg Road. Knife Lake is also well traveled. Find a campsite in the South Arm, as camper congestion is common in the southwest end of this very clear lake. The west end of the peninsula separating the South Arm from the main part of Knife Lake is known at Thunder Point. Take time to climb ¼ mile up the Thunder Point Trail to the scenic overlook. There you will be treated to a fabulous panorama of the international boundary from over 150 feet above the lake.

Then cast your line for one of the lake trout, walleyes or northern pike that live in this crystalline border lake.

DAY 6: **Knife Lake,** p. 200 rods, **Vera Lake.** This will be a relatively easy day, but your only portage is rough. It begins with a steep climb to an elevation of 80 feet above Knife Lake, follows a ridge for over ½ mile, and then rapidly descends to Vera Lake. Bears are notorious in the vicinity of Vera Lake, so be sure to hang your food pack up well.

During the summer of 1987 high water caused the old logging dam at the southwest end of Knife Lake, built in the early 1900s, to wash out. Consequently, the water level on Knife Lake has returned to its natural level, about three feet lower than it has been during this century. For the next few years, the exposed rocky shoreline may look strange to returning visitors.

Not far from the old dam, in a cluster of three small islands in Knife Lake, is the homesite of the BWCA's last permanent resident. Dorothy Molter, who sold home-made rootbeer to canoeing passersby for nearly half a century passed away in December of 1986. Two of her log cabins were then moved, log by log, to Ely and reconstructed as a memorial to her next to the Chamber of Commerce building.

DAY 7: **Vera Lake,** p. 180 rods, **Ensign Lake,** p. 53 rods, **Ashigan Lake,** p. 105 rods, **Gibson Lake,** p. 25 rods, **Cattyman Lake,** p. 55 rods, **Jordan Lake,** p. 5 rods, **Ima Lake.** You will be doing a lot of uphill walking this day. After the first long downhill carry, the remaining five are all uphill, including steep climbs from Ensign to Ashigan Lake and from Gibson to Cattyman Lake. You'll find many good campsites on Ima Lake.

DAY 8: **Ima Lake,** p. 50 rods, **Hatchet Lake,** p. 10 rods, **Thomas Creek,** p. 10 rods, **creek,** p. 10 rods, **pond,** p. 5 rods, **Thomas Lake,** p. 25 rods, **Kiana Lake,** p. 179 rods, **Lake Insula.** If the water level is high enough, you may be able to eliminate the first two 10-rod portages between Hatchet and Thomas lakes by pulling your canoe up the shallow rapids. On the other hand, if the water level is quite low, you may find it necessary to walk your canoe through portions of the shallow creek, in addition to taking all three 10-rod portages. The ½-mile carry from Kiana to Lake Insula is mostly downhill.

DAY 9: **Lake Insula,** p. 105 rods, **Hudson Lake, Kawishiwi River,** p. 10 rods, **river,** p. 25 rods, **river,** p. 20 rods, **Lake Four, Lake Three, Lake Two.** You will see more and more canoes the farther west you get this day. Find a campsite early, before they are all taken. If time permits, you may wish to continue on to Clearwater Lake, a peaceful and pretty lake that few people visit.

DAY 10: **Lake Two,** p. 45 rods, **creek, Rock Island Lake,** p. 242 rods, **Clearwater Lake,** p. 125 rods, **Camdre Lake,** p. 64 rods, **Pietro Lake,** p. 50 rods, **Gull Lake,** p. 41 rods, **Gull Creek,** p. 189 rods, **Bald Eagle Lake.** Your first three portages are generally uphill, while the last four are downhill. None is difficult, including the 242-rod path to Clearwater Lake, which follows a nearly level course most of the way. The campsites at the northwest end of Bald Eagle Lake are more attractive than those at the southeast end, but you will have to paddle out of your way on this wide-open lake to enjoy the better ones.

DAY 11: **Bald Eagle Lake,** p. 190 rods, **Isabella River, rapids, river,** p. 33 rods, **river, rapids, river,** p. 40 rods, **river,** p. 27 rods, **river,** p. 27 rods, **river,** p. 10 rods, **river, Rice Lake.** You can probably eliminate the final 10-rod portage before Rice Lake by pulling your canoe up the short rapids there. Watch for moose along the banks of this scenic river. If you arrive at Rice Lake early in the afternoon, you will have plenty of time to continue on to Isabella Lake and conclude this trip—but that makes a long day for the average group.

DAY 12: **Rice Lake, Isabella River,** p. 130 rods, **river,** p. 15 rods, **river,** p. 28 rods, **Isabella Lake,** p. 35 rods. Make sure you bear left at the junction of the Isabella and Island rivers, just before the 15-rod portage. You should have no trouble making it back to your origin at Forest Route 377 by noon.

Entry Point 36—Hog Creek

Permits: 251
Popularity Rank: 25
Daily Quota: 7

Location: Hog Creek is located about 35 miles southeast of Ely, midway between Ely and the Gunflint Trail, accessible from the Sawbill Trail to the east as well as from Highway 1. From Highway 1 at Isabella, follow Forest Route 172 east for 12 miles to County Road 7. Turn left and follow 7 north for 11 miles to the junction with Forest Route 354. Then go 2 miles north on 354 to Hog Creek.

Just before arriving at the creek (0.1 mile), you'll come to a spur road leading a short distance west (100 yards) to a newly constructed parking area that accommodates up to a dozen vehicles. A short (15 rods) portage trail leads downhill from the spur road, starting 20 rods from the north end of the parking lot.

Description: Parent Lake was named after a trapper who worked this area in the early part of this century. Beavers, muskrats, wolves and other fur-bearing animals trapped by Parent are still common in this region. With the densest concentration of moose in all of Minnesota nearby, moose are occasionally seen browsing along the shoreline or swimming across the lake. There is also a nesting pair of bald eagles in the Parent Lake area.

There is also a variety of bird life that is unique to this area. The only record of a nesting Wilson's Warbler in the state was made here. Other unique species include the Rusty Blackbird and the Virginia Rail, both of which were found nesting near Hog Creek.

Over the years Hog Creek has become more and more popular among canoeists. This may be attributed, in part, to the fact that motorboats were banned from this entry point in 1978. Most of the traffic on Hog Creek goes no farther than Parent Lake, a good source of walleyes and large northern pike. There are 23 campsites on the lake.

A nice public campground is located 2.4 miles north of Hog Creek on Forest Route 354, adjacent to the Kawishiwi Lake access. There are only 5 campsites, however, so plan to arrive early if you wish to spend the night there before your departure into the Boundary Waters Canoe Area. There is no fee assessed to camp there.

Route #49: The Perent Lake Route

2 Days, 10 Miles, 1 Lake, 1 Creek, 4 Portages
Difficulty: Easy
Fisher Map: F-5
Travel Zone: 27

Introduction: This very easy route simply takes you down Hog Creek to Perent Lake, and then returns you via the same creek to your origin at Forest Route 354.

Intended for the weekend angler or the BWCA neophyte, this trip will provide you with a quick yet satisfying taste of what canoeing in the Boundary Waters is all about.

DAY 1: P. 15 rods, **Hog Creek,** p. 15 rods, **creek, Perent Lake.** Hog Creek is barely wide enough to carry a canoe, but plenty deep enough. You will feel as if you were on an African safari as you meander through the dense vegetation. In addition to the 15-rod portage near the road, small beaver dams may occasionally create obstacles that require quick liftovers. The point at which the creek enters Perent Lake is not shown on some Fisher maps. No problem, though. Simply bear right and follow the shoreline to the main part of the lake where most of the campsites are located, which *is* on the map.

Grab a good campsite. Then paddle west and explore the primitive region into which the Perent River flows. There you are likely to see moose, or at least fresh tracks, and eagles are not an uncommon sight overhead.

DAY 2: **Perent Lake, Hog Creek,** p. 15 rods, **creek,** p. 15 rods. Now, wasn't that a pleasant weekend?

Route #50: "Three Rivers" Route

7 Days, 88 Miles, 20 Lakes, 3 Rivers, 1 Creek, 51 Portages
Difficulty: Challenging
Fisher Maps: F-5, F-4, F-3, F-10, F-11
Travel Zones: 27, 26, 25, 24, 22, 28, 33, 34

Introduction: This fascinating route follows nearly the same course as the Four Rivers Route (#46)—minus the Island River. It will take you west from Forest Route 354, down the narrow meandering channel of Hog Creek, across Perent Lake and into the pristine wilderness of the Perent River, across Isabella Lake and on down the lovely Isabella River to the base of Bald Eagle Lake. From there you'll point northwest and navigate the open waters of Bald Eagle and Gabbro until you intersect the South Kawishiwi River. Up the beautiful pools and rapids of the Kawishiwi River, you'll paddle, pull and carry your canoe, north and east across the popular "numbered lakes" and island-studded Lake Insula. On up the Kawishiwi River you will pause to view a display of ancient Indian pictographs decorating the vertical cliffs along its shore. At Malberg Lake you'll turn south and continue on up the system of lakes, ponds and creeks that compose the upper reaches of the Kawishiwi, until you reach its source at Kawishiwi Lake. From there, a two-mile trek on Forest Route 354 will return you to your origin at the Hog Creek Entry Point. (See Introduction, Route #46.)

DAY 1: P. 15 rods, **Hog Creek,** p. 15 rods, **creek, Perent Lake,** p. 61 rods, **Perent River,** p. 31 rods, **river,** p. 25 rods, **river,** p. 33 rods, **river, rapids, river,** p. 17 rods, **river,** p. 39 rods, **river, rapids, river,** p. 22 rods, **river,** p. 16 rods, **river,** p. 40 rods, **river,** p. 22 rods, **river,** p. 16 rods, **river, Boga Lake,** p. 26 rods, **Isabella Lake.** (See comments for Days 6 and 7, Route #46.)

DAY 2: **Isabella Lake,** p. 28 rods, **Isabella River,** p. 15 rods, **river,** p. 130 rods, **river, Rice Lake, Isabella River,** p. 10 rods, **river,** p. 27 rods, **river,** p. 27 rods, **river,** p. 40 rods, **river, rapids, river,** p. 33 rods, **river, rapids, river,** p. 190 rods, **Bald Eagle Lake.** (See comments for Day 1, Route #45.)

DAY 3: **Bald Eagle Lake, rapids, Gabbro Lake, Little Gabbro Lake,** p. 122 rods, **South Kawishiwi River,** p. 28 rods, **river,** p. 18 rods, **river,** p. 12 rods, **river, Kawishiwi River,** p. 8 rods, **river,** p. 40 rods, **river,** p. 20 rods, **river,** p. 19 rods, **Lake One.** (See comments for Day 2, Route #46.)

DAY 4: **Lake One,** p. 30 rods, **pond,** p. 45 rods, **Lake Two, Lake Three, Lake Four,** p. 20 rods, **Kawishiwi River,**

p. 25 rods, **river,** p. 10 rods, **river, Hudson Lake.** (See comments for Day 3, Route #46.)

DAY 5: **Hudson Lake,** p. 105 rods, **Lake Insula,** p. 18 rods, **Kawishiwi River, Alice Lake,** p. 20 rods, **Kawishiwi River,** p. 90 rods, **Kawishiwi River,** p. 15 rods, **river.** (See comments for Day 4, Route #46.)

DAY 6: **Kawishiwi River,** p. 60 rods, **Malberg Lake,** p. 24 rods, **Koma Lake,** p. 127 rods, **Kawishiwi River,** p. 48 rods, **river,** p. 19 rods, **Lake Polly,** p. 91 rods, **Townline Lake,** p. 181 rods, **Kawasaschong Lake.** (See comments for Day 5, Route #46.)

DAY 7: **Kawasaschong Lake, Kawishiwi River,** p. 11 rods, **river,** p. 20 rods, **Square Lake, Kawishiwi River, Kawishiwi Lake, Forest Route 354 to Hog Creek.** When the water level is low, the 20-rod portage could extend to 25 or 30 rods. Keep an eye out for moose; they are thick in this area, in spite of the summer influx of canoeists. Unless you have made prior arrangements to have your vehicle waiting at the Kawishiwi Lake access, the final 2.5 miles of your trip will have to be on foot.

Entry Point 37—Kawishiwi Lake

Permits: 583
Popularity Rank: 12
Daily Quota: 9

Location: Kawishiwi Lake is located about 35 miles southeast of Ely. From Highway 1 at Isabella, follow Forest Route 172 east for 12 miles to County Road 7. Turn left and follow 7 north for 11 miles to the junction with Forest Route 354. Kawishiwi Lake is at the north end of Route 354, 4 miles from County Road 7. It is also accessible from the Sawbill Trail to the east.

Description: In spite of its remote location, about midway between Ely and Lake Superior, the Kawishiwi Lake entry point is quite popular among canoeists. There are nearly 50 designated Forest Service campsites from Kawishiwi to Malberg Lake to accommodate the use. And much of the traffic goes no further than Malberg. In spite of the heavy use, moose are not an uncommon sight throughout the area. In fact, the densest population of moose in all of Minnesota is found in the region just west of Kawishiwi Lake.

A nice public campground adjacent to the Kawishiwi access provides a good spot to spend the night before your trip into the Boundary Waters. There are only 5 campsites, however, so plan to arrive early, and avoid the busier weekends. No campsite fee is charged there.

Route #51: The "Gabi-Gishke-Kabic" Loop

6 Days, 68 Miles, 34 Lakes, 1 River, 1 Creek, 56 Portages
Difficulty: Rugged
Fisher Maps: F-5, F-11, F-12
Travel Zones: 34, 33, 37, 32, 29

Introduction: This portage-laden route will lead you north through the lakes and streams of the upper Kawishiwi River system to the fishing paradise on Malberg Lake. From Malberg you'll angle to the northeast through the seldom-traveled interior of the Boundary Waters to popular Little Saganaga Lake, and north to breathtaking Gabimichigami Lake. You'll exit "Gabi" to the northwest, cross the famous Kekekabic Trail and visit the ever-popular Ogishkemuncie Lake. Eight portages to the west, you'll welcome the inspirational sight of big Kekekabic Lake, bordered with beautiful, towering bluffs, and surrounded by hills rising as high as 400 feet above the water. You will portage out of "Kek" to the south and soon re-enter the part of the BWCA that is seldom penetrated by the casual canoeist, before returning to Malberg Lake and retracing your path back to Kawishiwi Lake.

Motors are banned from the entire loop. Although the southern and northern sections are heavily used, you'll find an adequate degree of solitude in the central portion, north of Malberg Lake. Some of the most spectacular scenery in the central region of the BWCA will be viewed along this route. And even though portaging is all too frequent, only five carries exceed 100 rods.

This is a good route for the wildlife enthusiast. Evidence

of beaver will be found all along the way, and moose are not uncommon, especially in thr region south of Little Saganaga to Kawishiwi Lake.

Walleye and northern pike fishing may be excellent in Polly, Koma, Malberg, Kivaniva and Fraser lakes. Lake trout may also be caught in Little Saganaga, Gabimichigami, Eddy and Kekekabic lakes. A fishing rod and license are a must for this trip. Although an experienced group of strong canoeists could easily complete this route in 5 days or less, I suggest 6 for the "average" voyageurs.

DAY 1: **Kawishiwi Lake, Kawishiwi River, Square Lake,** p. 20 rods, **Kawishiwi River,** p. 11 rods, **river, Kawasaschong Lake,** p. 181 rods, **Townline Lake,** p. 91 rods, **Lake Polly,** p. 19 rods, **Kawishiwi River,** p. 48 rods, **river,** p. 127 rods, **river, Koma Lake,** p. 24 rods, **Malberg Lake.** Your first day will take you through the lovely small lakes and streams that compose the upper part of the Kawishiwi River system. The portages are fairly well scattered throughout the day and not difficult. Even the 181-rod portage leading from Kawasaschong Lake is an easy, slightly downhill trek. Campsites are plentiful from Lake Polly to Malberg Lake. Since Malberg is the apparent destination of many fishermen using this popular route, however, you might be wise to stop on Koma. The 20-rod portage on the river between Square and Kawasaschong lakes may be as long as 25–30 rods when the water level is low. Keep your eyes open for moose in this area.

DAY 2: **Malberg Lake,** p. 48 rods, **Kawishiwi River,** p. 40 rods, **Kavaniva Lake,** p. 14–35 rods, **Anit Lake,** p. 25 rods, **pond,** p. 19 rods, **Pan Lake,** p. 55 rods, **Panhandle Lake,** p. 89 rods, **pond,** p. 65 rods, **Makwa Lake,** p. 45 rods, **Elton Lake,** p. 19 rods, **pond,** p. 19 rods, **Little Saganaga Lake.** None of the portages this day is difficult, but their frequency will slow travel somewhat. You won't see as many people between Malberg and Little Saganaga as north or south of this section of the route. However, Little Saganaga Lake itself is quite popular, and many of the campsites here may be taken if you arrive late in the day. If time permits, you may wish to proceed to one of the pleasant campsites on the southeast shores of awesome Gabimichigami Lake. Most of these sites are outstanding for any size of group, and the view is breathtaking from those that border the main body of the lake.

DAY 3: **Little Saganaga Lake,** p. 30 rods, **Rattle Lake,** p. 25 rods, **Gabimichigami Lake,** p. 15 rods, **Agamok Lake,** 3 portages, **Mueller Lake,** p. 80 rods, **Ogishkemuncie Lake,** p. 15 rods, **Annie Lake,** p. 15 rods, **Jean Lake,** p. 15 rods, **Eddy Lake,** 5 portages, **Kekekabic Lake.** On this day you will find yourself canoeing through some of the most scenic terrain in all the BWCA. Each part of the route offers a unique form of beauty, from island-studded Little Saganaga and Ogishkemuncie lakes, to the large open expanses of Gabimichigami and Kekekabic lakes. A favorite section of mine is between Gabimichigami and Ogishkemuncie. Agamok is more like a river than a lake, connecting Gabi with a series of ponds and rapids that flow into Mueller Lake. Here you have a choice: either three short portages around three sets of rapids, or one continuous portage of about 100 rods from Agamok directly to Mueller. If time is of the essence, choose the latter. But you will not regret taking the time for the other alternative. All three portages are rocky and somewhat steep in places, but none exceeds 25 rods. The second portage crosses the Kekekabic Trail, which utilizes a wooden bridge to pass over a picturesque waterfall flowing parallel to the portage. Those who bypass the area via the longer portage are missing a real treat.

The 80-rod portage from Mueller into Ogishkemuncie Lake looks innocent on the map, but it's not. It makes a steep uphill climb before descending to lower Ogishkemuncie Lake. Several canoe rests along the way will be a welcome relief if you find that you are not in as good shape as you had thought.

Ogishkemuncie is a pretty lake and, consequently, quite popular among canoeists beginning their trip from the Gunflint Trail or the Fernberg Road. So is Kekekabic Lake, which is more difficult to reach, but well worth the effort. The five short portages into the Kekekabic ponds are barely more than "liftovers." Though neither long nor difficult, they are a nuisance at the end of a day already filled with portages.

Few other experiences will awaken your feeling that you

have discovered Paradise more than entering Kekekabic Lake
from the east after a long, hard day. As you leave the last of
the five portages from the ponds, the narrow entrance to the
lake will gradually widen as it winds to the west. The evening
sun hovering over the far-distant shoreline accentuates the
high-rising bluffs that encircle this magnificent lake. And in the
distance, you'll see hills rising as high as 400 feet. Several
campsites are located near the east end of the lake, and you
would be wise to grab the first one you see, because Kekekabic
attracts many visitors.

DAY 4: **Kekekabic Lake,** p. 85 rods, **Strup Lake,** p. 10
rods, **Wisini Lake,** p. 90 rods, **Ahmakose Lake,** p. 30 rods,
Gerund Lake, p. 15 rods, **Fraser Lake,** p. 65 rods, **Sagus
Lake,** p. 42 rods, **Roe Lake,** p. 60 rods, **Cap Lake,** p. 220
rods, **Boulder Lake.** You'll find three campsites from which to
choose on Boulder Lake, without much competition for them.
This is in one of the least traveled parts of the Boundary
Waters, and here you will more than likely find the solitude
that you desire. The five portages between Kekekabic Lake
and Fraser don't appear as much on the map, but don't under-
estimate them! The 85-rod portage out of Kekekabic climbs
over 100 feet before descending 21 feet to Strup Lake. The
next short portage ascends 17 feet in its 10-rod length. And,
although Wisini and Ahmakose lakes lie at nearly the same
elevation, the 90-rod portage climbs 54 feet above them. But
after that it's all downhill. The 220-rod portage from Cap into
Boulder is the longest of the trip, but level. As you approach
the east end of Cap Lake, you will see two portages leading
into the woods. The one on the left leads to Ledge Lake; the
right one leads to Boulder Lake. After walking 85 rods toward
Boulder Lake, you'll come to a split in the trail. Be sure you
take the *right* trail here, or you may find yourself on Ledge
Lake, 280 long rods from your target.

DAY 5: **Boulder Lake, liftover, Boulder Creek,** p. 15
rods, **creek, Adams Lake,** p. 90 rods, **Beaver Lake,** p. 30
rods, **pond,** p. 15 rods, **Kawishiwi River,** p. 60 rods, **Malberg
Lake,** p. 24 rods, **Koma Lake, Kawishiwi River,** p. 127 rods,
river, p. 48 rods, **river,** p. 19 rods, **Lake Polly.** Your fifth day
will bring you out of the more isolated interior of the BWCA
and back to the more heavily used Kawishiwi River system

feeding Malberg Lake. There are many good campsites on Lake Polly, but once again there are many more people with whom to compete. Hang your food pack carefully this night; bears are a common nuisance around Polly Lake. Take advantage of the fine fishing available in Polly, Koma and Malberg, where walleye and northern pike abound, and try to make camp early this day.

Low water may seriously hinder navigation of the creek between Boulder and Adams lakes. Beaver dams may also interfere. But under normal conditions you should be able to paddle all but about 15 rods of this half-mile stream.

DAY 6: **Lake Polly,** p. 91 rods, **Townline Lake,** p. 181 rods, **Kawasaschong Lake, Kawishiwi River,** p. 11 rods, **river,** p. 20 rods, **Square Lake, Kawishiwi River, Kawishiwi Lake.** This is, of course, familiar territory to you now. This final part of your trip could be completed on the fifth day, but the pressure would no doubt detract from your enjoyment of this pretty route.

Route #52: Three Rivers Route

8 Days, 88 Miles, 21 Lakes, 3 Rivers, 1 Creek, 51 Portages
Difficulty: Challenging
Fisher Maps: F-5, F-11, F-4, F-10, F-3
Travel Zones: 34, 33, 28, 22, 24, 25, 26, 27

Introduction: This delightful route will take you north from Kawishiwi Lake through the lakes, streams, pools and rapids that compose the Kawishiwi River system. From Malberg Lake you'll head southwest down the Kawishiwi River, taking time out to view ancient Indian pictographs along its shore, through Lake Insula and the "numbered lakes" chain to the South Kawishiwi River. Here, you'll have an opportunity to shoot rapids. Turning southeast, you'll encounter the greatest amount of "open water" on Gabbro and Bald Eagle lakes. From there you will portage into the Isabella River and paddle up this beautiful stream to Isabella Lake. Continuing east, you'll soon enter one of the wildest and most interesting regions within the BWCA—the Perent River, where you will portage between towering virgin pines, stepping on terrain only recently vacated by moose and sighting bald eagles overhead. Across Perent Lake and through the winding wilderness of Hog Creek, you will return to Forest Route 354, just 2.4 miles south of your origin.

Wildlife abounds in this region. Beaver homes abound along the Kawishiwi River and moose are also a common sight, especially in the region through which flow the Isabella and Perent rivers. My wife and I saw eight moose along this route during the Summer of 1977, and we're not among the quietest of paddlers. So, with a little effort, you can hardly miss!

Fishing is generally excellent throughout the loop. Walleye and northern pike, in particular, are plentiful in Perent and Isabella lakes, in all parts of the Kawishiwi River and in Malberg, Koma and Polly lakes. Crappies and bass can also be found in several of the lakes.

Motors are not allowed on any of the route, but the region around Lake One is quite heavily used during much of the summer. The Kawishiwi-Polly-Malberg chain of lakes is also very popular. But the variety of beauty that exists along the Three Rivers Route more than compensates for the number of people encountered along the way. A good blend of lakes with rivers and small creeks eliminates any chance of boredom. And although portages are frequent, most are quite short and easily traversed: the longest is 190 rods.

Allow eight full days to complete this challenging route. Nine would permit more time to fish. Low water and occasional beaver dams may slow travel considerably, especially on the Perent River and Hog Creek, as well as eliminate the possibility of running rapids on the South Kawishiwi River. An efficient crew of experienced canoeists could complete the route in seven days, or even less.

DAY 1: **Kawishiwi Lake, Kawishiwi River, Square Lake,** p. 20 rods, **Kawishiwi River,** p. 11 rods, **river, Kawasaschong Lake,** p. 181 rods, **Townline Lake,** p. 91 rods, **Lake Polly,** p. 19 rods, **Kawishiwi River,** p. 48 rods, **river,** p. 127 rods, **river, Koma Lake.** (See comments for Day 1, Route #51.)

DAY 2: **Koma Lake,** p. 24 rods, **Malberg Lake,** p. 60 rods, **Kawishiwi River,** p. 15 rods, **river,** p. 90 rods, **river,**

p. 20 rods, **Alice Lake, Kawishiwi River,** p. 18 rods, **Lake Insula.** Fishing for walleye and northern pike may be excellent in Malberg and along the Kawishiwi River, as well as in Lake Insula. Take time to make a short side trip to the Indian pictographs, just south of the 90-rod portage approaching Alice Lake. A careful examination of the vertical cliffs bordering the river on the west side will yield reminders of a civilization that once flourished in this water wilderness.

DAY 3: **Lake Insula,** p. 105 rods, **Hudson Lake, Kawishiwi River,** p. 10 rods, **river,** p. 25 rods, **river,** p. 20 rods, **Lake Four, Lake Three, Lake Two,** p. 45 rods, **pond,** p. 30 rods, **Lake One.** You will be traveling the entire day on a heavily used route as you approach the second most popular entry point into the BWCA—Lake One. Island-studded Lake Insula is beautiful, but may provide a challenge to the novice map reader. You would do well to plan your trip so that you do not arrive at Lake One on Saturday, Sunday or Monday, when campsites may be at a premium. If supplies are in need of replenishing, a brief stop may be in order at Kawishiwi Lodge, located just outside the BWCA on the northern tip of Lake One.

DAY 4: **Lake One,** p. 19 rods, **Kawishiwi River,** p. 20 rods, **river,** p. 40 rods, **river,** p. 8 rods, **river, South Kawishiwi River,** p. 12 rods, **river,** p. 18 rods, **river,** p. 28 rods, **river,** p. 122 rods, **Little Gabbro Lake, Gabbro Lake.** If desired, you may bypass the "civilized" northern part of Lake One, where the Kawishiwi Lodge and the public landing are located, by portaging 41 rods into Confusion Lake and then 25 rods back into the Kawishiwi River. This eliminates about three miles of paddling, but increases portaging by 47 rods. For those who prefer a little white water to the drudgery of a portage, four of the six portages on the Kawishiwi River this day can be avoided (20, 12, 18 and 28 rods) by shooting, lining or walking the respective rapids, depending on the water depth. Be sure to check them out first, however, because, although the rapids are not considered dangerous, sharp rocks could damage your canoe. The true adventurer with time to kill can also avoid the 122-rod portage from the South Kawishiwi River to Little Gabbro Lake by walking up two sets of gentle rapids, and portaging a small waterfall and an old logging dam.

The map won't show this, so here is what to look for: just beyond the 122-rod portage you'll encounter a short stretch of rapids that must be walked up (no portage). Bearing to the left shoreline, you'll soon come to a picturesque little waterfall that must be passed on the left by a steep, overgrown 10-rod portage that appears to have been used only once or twice since the last Chippewa Indians moved out of the region. Soon after, you will again have to walk up a somewhat longer stretch of rapids, until you arrive at the old dam, which can be passed on the right via an even less traveled path. *Viola:* the back door to Little Gabbro Lake. It is kind of fun, but takes much longer than the 122-rod portage.

DAY 5: **Gabbro Lake,** p. 2–5 rods, **Bald Eagle Lake,** p. 190 rods, **Isabella River, rapids, river,** p. 33 rods, **river, rapids, river,** p. 40 rods, **river.** A small but swift rapids separates Gabbro and Bald Eagle lakes. Your canoe could be pulled through it, if you prefer to avoid the short but tricky portage on the right. Fishing is good here, below the rapids. The Isabella is an attractive river, along which moose may be seen. But campsites are few, and none is large enough to adequately accommodate a large group. If necessary, you can leave the Isabella River for the night by portaging 99 rods to Quadga Lake, where three Forest Service campsites are located. Although this day may appear short on a map, remember that you will be traveling upstream and meandering considerably. It is longer than it looks.

DAY 6: **Isabella River,** p. 27 rods, **river,** p. 27 rods, **river,** p. 10 rods, **river, Rice Lake, Isabella River,** p. 130 rods, **river,** p. 15 rods, **river,** p. 28 rods, **Isabella Lake.** You can avoid the 10-rod portage before Rice Lake by pulling your canoe up this short rapids. Be sure to bear left as you pass the junction of the Island River with the Isabella River. Several good campsites are located on Isabella Lake.

DAY 7: **Isabella Lake,** p. 26 rods, **Boga Lake,** p. 16 rods, **Perent River,** p. 22 rods, **river,** p. 40 rods, **river,** p. 16 rods, **river,** p. 22 rods, **river, rapids, river,** p. 39 rods, **river,** p. 17 rods, **river, rapids, river,** p. 33 rods, **river,** p. 25 rods, **river,** p. 31 rods, **river,** p. 61 rods, **Perent Lake.** This day will find you in one of the wildest parts of the Boundary Waters, an area containing a high moose population. Although both

Isabella and Perent lakes are easily accessible to canoeists, it seems that few navigate the winding river between. (See detailed sketch of the Perent River region in Route #46.)

DAY 8: **Perent Lake, Hog Creek,** p. 15 rods, **creek, Forest Route 354.** This final leg of your trip could be completed on the seventh day. But be sure to allow enough time to negotiate the meandering path of Hog Creek. And, unless you have made prior arrangements to have a vehicle at the Hog Creek parking lot, you will have to walk the last 2.4 miles to your origin on Kawishiwi Lake.

The southeast corner of Perent Lake and the mouth of Hog Creek are not shown on Fisher map #113. The creek is not difficult to find, however. While paddling southeast past the point at which the map ends, stay along the left shoreline and you will find the entrance to Hog Creek just past a small bay in which a campsite is located. (See detailed sketch of Perent River region in Route # 46.)

Appendix I
Routes Categorized by Difficulty and Duration

Duration	Route #	Entry Point Name (and #)
Easy Trips		
2 Days	#23	South Hegman Lake (#77)
2 Days	#42	Little Gabbro Lake (#33)
2 Days	#49	Hog Creek (#36)
3 Days	#1	Trout Lake (#1)
3 Days	#32	Wood Lake (#26)
3 Days	#34	Snowbank Lake (#27)
3 Days	#44	North Kelly Road (#75)
5 Days	#29	Fall Lake (#24)
Challenging Routes		
2 Days	#26	Range Lake (#22)
2 Days	#38	Farm Lake (#31)
2 Days	#43	Snake River (#84)
3 Days	#24	Mudro Lake (#21)
3 Days	#36	Lake One (#30)
3 Days	#40	South Kawishiwi River (#32)
4 Days	#28	Fall Lake (#24)
4 Days	#30	Moose Lake (#25)
4 Days	#33	Wood Lake (#26)
4 Days	#39	Farm Lake (#31)
5 Days	#37	Lake One (#30)
5 Days	#41	South Kawishiwi River (#32)
5 Days	#45	Island River (#34)
5 Days	#47	Isabella Lake (#35)
6 Days	#16	Little Indian Sioux River-North (#14)

Duration	Route #	Entry Point Name (and #)
7 Days	#14	Little Vermilion Lake (#12)
7 Days	#25	Mudro Lake (#21)
7 Days	#35	Snowbank Lake (#27)
7 Days	#46	Island River (#34)
7 Days	#50	Hog Creek (#36)
8 Days	#19	Moose River-North (#16)
8 Days	#31	Moose Lake (#25)
8 Days	#52	Kawishiwi Lake (#37)
9 Days	#17	Little Indian Sioux River-North (#14)
9 Days	#27	Range Lake (#22)
10 Days	#5	Crab Lake (#4)
12 Days	#15	Little Vermilion Lake (#12)
12 Days	#48	Isabella Lake (#35)

Rugged Expeditions

3 Days	#4	Crab Lake (#4)
3 Days	#6	Slim Lake (#6)
3 Days	#8	Big Lake (#7)
4 Days	#2	Trout Lake (#1)
4 Days	#10	Moose River-South (#8)
4 Days	#20	Stuart River (#19)
4 Days	#22	Angleworm Lake (#20)
5 Days	#12	Little Indian Sioux River-South (#9)
5 Days	#18	Moose River-North (#16)
6 Days	#9	Big Lake (#7)
6 Days	#51	Kawishiwi Lake (#37)
7 Days	#3	Trout Lake (#1)
7 Days	#7	Slim Lake (#6)
7 Days	#21	Stuart River (#19)
8 Days	#11	Moose River-South (#8)
10 Days	#13	Little Indian Sioux River-South (#9)

Appendix II
BWCA Travel Zone Data
(Western Region)

#	Travel Zone Name	Groups Entering No.	Rank	No. of Campsites	Campsite Occupancy Rate
1	Little Vermilion Lk	1059	29th	7	22%
2	Lac La Croix Lake	1991	12th(T)	79	41%
3	Pauness Lakes	941	36th	8	70%
4	Loon Lake	1451	21st	17	40%
5	Moose River	1238	25th	30	36%
6	Shell Lake	902	37th	42	27%
7	Gabeonequet Lake	623	40th	49	19%
8	Trout Lake	1854	15th	61	29%
9	Cummings Lake	552	42nd	28	25%
10	Schlamm Lake	247	49th	16	14%—Lowest
11	Big Moose Lake	508	43rd	16	21%
12	Stuart Lake	306	48th	14	26%
13	Crooked Lake	1521	20th	43	58%
14	Angleworm Lake	609	41st	29	23%
15	Horse Lake	998	32nd	32	40%
16	Basswood River	1565	19th	20	37%
17	Jackfish Bay	5527	2nd	92	42%
18	Basswood Lake	4856	4th	90	38%
19	Moose Lake	8248	*1st*	49	47%
20	Ensign Lake	3010	5th	53	45%
21	Snowbank Lake	2347	11th	67	33%
22	Lake One	2959	6th	82	37%
23	Clearwater-Pietro	371	45th	20	16%
24	South Farm Lake	1001	31st	21	30%
25	Gabbro Lake	1228	27th	45	29%

#	Travel Zone Name	Groups Entering No.	Entering Rank	No. of Campsites	Campsite Occupancy Rate
26	Isabella Lake	635	39th	29	18%
27	Perent Lake	368	46th	24	18%
28	Insula Lake	2544	10th	91	43%
29	Kekekabic Lake	1991	12th(T)	56	35%
30	Knife Lake	2663	8th	70	52%
31	Hanson Lake	967	34th	26	45%
32	Ogishkemuncie Lake	1856	14th	30	71%—Highest
33	Adams Lake	1233	26th	46	32%
34	Kawishiwi Lake	1029	30th	49	34%
35	Alton Lake	1584	18th	44	38%
36	Mesaba Lake	1150	28th	24	40%
37	Little Saganaga Lake	1599	17th	89	35%
38	Seagull Lake	2699	7th	63	41%
39	Saganaga Lake	4896	3rd	85	46%

Groups Entering: No.—The total number of groups that entered this zone in 1977. (In all, 41,857 groups entered the BWCA in 1977.)

Groups Entering: Rank—With "1" being the most visited travel zone of the 49 designated.

No. of Campsites—Designated US Forest Service sites throughout the travel zone.

Campsite Occupancy Rate—Campsites occupied ÷ sites available in the travel zone during the 105 nights of the Visitor Distribution Program.

Appendix III
BWCA Travel Permit Data
(Western Region)

EP#	Name of Entry Point	Quota	Permits	Rank	Motor Use	First Zone
Echo Trail Region:						
1	Trout Lake	18	736	9th	25 hp	8
4	Crab Lake	6	286	22nd	No	9
6	Slim Lake	2	58	45th	No	11
7	Big Lake	2	12	67th	No	11
8	Moose River-South	3	40	51st	No	11
9	L. Indian Sioux River-South	2	18	62nd	No	11
12	Little Vermilion Lake	20	265	24th	No limit	1
14	L. Indian Sioux River-North	8	569	13th	No	3
16	Moose River-North	13	966	7th	No	5
19	Stuart River	3	60	43rd	No	12
20	Angleworm Lake	2	49	49th	No	14
77	South Hegman Lake	2	103	38th	No	14
21	Mudro Lake	4	911	8th	No	15
22	Range Lake	3	911	8th	No	15
Fernberg Road Region						
24	Fall Lake	33	1233	6th	25 hp	17
25	Moose Lake	40	3361	1st	25 hp	19
26	Wood Lake	4	104	37th	No	18
27	Snowbank Lake	7	671	10th	25 hp	21
30	Lake One	23	2200	2nd	No	22
31	Farm Lake	4	236	27th	No limit	24
State Highway 1 Region						
32	South Kawishiwi River	4	250	26th	No	25
33	Little Gabbro Lake	3	231	28th	No	25

EP#	Name of Entry Point	Quota	Permits	Rank	Motor Use	First Zone
84	Snake River	2	46	50th	No	25
75	North Kelly Road	2	30	54th	No	26
34	Island River	6	110	36th	No	26
35	Isabella Lake	7	277	23rd	No	26
36	Hog Creek	7	251	25th	No	27
37	Kawishiwi Lake	10	583	12th	No	34

Quota: The maximum number of overnight travel permits issued at the entry point each day.

Permits: The total number of overnight travel permits issued in 1986 for all modes of travel, including canoes, motorboats, hikers and all other means.

Rank: With "1" being the most popular entry point, this is based on the total number of travel permits issued for each of the 84 entry points.

Motor Use: Whether or not motors are allowed through the entry point, and, if so, the horsepower limit.

1st Zone: The first travel zone to which the entry point leads.

Appendix IV
Canoe Trip Outfitters

Canoe trip outfitters provide a valuable service to the first-time visitor to the Boundary Waters Canoe Area. For a reasonable fee, an outfitter will provide you with EVERYTHING needed for a wilderness canoe trip. All you must do is show up with your toothbrush—the outfitter will take care of the rest.

Not all people are "cut out" for wilderness tripping. If you are not sure of yourself, it is foolish to invest hundreds of dollars in your own gear and outdoor clothing. After you have tried it, if it seems likely that you will return to the BWCA at least once every year, THEN you may want to own your own gear, to save money in the long run.

To obtain current brochures from the outfitters in the Western Region of the BWCA, write to any (or all) of the agencies listed below:

> Cook Chamber of Commerce
> Cook, MN 55723
>
> Crane Lake Commercial Club
> Crane Lake, MN 55725
>
> Ely Chamber of Commerce
> 1600 East Sheridan Street
> Ely, MN 55731
>
> Tower-Sudan Chamber of Commerce
> Tower, MN 55790

VOLUNTEER! Interested in doing more to help preserve the area? The Forest needs your help. Volunteer jobs range from carrying out extra litter and garbage on a canoe trip to spending a weekend building a ski-hiking trail to spending a summer cleaning and maintaining campsites in the BWCA Wilderness. To learn more about volunteering, write or call: Forest Supervisor; P.O. Box 338, Duluth, MN 55801; 218/720-5324.

Index